AI + The New Human Frontier

AI + The New Human Frontier

Reimagining the Future of Time, Trust + Truth

ERICA ORANGE

WILEY

To Jared and Zane. . .
and a future filled with adventure, discovery, and wonder

Contents at a Glance

Contents

PART IV   Augmented Intelligence   68

Foreword

Everyone is talking about artificial intelligence (AI) today. The topic is all over coverage on legacy media and chatter on social media. And, as futurists, AI comes up in many conversations we have with friends and colleagues. The rising prominence of AI is obvious, but real questions remain about how much impact it will truly have in many different aspects of both our work lives and our personal lives. Around the world, people are attempting to separate the signal from the noise in a world of extreme hype around the future of this technology. Some areas of our lives will be profoundly impacted by AI, while others, not as much.

As we look toward the future of AI, perhaps the two most important areas for consideration are the *why* and the *who* of AI.

The *why* revolves around the reasons we should use AI in the first place. Together, those reasons should serve as the guiding principles for all AI research and deployment in the future. Why are we investing in it? Is it merely the next step in the evolution of technology, or can it do things far better than other current technologies? At the *enterprise* level, how can it make our work and businesses more productive?

And at the *human* level, what are the many ways that AI could impact our lives? Will it do so for the better? Will we even be aware of AI as it's being incorporated into our day-to-day experiences? Will we be able to trust it?

Today, most innovators and business leaders are determining *how* to strategically pursue AI, *when* to invest, and *where* to invest. But the *who* relates to a fundamental, and often overlooked, aspect of the future of AI: the *human* implications of all of this.

Which people will we need to hire more of in the future? Who will specialize in AI? Which human skill sets will be required? What will the human/machine interface look like in the years ahead? Which human jobs will disappear? And which new jobs—and career fields—will rise like phoenixes from all of this transformation? What will the future of humanity look like in the face of all this technological change? How will we adapt? How will we best optimize those things that make us uniquely human? Will AI soon overtake our capabilities and possibly our intelligence? What about in the long term? Or. . .ever?

This book addresses these critical questions at precisely the time when it's needed the most. We are at a civilizational inflection point right now—at this very juncture in our coevolution with technology.

This book is also a realistic and pragmatic assessment of the AI landscape—something that is far too often absent in a world characterized by attention, clicks, and sensationalism. For example, while AI will impact *many* things about the world around us, it certainly won't impact *everything*. Many of the loudest voices in the room tend to fall into one of two camps, both of which assign almost godlike characteristics to AI. In one camp are those who promote the universally transformative power of AI, and thus believe that we should be pursuing the development of this technology as aggressively as possible, with few—or no—guardrails. In the other camp are those who tend toward more dystopian perspectives on the future of this technology. They believe that AI could destabilize human labor and other aspects of the economy—and that once we open "Pandora's box," we'll never be able to control the unintended consequences of it. Both camps will be proven right. . .and both camps will be proven wrong. There are no absolutes in any of this. It should never be considered a zero-sum game.

As futurists, we can't predict the future with absolute certainty, but we can make enlightened projections based on studying past patterns, current trends, and technological shifts. This book will be relevant not just now, but in years to come, because it seeks less to make bets on different versions (or iterations) of AI as it exists today. This book, instead, seeks to answer the fundamental questions that will impact the newly emerging human frontier—the somewhat uncharted and evolving nexus between us and the technology around us. The book does this by breaking down the future into three fundamental areas that will impact this new human frontier: time, truth, and trust—three things that are more important than ever but which are perhaps also at a greater premium than ever before. This book will be just as relevant 3, 5, or 10 years in the future as it is today.

And it is written by someone who has dedicated many years of her life, both personally and professionally, to the understanding of all of this. I know this not just because Erica is my partner in business but also because she's my partner in life. I see her passion for these subjects every day, and I marvel at her innate curiosity and determination to always evolve her own understanding. She also has the unique ability to transform highly complex information into more relatable concepts, and she has done exactly that within this book.

She and I often end our days with a drink, sitting and discussing our perspectives on technology, culture, the universe, and all things existential and interesting to us. We bounce thoughts off one another, challenge each other, and consider what things could look like for us, our family, and for society in the future. And we have these constant conversations because they're fun . . . and because they're important.

To the future.

Jared Weiner

EVP + Chief Strategy Officer

The Future Hunters

Introduction

My now 7-year-old son's favorite "relaxing" bedtime book is *Who Would Win? Extreme Animal Rumble*. Sixteen creatures in a bracketed battle. Single elimination. Nothing like a fight to the death between sharks, dinosaurs, deadly insects, and jungle animals to lull him into a peaceful sleep at night. He's so inspired by these rumbles, he has taken to writing his own version, which he calls "The Intelligence Rumble"—smart animals vs. smart animals. (He excitedly gave me the full rundown on the list of competitors, which include the highly anticipated matchups of giant squid vs. octopus and crow vs. raven.)

"The Intelligence Rumble?" I asked, as thoughts swirled in my head. "What do you think about *this* intelligence rumble: humans vs. robots. What would a matchup look like? Who would win?"

"Well, humans are smarter than robots because they invented robots; robots did not invent people," he reasoned. "People can control what robots do, but robots cannot control what people do. Some people are smarter than robots, and some robots are smarter than people. Both minds are getting smarter and smarter, but robots are catching up a little bit to humans."

"Oh, and add this part," he later added over one of our breakfast chats. "Humans have been evolving and have been on this planet for a lot longer than robots. So, they *must* be smarter."

It's amazing to see how new perspectives of the future can unfold when the world is seen through the eyes of a child. And once I got over my budding futurist-in-training's mini soliloquy and let his words and insights sink in, it got me thinking about several questions worth pondering: Will there ever be a clear victor in an artificial intelligence (AI) vs. human rumble? Will we be constantly jockeying for position? Or, will we coevolve less in competition and more in collaboration with each other? AI is evolving exponentially faster than humans are. Will our evolution speed up as an adaptation? Is this already happening over just a few generations?

The future holds incredible promise—and the promise of myriad technological advancements, the biggest of which, right now, is AI. Revolutionary breakthroughs in AI will transform our lives in ways never thought possible. It will likely become a more integral part of our existences, opening entirely new vistas of human possibility and ushering in a world that is anchored more around human capabilities. Its applications are limitless. And this is an existential paradox. Could we (and would we) invent technology that could render us obsolete? If so, the societal (and civilizational) shift would be profound. In the near term, however, we are just beginning to grapple with the implications of what should perhaps be reframed as artificial *smart* versus true artificial intelligence.

I, for one, would like to be a cheerleader for humanity. I believe AI will not decide how AI is used. *We* will decide how AI is used. In the end, however, there are other indications that perhaps we won't be in control of those decisions. Ultimately, we will have to decide—if and/or when we maintain control—whether AI is used for constructive or destructive ends.

The rules that once governed much of our day-to-day realities are being rewritten as AI reshapes industries and disrupts traditional business models. As we seek to shed light on our interrelationship with AI, it will increasingly be one that is less about "us *vs.* it" and more about "us *and* it." AI will continue unabated to challenge older (and outdated) frontiers of human knowledge. As it does so, it may also allow us to expand to entirely new ones. New understanding, insight, and knowledge could challenge us to rethink our unique value proposition in a changing world. While concerns about obsolescence are normal, humans will not face a robotic takeover; rather, we will all be faced with navigating a reality in which many facets of our lives are symbiotically interwoven with technology. AI is—and will continue to be—a beacon of transformative power, but its abilities will be revealed only when combined with human ingenuity. The fusion of the two will not serve as a harbinger of human obsolescence but rather as a magnifier of human capability. AI's true revolutionary potential as both an accelerator and an amplifier lie in its ability to unlock new frontiers of human creativity and thought.

Change is inevitable and constant. It has always been a driving force as it has long helped enable progress in many, if not all, aspects of life. Right now, there is a split between nostalgia for what was and enthusiasm for what could be. We are standing at a crossroads. Finding one's purpose and employment in life will become a self-reliant, ever-shifting journey, especially as traditional safety nets are no longer guaranteed in an age of ever-advancing AI. It is easy to get caught up in fear and doubt about what lies ahead. I get it, and I feel it, too. I think about this as a parent, going down rabbit holes about the existential threats that will face my son's generation and those that will come after. I think about the things he'll need to navigate that other generations never faced—all those threats that only existed once in sci-fi novels or were posited as academic conjecture about a more distant time.

No matter how often we may dwell in these thoughts and ponder the personal effects of these emerging realities, this book is here to offer a different perspective: one of hope. Hope for the future, hope for the next generation, and hope for humanity. The future may seem daunting at times, but it is filled with endless pathways ripe for discovery. It is a blank canvas. This book aims to inspire readers to embrace their role in shaping the future. It reminds us that despite the challenges we may face, we possess an innate ability to adapt and overcome.

Do we believe in the potential of people with as much certainty as we believe in the potential of AI?

If so, this means that we cannot be entrenched in the old ways of doing things and the old ways of solving problems. Because in the future we are rapidly moving into, we shouldn't be afraid of new ideas. We should be afraid of the old ones that no longer work. Today's global challenges cannot be addressed with yesterday's thinking.

Overview

This book has six parts:

- **Part I (Translating the Future)** focuses on contextualizing the future and beginning to see it through new eyes. It's about leaving past assumptions behind and approaching the ways in which we see the world, our lives, our jobs, and our organizations in a new light.

- **Part II (Time + Templosion)** focuses on a term that we, as a firm (The Future Hunters), coined almost a decade and a half ago: *Templosion*. . .the implosion of time. Templosion refers to the idea that the biggest of things and the biggest of events are happening in shorter periods of time. Time horizons are being reduced, and our experience of time is in overdrive. It is creating a world that is more nonlinear and boundaryless.

- **Part III (Technology: Artificial Intelligence)** focuses on the exponential explosion of AI and how it is forcing older ways of working to evolve. It highlights both the opportunities and the threats and separates the hype from reality.

- **Part IV (Augmented Intelligence)** focuses on the human experience and how it will be transformed in an age of AI. We are quickly being catapulted into a world defined not just by automation but by *augmentation*. This is creating a dynamic that is less about replacement and more about enhancement. Human elements such as intuition, empathy, sensemaking, and lived experience will become more valued than ever before.

- **Part V (Trust + Truth)** highlights the growing vacuum of trust and how that vacuum is giving new urgency not just to transparency but to honesty. Building trust will be an ongoing process, particularly as AI makes it harder to know who or what to trust. We are also navigating a macro-environment where it is getting harder to decipher between what is real, fake, true, and false. The distortion of the truth is being exacerbated by a climate of rampant distrust and mis-, dis-, mal-, and digitally derived information (MDMD).

- **Part VI (Tomorrow)** is about the future frontiers of human thought . . . and humanity, at large. It also addresses some of the other current states of AI that may impact the future of human experience. Ultimately, it seeks to answer how we can create a future where progress prevails over stagnation. How can possibility prevail over pessimism? How can action prevail over apathy? How can creation prevail over crisis? And how can imagination prevail over inertia?

PART I

Translating the Future

Technology has long captivated us with the promise of change. But a more dynamic understanding of why technology changes, how we change with it, and how we might govern it is needed. Part I focuses on how to better translate the future and make sense of the shifts many of us are feeling and experiencing—both in our own lives and in the world at large. We will start by contextualizing the pace of change and challenging many of the assumptions we make about how the future operates.

CHAPTER 1

A Voyage into the Future

It's a tale as old as tech. Radio Shack. Neon phones. Game Boys. VHS tapes. Dial-up Internet. In 1999, I left for college with my bright purple Space Age iMac. With its sleek design and vibrant colors, it became more than just a computer—it felt like a statement piece. And let's not forget those coveted .edu email addresses. They were like badges of honor and status symbols. As were our now cringe-worthy AOL Instant Messenger names. Ah, nostalgia. It's a feeling that takes us back to what seemed like simpler times, reminding us of the moments when technology was just beginning to shape our lives and shape our memories.

Many of our memories are also defined through the music from our youth and the technologies that shaped the way we experienced and consumed it. From vinyl records to cassette tapes, CDs to MP3 players, and now streaming platforms, each advancement has brought with it a sense of nostalgia for the previous era. Whether it's hearing a song from our childhood or rediscovering an album that defined a specific moment in our lives, music has the power to connect us with memories and emotions like nothing else. And for 8th grade me, this cassette single was in my boombox rotation: "Fantastic Voyage." It's a song that instantly brings you back to the 1990s. I would sing this funkadelic hook on repeat. (For anyone of the same generation, you're probably swaying to it in your head right now.) Coolio's catchy chorus was a song, when you got down to it, about people coming together. Coming together for a fantastic voyage in search of something better.

When taken more broadly, humanity has always been on a fantastic voyage. Life is a journey of unknowns. Of risks. Of challenges. Of chaos— some of it stressful, some of it beautiful. It is easy to get caught up in all the different ways we experience chaos because it can be both thrilling and deeply discomforting at the same time. But we have a choice: we can be more passive, adopting a wait-and-see approach to help to define the future, or we can embark on a voyage where we seek to drive new frontiers of human progress and push the boundaries of what we believe . . . and believe to be possible.

We, in many ways, are moving away from the familiar, and it is forcing us to define and redefine what it truly means to be human in a world of complexities. We are entering a period of transformation, moving from the world as we have always known it to a profoundly new one—a world with new dimensions, boundaries, and delineations. Our macro environment is in flux and forcing us to continually challenge our long-held assumptions about how the world works and what it takes to succeed in it.

As these complexities multiply, thinking about the future can be overwhelming. And what's more is that thinking about *our* role, as humans, in this ever-changing world can be overwhelming. One reason for this is because we are entering a future in which decisions in the home, in the marketplace, in the workplace, and perhaps even in the voting booth, will increasingly be made by smarter and more sophisticated forms of technology. These technologies—most notably, AI—will increasingly instruct us about aspects of behavior, security, risk, education, and work. AI will undoubtedly yield greater influence across many facets of our lives—both personally and professionally.

These evolutions, however, when taken in their totality, represent not just challenges (and there will be significant challenges) but opportunities. Opportunities that, if we approach the future without all the baggage of outmoded thinking, will outweigh the challenges. By zeroing in on the opportunities, we are given a chance to rethink and reimagine the way we've always done things.

So, rest assured: the future *is* there for humanity. We will never be obsolete. But we're at a tip of the iceberg moment. Seismic shifts in AI are forcing us to double down on how to coevolve alongside of it, and it's forcing us to double down on our own humanity. We also must remember this: the future does not belong just to AI, nor does it belong just to humans; rather, we will coexist with the technology that increasingly surrounds us. Just as we always have . . . and just as we always will. As we have seen throughout history, from prehistoric times to modern times, humans have always adapted and evolved alongside their tools and technologies. The emergence of AI should be viewed as another step in this ongoing process.

This goes back to the earliest of humans. From the discovery of fire to the invention of the wheel, our ability to harness tools has propelled us forward. Archaeologists recently reported a discovery on South Africa's Cape Coast that upends our prevailing assumptions about the use of one of humankind's oldest forms of "wearable technology." Ancient humans may have worn shoes as early as the Middle Stone Age, a period believed to date between 75,000 and 150,000 years ago. While this doesn't conform to modern definitions of wearable technology (e.g., fitness trackers and smartwatches), that is very much what they were. They also represent one of humankind's earliest technological innovations.[1] And it certainly captures the essence of how humans and technology have progressed together. Our evolution and technology's evolution are intertwined. The only thing that makes this dynamic different from other periods of time is that this coevolution is happening at a faster pace and is driven by more complex and sophisticated systems and tools.

Change has always been with us. It is as old as human history and is a constant in our existences. What is new is the *pace* of change. Change that is driven in large part by the rate of technological innovation around the world. It is human nature to view some change as scary. We all do. It is why we have an inborn response to fear. A core part of human nature—and our biological makeup—consists of self-preservation. It is an instinctive tendency to ensure survival. While it is normal to view these changes as frightening, they also represent tremendous chances to rethink our approaches toward the future. People always ask me: "How can I get better at embracing change?" I wish I had a crystal ball to answer that one. But life—and the future—isn't about simply embracing change. It's about learning how to navigate it. Hope serves as an anchor during turbulent times, reminding us of our resilience and capacity for growth. It fuels our belief in the power of collaboration and collective action.

Note

[1] https://thedebrief.org/middle-stone-age-discovery-may-extend-earliest-use-of-ancient-wearable-technology-as-far-back-as-150000-years

CHAPTER 2

The Sky's the Limit

"Are you ready?" asked the instructor harnessed to my back. Without me even attempting to utter a response, we shuffled out of the prop plane and began our free fall. Terminal velocity. That is the fastest speed you can reach on a skydive. As I fell 120 miles an hour through the air, aerial images captured that simultaneous feeling of fear and elation. Those images also somehow managed to capture me looking like a baby pterodactyl with crooked dangling arms, wide eyes, and a gaping mouth. I looked completely scared.

I was gasping for air, repeating not-so-reassuring mantras in my head on loop, and hoping that the New Zealander on my back knew what he was doing. All of this in probably only 45 seconds. A mere snapshot in time. But a moment of significance. No matter how quickly the adrenaline was pumping, I still felt oddly reassured. Why? Because I knew I was secure. I was both free and secure at the same time. My free fall through the sky felt risky, but I always knew I had the safeguard of a parachute. The parachute gave me the comfort that I would eventually slow down. It gave me a semblance of control. I could steer my own direction and navigate my own path. I trusted it, and that sense of trust gave me a sense of safety.

Skydiving is the ultimate trust fall. The entire thing depends on trust. When you approach the open door and wait for the go-ahead, the only thing you can do is trust. Trust between the diver and the instructor. Trust in the equipment. Trust in the entire experience. Without trust, skydiving would feel incredibly risky and daunting.

Remember the "trust fall" game when you were young? I remember playing this on the playground and always trying to assess the presumed physical strength of the kid next in line who would be trusted with catching my body weight. Intentionally falling backwards requires a great deal of trust. We placed our trust in the tiny people we believed could carry our weight. Now, as adults, we reflect on the concept and realize that at its core, it is about abandoning your sense of control. It's about being vulnerable. Having confidence in people. Trusting that you will be caught.

Just like with skydiving, the future, in many ways, feels like a trust fall. And increasingly, it feels like a free fall. Turn on any news channel or go on social media and it will elicit this same feeling. Dread. Anxiety. Fear. We have all felt it—we still feel it. The pandemic. Gun violence. The politicization of everything. Tribalism. Climate change. Income inequality. Trade wars. Threats to our democratic institutions. The destruction of the natural habitat. The rapidly growing and often unchecked powers unleashed by modern technology. The weaponization of social media. The mental health epidemic. Escalating geopolitical conflicts. And the list goes on and on. When taken in sum, these examples—along with countless others—signify tremendous challenges. Challenges that make it seem as if we are collectively maneuvering through some type of dystopian sci-fi movie. Each one of us is trying to make sense of things. Trying to understand where the world is moving. Trying to figure out what it all means. And the feeling that we are coming up short is a common one.

Many of us feel this way because we are constantly hammered over the head with new and conflicting information. We are being bombarded by a steady and never-ending flow of information, and this is making us feel like we are swimming upstream against a tide of information overload. And as this information overload fights harder and harder to gain our attention, we might feel like we are not just swimming upstream but drowning in it. Anxiety and stress are on the rise globally, and many people feel as if they are losing a sense of control.

From Headwinds to Tailwinds

When seen through this lens, change can be viewed as . . . well, a lot. We only have a finite amount of mental bandwidth. That's why it's natural to focus on the external difficulties we are faced with today. We can refer to those external factors as the *headwinds*. At times it can feel quite dizzying to try and navigate these different pathways. It might seem as if we have lost agency over our own lives.

We are being catapulted into a future that is growing more complex by the day. The expectations, the risks, the challenges—all of these have escalated. We can try as hard as we want to slow down time, but things never operate this way. We can attempt to cut ourselves off and shield ourselves from the myriad headwinds, but those headwinds are hard to ignore and hard to silence—especially when we are in free fall.

But our parachute—the one to help make us future-ready—is this: it's learning how to move our focus away from the headwinds and toward the tailwinds. The tailwinds push us; they don't push up against us. Recognizing the opportunities isn't always easy, especially when there is so much uncertainty out there. But a part of our collective trust fall resides in identifying the opportunities: those tailwinds that can propel us forward.

Today we sit at an inflection point. Societally. Culturally. Technologically. Economically. Environmentally. Politically. Organizationally. Individually. We are living through a time of profound transformation, which is leading us to look for ways to be more agile, resilient, and ready for future disruption. We will all need the courage to take on challenges and embrace the ambiguity of the future.

Developments in AI are shifting daily. There are new applications, new chatbots, new tools, new corporate pivots, new capabilities, new entrants into the market, new job projections, new . . . everything. It's overwhelming. You feel as if you can't keep up. Not only do we need a parachute, but we need a roadmap, too.

When I was talking about this recently with a wise friend, she said to me: "Irritated oysters make pearls." Something beautiful and valuable can come from pain points and periods of uncertainty. Pearls are made as a natural defense. As we face irritants of various kinds and of various magnitudes in our own lives, how do we transform them? How do we take our own natural defense mechanisms and form a "gemstone"? An oyster spends almost its entire life stuck in a single spot. It opens its shell only to filter food from the water. It also builds its pearls slowly—layer by layer. We, too, need to take the time to address our responses and reactions to the external irritants—the headwinds—in our collective lives. Because not only can we not afford to stay stuck, but also much of the growth we experience—both individually and collectively—is caused by the various factors that ultimately make us stronger and more resilient.

CHAPTER 3

How To Think about the Future

Too often, pundits and strategists assume that the world will return to the point of known stasis from which it began. As a case in point, witness the seemingly endless stream of predictions from trusted sources who speculated during the COVID-19 pandemic about when the world would return to "normal." To assume that there is a fixed baseline to which the world and its institutions will return is an oversimplification—and likely a heuristic that allows for many people to feel more secure about a "predictable" future for themselves.

The world doesn't operate according to the principles of a pendulum. The mental image we have for cycles is that whatever the object of attention, activity will go in one direction for just so long—perhaps too long—and then swing back, past center, to its original point, and then the process will begin all over again. When we see emotions of a society swing too far out to an extreme, we anticipate a course correction and a swing back to center and then to the opposite extreme and then back again. When we see stock prices rise dramatically and then fall dramatically and then rise and fall, over time we expect the same conditions to prevail, causing the pendulum to continue swinging back and forth around some central point.

Things cannot possibly retrace their path back to where they have been. The context has changed. Places are not the same; people are not the same; nothing is exactly the same as it was before. Everything from global employment and unemployment, economic transition, workforce migration, and technological innovation can best be understood within this context. Clearly, where we end up will not be where we started.

The Drunkard's Search Principle

The streetlight effect, or the drunkard's search principle, is a type of observational bias that occurs when someone's expectations, opinions, or prejudices influence what they perceive.[1] This principle refers to a well-known joke: A policeman sees a drunk man searching for something under a streetlight and asks what the drunk has lost. He says he lost his keys, and they both look under the streetlight together. After a few minutes, the policeman asks if he is sure he lost them here, and the drunk replies, no, and that he lost them in the park. The policeman asks why he is searching here, and the drunk replies, 'This is where the light is.'[2]

The point of the story? People only search for something where it is easiest to look. It is harder to find something on the part of the floor that is not well lit. In a world where information is abundant and attention spans are short, people tend to search for things in the easiest and most accessible places. It's a natural tendency to look where it's convenient and familiar, just like in the joke. This concept applies not only to physical objects but also to our thinking patterns. We often rely on what is readily available or easily observable, leading to biased perspectives or overreliance on our own value judgments. We may overlook alternative viewpoints or dismiss unconventional ideas simply because they require more effort.

The drunkard's search principle challenges us to think differently when it comes to observation and personal bias. That's because our observations are not always objective. Our perception filters and selects information based on various factors such as attention, memory, and personal experiences. Human perception can be subjective and influenced by our individual interpretations.

This conjures up a similar story: that of the "invisible gorilla." There is a famous psychological experiment in which subjects were shown a one-minute video and told to focus on how many passes a basketball team made. About halfway through the video, a gorilla emerged and walked across the basketball court. Half the participants in the experiment did not see the gorilla. Why is that? I participated in this experiment in college and admittedly never saw the gorilla. Psychologists call this *inattentional blindness*—in other words, the phenomenon of not being able to perceive things that are in plain sight. How our minds see and process information is at the heart of this. The more you focus on something, the less able you become to see unexpected or unanticipated occurrences elsewhere. In this case, subjects were concentrating on the ball and unable to see the gorilla. The lesson is this: depending on your focus, your entire perspective can shift.

No matter who we are, we all carry around a load of mental baggage that we've accumulated over time. While this "knowledge" helps to shape our views of the world, it can also cloud our vision and make it near impossible to spot things that are unforeseen and new. For many unknowns, we rely on inferences made from what we *do* know. But are our extrapolations correct? Are the heuristics we use sufficient? How many times do we do this in our own lives, in our businesses, or when looking for a job? Just like we would never drive using only the rearview mirror, we shouldn't navigate through the future this way either.

As the early 20th-century French novelist Marcel Proust once said: "The true voyage of discovery consists not in seeking new landscapes, but in having new eyes." Truly meaningful discovery doesn't come just from learning new things, but from discovering new aspects of things that are already familiar to us.

So, how do we shed the "invisible gorilla" that we all carry around with us? For starters, we need to question the ways we look at the future and begin seeing it through a new lens. We must recognize and revel in what we don't know as a pathway to discovering new things, new possibilities, new realities, and new futures.

The Interconnectedness of the Future

Math. A four-letter word that still haunts me. It was a subject in school I tried to pretend did not exist, and a grade I tried to pretend did not count. Trying to comprehend it was like learning a foreign language in a foreign language. I could not wrap my brain logically around it.

After years in school of feeling mathematically inadequate, I came to the realization in my adult years that perhaps my brain is just not wired to think that way. Comprehension, for me, comes in more abstract forms. Teachers were never able to recognize this, but I knew that my thinking and cognition did not follow a linear path. I have always been a visual learner. I like to *see* what I am learning. Many people are wired this same way.

The pop psychology theory is that people are either left-brained or right-brained, meaning that one side of their brain is dominant. If you are mostly analytical and systematic in your thinking, you are said to be left-brained. If you tend to be more creative or artistic, you are thought to be right-brained. The two brain hemispheres are unique, yet brain imaging technologies like functional magnetic resonance imaging (fMRI) suggest that, on average, we use both sides of our brain equally.

We need to stop dividing ourselves as "right brainers" or "left brainers" and instead begin embracing the notion that we are all "brain-ambidextrous." Or, at the very least, start training our brains to be. The better the different parts of your brain communicate with each other, the more integrated your brain. A vast network of interconnected neurons is constantly firing in a way to inform all parts of the brain of what is happening so we can respond from a whole-view perspective.

That, ultimately, is what the future will require. A whole-view perspective. A fully integrated approach to understanding how all the individual puzzle pieces fit together to build one larger, unified view of where the needle is moving. Rarely do things operate in silos. And trends never operate this way. A technological trend never stands on its own. Nor does an economic trend. Or a sociocultural trend. Or a geopolitical trend. Or a demographic trend. They are all interconnected. They inform and influence each other. Often the connections between the trends tell us more about where things are moving versus simply looking at a trend in isolation. Everything is overlapping.

The interconnectedness of our external environments creates a dynamic landscape where each trend influences and shapes others. For instance, technological advancements have accelerated the pace of change across multiple domains. The rise of AI has not only revolutionized industries like health care, finance, and transportation but has also altered the way we interact with technology itself. The intersection of AI with other trends such as automation, data analytics, and machine learning paints a more comprehensive picture of how our world is evolving. Similarly, societal changes are intertwined with technological progress. The increasing focus on sustainability has spurred innovations in renewable energy sources, eco-friendly products, and circular economies. Trends are about their collective—not singular—impacts.

Looking at trends solely in isolation only scratches the surface of understanding. That is when, early in my career, I came to the realization that math did, in fact, play a role in my thinking about the future. It might be the most simplistic type of math, but it informs all that I do. It comes down to one thing: logic. Logical relations between things, sets of ideas, and concepts. Logical relations as best illustrated by my all-time MVP . . . the Venn diagram. Anyone who knows me well knows that I love geeking out on a good old Venn diagram. It has helped me learn a simple yet foundational overarching lesson: it is often in the intersection between trends where the biggest sparks can occur. Straight-line extrapolation based on what we know—or think we know—will not lead us to the new types of thinking that the future requires. So, we must start digging deeper to reveal the possibilities in the white space. The white space exists in the intersections and is where unmet needs and unspecified ideas are unearthed to create new, leverageable opportunities. To truly unlock new types of thinking (and the innovations those new types of thinking could spawn), we must explore the intersections—and in a world of quickly advancing AI, this becomes an even more critical imperative.

The Future Is a Rorschach Test

Almost two decades ago, two visionary pioneers of the field and founders of our firm (then Weiner, Edrich, Brown, Inc. in 1977), Edie Weiner and Arnold Brown, gave me the unique opportunity to delve deeper into the world of futurism. They served as my mentors and taught me, at the very beginning of my career, how to begin spotting patterns, seeing connective threads, training my eye, and thinking critically.

And perhaps most importantly, they taught me two central lessons:

1. Imagination is an extension of long-term strategic foresight.
2. The future is a Rorschach test—our perception of it informs our reality.

Much of our reality can be likened to a Rorschach test—an inkblot that we interpret based on our own perceptions and beliefs. (And fast-forward to today and that knowledge and awareness informs much of how I approach my work.) Our mindset toward the future can be either limiting or empowering. If we view it with fear and uncertainty, we may become paralyzed by the unknown, unwilling to take risks or embrace change. On the other hand, if we approach it with curiosity and optimism, we open ourselves up to new realities. We must also remember that the future is not predetermined; it is malleable and dependent on our collective actions. Some may see atrophy and decline, while others see betterment and advancement. We have a choice in which path we choose and which version of the Rorschach test we choose to see.

Notes

[1] https://freedman.com/2010/10/20/the-streetlight-effect.
[2] Freedman, D. (2010). *Wrong: Why experts keep failing us—and how to know when not to trust them*. New York: Little Brown and Company.

PART II

Time + Templosion

P art II is about time—time as a currency, time as a luxury, and time as a new value proposition. Time doesn't operate linearly; rather, it goes off in multiple directions, and its compression will affect many different facets of our lives.

CHAPTER 4

The Speeding Up of Time

"Are we there yet? Are we there yet? Are we there yet?"

"What?! 40 more minutes? I can't wait that long!"

"Tomorrow?! Tomorrow is forever!!"

That is time through the eyes of my first grader (at the time of writing this book). With the short answers to each of those repetitive questions being: *"Nope," "Yes, you can,"* and *"Not quite. Let's try that again."* Long, drawn out, laborious. Each day seems to contain its own lifetime when you are young.

Time is an integral part of our daily life, and our perception of it fluctuates with age. It governs the rhythm of our days, dictating when we wake up, eat, work, and rest. The older we get, the more minutes become a smaller fraction of our overall lifetime, so the more quickly we feel them moving forward. We often find ourselves wishing for more time or lamenting its fleeting nature. And our emotions color the way we perceive it, as time becomes intertwined with our experiences and memories. As children, we try to understand the world around us and make sense of the people in it. This may be one reason time moves slower when we are younger.

Time is also experienced linearly—the arrow of time points forward, not back. But even though the fundamental laws of physics do not distinguish between past and future, in our experience, time always points into the future. We still experience reality through linear time. In the agricultural age, we experienced it as unfolding seasons. In the industrial age, we measured time with clocks. By observing a clock, we have an impression that time is running forward. Ticking away toward some end point. When experienced this way, time seems to have a duration. It informs our experience of past, present, and future. And our society cannot function without a linear concept of time. Without thinking of time as horizontal, it would turn everything upside down, from religious holidays to work schedules to financial planning to birthdays.

Now, in our long-past industrial environment, digital time is showing that it is capable of not only speeding up but also sweeping us up along with it at a remarkable pace. We now measure time in billions and trillions of seconds. So, to my son's question *"Are we there yet?"* the answer is clearly subjective. But the journey with which to get there—whatever and wherever "there" is—is happening faster than ever before. Everything is beginning to speed up. We are being slingshot into a future that is unveiling itself to us at record speed.

We are witnessing a constant stream of technological advancements and societal shifts that are not only transforming our lives but also reshaping the way we perceive and experience time itself. We no longer experience time strictly linearly and sequentially. Rather, the current landscape is characterized by a simultaneous unfolding of events. We no longer have the luxury of simply choosing just one path to go down. We have to get comfortable operating in many different scenarios, many different realities, and exploring many different pathways. All at once. Technologies like AI, automation, robotics, big data, and digitalization have revolutionized industries, enabling businesses to operate with greater efficiency and agility. As a result, traditional notions of time constraints are being challenged as processes become faster and more streamlined.

Simultaneous Time

Time has become a more fluid entity, allowing us to exist in multiple dimensions. We can live one life in the real world, where we interact with people face-to-face and experience physical sensations. Simultaneously, we can have another life and persona in the digital world, where we communicate through screens and engage with others virtually. Then there is yet another life in extended realities, e.g., metaverse realms that push our imaginations even further. And as our day-to-day reality becomes more uncertain and complex, we are evolving to navigate these complexities with greater skill. We are learning, almost in near real time, how to seamlessly transition between different roles, personas, and environments. Living these multifaceted lives allows us to explore various aspects of ourselves and tap into diverse experiences. For younger generations, and many others, the boundaries between these different realities, identities, and personas are no longer clear-cut.

We have now become accustomed to shopping at all hours of the day and night, any day of the year, as retailers battle it out around the world for access to customers online. Customer expectations are rising each year, and an important component is the speed of response. Influencers have followers around the world watching their entire lives all the time, immediately affecting purchase decisions. With today's constant news cycle, there is no place for businesses to hide. When a company does environmental damage, or has a scandal, or comes up with an invention, it is instantly news all over the world. Security, privacy, integrity, reliability, and responsiveness will be increasingly tested as all professions grapple with the many ways fast, mobile, decentralized, and smart systems will change the work they do, where they do it, how they do it, and for whom they do it.

The term *24/7/365* has long been used to describe a world where communications and commerce never stop. With the rise of mobile technology, globalization, and just-in-time production, there seemed to be no limit to what could be achieved at any given moment. However, the global pandemic forced us to reevaluate our relationship with time. The pressures brought on by COVID-19 challenged the notion that we can always be available and productive around the clock. The traditional 9-to-5 work model for many knowledge jobs is being questioned as remote work becomes more prevalent. More of us are also feeling enormous pressure to completely give up on the traditional concept of "weekday" and "weekend." As day and night converge, the 7 days of the week morph into one another, and our sense of boundaries where time is concerned becomes weakened. For many, the rhythm of the workweek is disappearing, and Friday has increasingly become a day to skip the office altogether. The idea of part-time and gig work being as acceptable as full-time and permanent work is working its way up the structural ladder.

Ultimately, time is melting much as it is in Dali's paintings. It is not unusual now to hear people wonder what day or time it is. Big chunks of our time-driven lives are fading along with an industrial era that no longer exists. But we must understand that all of this is part of a well-understood cycle of economic transition and transformation. To contextualize these monumental shifts in our experience of and relationship to time, let's rewind the clock and travel briefly back through history.

Transformations of the Economy

2008. This was a year that was defined, in many ways, by a major global recession. Housing prices increased, then fell, due to the subprime mortgage crisis. Banks went into crisis. The stock market plummeted, erasing wealth. The economy fluctuates and experiences ebbs and flows—whether predictable or not. But when you begin to peel back the layers and look more deeply at what happened, you can see that what we experienced was far more than just an economic recession. It was (and still is) a fundamental global economic transformation. The story here is the collapsing of the time frames that separate major transitions between economies, from thousands of years to decades. These transformations are brought about by the convergences of new technologies that create efficiencies in existing businesses, create whole new ones, replace work and workers, and open entirely new vistas. Economies are not replaced; they layer on top of each other. The goods and services of past economies are still important, but their manner of production, pricing, and delivery change considerably. When technologies become commoditized, businesses must find the next higher value proposition to court the consumer.

The year 2008 was also unique in that it was the first economic transformation to not reabsorb human labor back into the traditional workforce. Much of that was due to advancements in AI and automation. Anything that can be digitized can be outsourced for less or done by AI. As we saw then—and continue to see today—those jobs aren't coming back. And the idea that we can have the government step in, throw money at it, and bring them back is a deep part of believing that we can go back to how we operated in the past. That is magical thinking that doesn't serve us anymore. But for those who truly see it for what it is—a fundamental transformation—you can see the opportunities in the future. For those who struggle to see that, they will be stuck trying to fix something to bring it back to what was instead of what could be.

This brings us to where we are today. Another time of transformation—this time driven by the exponential changes occurring in and around AI. The future of AI isn't predetermined. It is molded by the decisions and actions we take today. As humans, we have the power to shape the course of AI development and its impact on our economy and our collective futures. AI can automate tasks, improve efficiency, and generate new opportunities. But it is up to us to ensure that these advancements are used responsibly and ethically. When it comes to predicting the exact role AI will play in our future job landscape, we must remember that we are still in the very early stages of this transition. Many job categories will undoubtedly be effectively eliminated . . . but this is not new. This is a central part of understanding the evolution of economies. The same thing happened previously as we moved from the agricultural economy to the industrial economy to the postindustrial economy to the knowledge/ information economy and so on. As part of this transformation, job loss will be a natural byproduct. As has been the case with every economic transformation. But so will job creation. As the cycle continues, new jobs—and careers—that we could hardly have imagined will be created, with those new jobs creating offshoots for other new jobs, and so on and so forth. Some of those jobs will stay and begin to define a new future. Others will be fleeting and serve as Band-Aid solutions for a world in transition. As it has been said: the future is not evenly distributed. Not everyone will reap gains in efficiency. We will need the foresight to determine which jobs will be the ones to have long-term value.

We are the first generation of humans going through this transition. We are the experimenters. We are the shapers. We will make mistakes. We will confront major challenges. We will innovate around them—then reiterate. We will envision new ideas just as quickly as we scrap them in favor of others.

We will navigate pain points. We will pilot new frontiers of imagination. We will both challenge the status quo as well as rely on it as a source of stability. And all of this will take time to sort out.

As the tectonic plates of change increasingly collide, we may feel as if we are swept up in a flurry of aftershocks. The speed of change has magnified the uncertainties, disruptions, and risks. It's also magnified the need to accurately identify first-order unintended consequences—let alone second- and third-order ones. But this is becoming more futile. Governing, regulatory, and commercial bodies will struggle not only to anticipate the ripples of vast change, but also to adapt. Regulation is uneven and different around the globe, meaning that the rapid spread of technology is spawning positive unintended consequences that are being rapidly commercialized without much foresight, and negative unintended consequences that have no chance of being contained. The unintended consequences of rapid change, and the reversals of knowledge we thought we had, are more quickly presenting unforeseen opportunities and hazards at a time when global geopolitics and governing bodies are in major flux. Who will manage—and be responsible for—the consequences of labor optimization and human displacement? Who is responsible if the AI-recommended course of action impairs organizational performance?

Yes, the future is uncertain. Yes, we are entering a new phase of human development. Yes, AI and its algorithms will be interwoven into many aspects of how we interact with each other and the world around us. Yes, AI will impact us. The way in which we work in, live in, and benefit from this new economy will be markedly different from the past. It is currently difficult for us to conceive of time as malleable, rather than linear and constant. But as the 21st century progresses, we will be faced with alterations in this dimension that challenge our business practices as well as our personal behavior and expectations. As we navigate this, it will be crucial for us to adapt and embrace the concept of time as something dynamic rather than fixed. The speed at which technology advances and societal expectations shift requires us to be agile and open to new ideas. In terms of business practices, this means reevaluating our strategies and approaches to keep up with the changing times.

Technologies will not only continue to leapfrog each other at a breathtaking pace, but technological discovery and development is also outpacing, in some ways, our understanding of it. Are we fast approaching an absolute zero point, where we will no longer be able to adapt and respond to major disruptive moments in time because they will simply be happening too quickly? Traditional models may no longer be effective in a world where everything moves at an accelerated pace. This is a world of *templosion*.

CHAPTER 5

A World of Templosion

Economists define a *luxury* in basic economic terms as something in extremely high demand but extremely short supply. So, if I were to put on my Richard Dawson hat (or Steve Harvey for you current watchers) and play a game of *Family Feud* and I asked you what the number one answer would be to the question "What in your life is in the highest of demand and shortest of supply?" what would you say? My guess is that you'd say "time." For many of us, the biggest luxury is *time*. (Sidenote: I have asked this question many times, and some of the answers are as varied as "closet space," "love," "money," and "sex"—problems I am definitely not interested in attempting to solve!) But for many of us, time is something in higher demand and shorter supply—and that supply seems to be getting smaller. Time is a valuable currency, and people feel like they simply don't have enough of it. We are all time-starved and repeatedly trying to find ways to control it, maximize it, and spend it. Time is the ultimate currency today. And in turn, time has become our greatest asset.

All of this is leading to a world of what we in our firm (The Future Hunters) call *templosion*. Templosion refers to the implosion of time. In simpler terms, it is the idea that the biggest of things and the biggest of events are happening in shorter and shorter periods of time. Everything from corporate lifespans to financial planning cycles to the way in which we communicate is becoming more abbreviated. What once may have taken years of research and development, strategizing, and planning is now being done in months. What once took months is now taking weeks. Time is being truncated. It is being compressed. And our experience of time is operating as if it were on steroids. It's continually in overdrive. Time has become a precious commodity.

Templosion is taking its toll everywhere. A study by McKinsey found that, on average, Fortune 1000 companies now have lifespans of 15 years and the tenure of CEOs is at most half of that time. Genetic engineering is delivering outcomes in laboratories that nature would take hundreds of thousands of years to accomplish. We see the rapid rise of the consequences of climate change: unprecedented wildfires, ocean degradation, animal extinctions, pandemics, climate refugees, floods, and droughts. The Arctic is fast becoming a shipping lane. The creation of living computers and robots is a fast-developing possibility, and gaining direct access to our brains is a rapidly emerging reality. The year 2020 will go down in history not just for the challenges brought on by the pandemic but also as a remarkable period that condensed nearly a decade's worth of technological advancements into a mere 12 months. TikTok picked up more users in 6 years than most social media apps that were around for twice as long. And then along came ChatGPT in 2023, which surpassed one million users in its first 5 days of launching, the fastest any company has ever reached this benchmark. It amassed 100 million monthly active users just 2 months after its initial launch.

To understand templosion's effect on us, let's look at three examples of how it is impacting the human experience.

EXAMPLE #1 | THE RISE OF THE NONLINEAR LIFE TRAJECTORY

Templosion is leading to the blurring of traditional life stages. One-size-fits-all approaches to learning, work, and family are now becoming less the norm and more the exception. Over 5 decades ago, our firm introduced the concept of the nonlinear life trajectory. Traditional life stages are becoming harder to define (e.g., older people moving in with their children; having multiple careers in one lifetime; going back to school as adults or seniors; delaying having children; "unretiring" and going back into the workforce; going in and out of marriages and families; etc.). Life is increasingly less likely to follow a linear path. This will only become more common as the average lifespan grows longer.

The modern life cycle—as segmented by educators, marketers, and parents alike—has come to include multiple phases of youth. One of these phases is adolescence, a life stage that marks the transition years between childhood and adulthood. But beginning in the early 2000s, we began to see a blending of these phases and an extension of youth into what we might have considered full adulthood. In 2006, we saw a tidal wave of demographic and technological forces that were rapidly altering the workforce and reshaping the boundaries of communication and entertainment. At that time, we said that adolescence may not only extend to age 30 and beyond, but also fundamental economic shifts were taking a toll on children's maturation. Fast-forward, and this trend has only magnified in scope and scale. Children seem to be getting "older" more quickly, and young adults seem to be remaining "children" longer. The proverbial "midlife" crisis is occurring more often, with people in their 50s experiencing a new form of adolescence. Traditional markers of development need to be rethought and redefined.

The longer people live, the longer their work lives become. Advances in human longevity and life extension have become major factors in the nonlinearity of careers. People are switching careers—and jobs—more frequently than ever before, often having multiple careers in a lifetime (sequentially or simultaneously). While employers may frown upon this, workers themselves embrace this as part of their reclamation of their own power, their own preferences and work-life balance. This is now rapidly becoming the baseline for the youngest generations in the workforce today. Job hopping to increase salary and skills early in a career is increasingly common.

Templosion is also creating a dynamic where just-out-of-college young workers are on a highly sped-up work trajectory and are fast-tracking their way to more senior roles; and slightly older workers (in some cases by only 10 years) are struggling to stay relevant and compete. For millennials, a generation raised to view every moment through the lens of productivity, hustle culture is rooted in a "time is money" philosophy. For Gen Z, those born in 1996 and later, the move away from a linear life path is partially reflective of their expectations that you can invent your own story and not wait until the end for rewards. It is entirely possible that in the interconnected world in which they now live, they will continue to move away from linear narratives in many aspects of their lives.

As children and youth, with their more malleable brains, develop in an increasingly networked world, it does not seem unreasonable to assume that they will be comfortable creating and functioning in a culture where nonlinear narratives are the norm. If young brains start out processing information in a nonlinear fashion, then it may be possible that growing up in a networked world will encourage the brain to stay with that sort of processing.

Individuals, lacking a norm or standard to compare themselves to at various times in their lives, will question if they are doing the right thing at the right time. In the workplace, boredom is likely to increase for those who can't stick with a linear narrative. The gamer generation will require the reframing of tasks in a way that inspires them and allays their boredom and disinterest. This will present a challenge for managers unable to adapt to the nonlinear approach. Schools, too, must make changes—the old methods of teaching do not reach, or prepare, students living in an increasingly web-structured world.

As the lines become increasingly blurred, absolute demarcations between populations and generations will no longer exist. Demographic variables will be harder to quantify as the defining lines become more nebulous. Tangible definitions of household, income level, age, gender, race and ethnicity, employment status, religious affiliation, location, educational attainment, mobility, and marital status will all be inadequate for an increasingly nonlinear world.

Templosion will also force us to confront retirement and retirement planning in completely new ways. The trend toward longer lifespans throughout the developed world has been strong for a long time, and many of our most fundamental structures and systems have not sufficiently adapted to the changes. The 2023 French pension reform strikes, for instance, were a series of nationwide protests in opposition to a proposed bill that would increase the retirement age from 62 to 64. The government argued that raising the retirement age is needed to keep the French pension system afloat amid an aging

(continued)

EXAMPLE #1 *(continued)*

population. Opponents see the reform as an erosion of France's social safety net. Clashes like this will likely continue throughout much of the developed world, particularly because the traditional framework around the three-stage life of school, work, and retirement will no longer suit an age of unprecedented longevity and constant fluctuations in work and health outcomes.

We must all learn how to become better at embracing nonlinearity, as the future will reward those who are willing to think beyond traditional boundaries and constraints.

EXAMPLE #2 | THE BESPOKE LIFE

Throughout the developed world, there have long been accepted or expected pathways through education, work and career, and family planning. And while there has always been some element of variability, much of that has been dictated by factors at least somewhat beyond individuals' control (e.g., socioeconomic variables). But one-size-fits-all approaches to learning, work, and family are now becoming less the norm and more the exception. We are now undergoing a fundamental paradigm shift toward what we might call *the bespoke life*, a major evolution of the nonlinear life trajectory.

Individuals throughout much of the developed world now have more choice than ever before when it comes to how they learn, where they are educated, whether they go to school at all, where they work, how they get their work done, when to start a family, how their family might look, and whether to start a family at all. People have an increasing ability to customize their life experience to be uniquely theirs—tailored for their needs and preferences. Some of this is structural, in that external obstacles have been removed, allowing people more flexibility in their major life choices. Some of it is cultural, in that there is greater acceptance of, and less judgment toward, what would once have been perceived as unconventional life choices. Some of this is entirely voluntary, in that people retain the full locus of control. In other cases, the recent circumstances of the pandemic thrusted new realities upon people. But the bottom line is that the proliferation of choice ultimately decreases the chance that any two individuals' life experiences will look the same.

The bespoke life will not be equally attainable for everyone. The term *bespoke*, as used commonly in marketing today, connotes a luxury value proposition. The bespoke life is becoming a real luxury for large segments of the population. And income and/or socioeconomic status may not always be the primary determinants. Others include factors as diverse as geography, career field, and personal beliefs. Bespoke lives will materialize in an environment where each person will truly be an individual from early childhood on. Marketers and employers alike will have to treat them as such—and communicate with them accordingly.

Inevitably, some sectors are not going to have as easy a time accommodating bespoke work arrangements. While some companies are tinkering with the idea of reengineering physical labor to be remote, many physical jobs still require people to do the work—and that won't necessarily change anytime soon. This remains a major distinction between physical workers and knowledge workers. Many firms in spaces like manufacturing, transportation and shipping, logistics, and construction are going to have to face a very public reckoning with their stakeholders—and soon—about whether to push harder to induce people to continue to work (through enhanced benefits, etc.) or to simply eliminate the need for people and invest more aggressively in automation strategies.

In the 80s and 90s, a series of kids' books called *Choose Your Own Adventure* took readers on fun journeys filled with decision points that shaped the outcome of the story. This unique interactive format allowed readers to experience multiple possible endings, adding an element of excitement and personalization to their reading experience. Fast-forward to more recent times, and we see this concept being explored in the popular Netflix series *Black Mirror*. In 2018, with its interactive episode *Bandersnatch*, viewers were given the power to make choices that directly impacted the narrative and led to different outcomes. What if we now apply that type of narrative structure across all consumption categories and life choices?

EXAMPLE #3 | REDEFINING GENERATIONS

Generations have long been grouped in birth year cohorts of 15–20 years. While generations, by their very definition, are chronological groupings, they are now seemingly refreshing every 2–3 years. Technology is changing so rapidly that kids only a few years apart struggle to have the same cultural and technological frames of reference. For instance, an "early" millennial born in 1981 (example of one: me) did not have social media in college, whereas someone born just a few years later did. This minor chronological difference becomes profound because of the access to technological tools that define and shape experiences, communication, socializing, networking, access to information, etc. Extending that even further, a millennial born in 1981 has virtually no defining characteristics in common with a "tail-end" millennial born in 1995—other than the fact that they may both be the children of baby boomers. That is where chronology alone falls short. And, so, we must look deeper to truly understand the defining characteristics of a "generation."

Most brand execs have been clued into millennials (Gen Y) for quite some time. But Gen Z has distinguished itself from millennials in some meaningful ways. This generation will not only change the landscape for marketers and

(continued)

EXAMPLE #3 (*continued*)

advertisers, but they will also define the future. Gen Z is loosely defined as those born between the mid-1990s and the early 2000s. And, while we would argue that this generation should be further segmented into 2–3 *microgenerations*, we will consider them as a whole for our purposes right now in this book. Gen Z is growing up in a much more globalized and borderless world. While their digital connections may limit their interactions with the "real" world, the physical boundaries of time and space are disappearing, too. Distance does not have the same meaning to them as it does to previous generations. They are more exposed to other geographies (including outer space), ethnicities, cultures, and languages. As such, the physical environment has less of an impact on the Gen Z psyche, and Gen Z social circles are not restricted by geography. This is, indeed, the first truly boundaryless generation, whereby traditional boundaries, be they geographic or sociocultural, are not recognized as strongly as previous generations.

A better way to define this generation might be through its relationship with technology. Today's youth are not just "digital natives." They have had a fully symbiotic relationship with the digital world from the moment they were born. Recall that the Internet as we know it was first commercialized in the mid-1990s when the first of this generation were born. By the time the tail end of this generation were born, smartphones and social media had already mass-proliferated into the mainstream. The symbiosis with technology will profoundly affect how they think, feel, learn, socialize, relate, consume, and work. Technology is interacting directly with their brains, minds, bodies, and sensory systems in ways that we are still trying to fully understand.

Each microgeneration will also have very different ways of leveraging and working alongside technological tools. They will also have divergent attitudes toward AI that will lead to deeper generational divides, particularly in the workplace.

The increasing focus on time will have broad-sweeping social effects, and the leveraging of time-related value propositions will dramatically alter the future landscape of the workplace. The optimization of time itself will likely be *the* single most important value proposition for any business, employee, and consumer in the future. It will create entirely new business efficiencies through the acceleration of disruptive technologies. But it will also be a clarion call for us to ask ourselves fundamental questions about future human relevancy. These questions include: How will humans be economically relevant in a world that is rapidly being disrupted by advanced technology? How will templosion alter the human experience and transform our values? Templosion is advancing unabated and exponentially faster.

CHAPTER 6

Turning Templosion into an Opportunity

A ll of this serves as a backdrop. It's the foundation of the house upon which AI sits. We are about to delve into the revolutionary aspects of AI and take a much deeper look at how it has begun to transform various industries—and how it's going beyond mere automation to representing a fundamental change in how we approach problem-solving, decision-making, and creativity. But before we go there, we must first embrace a new way of thinking about change.

Change management is an essential aspect of growth and development. In a future that demands a more agile and adaptable approach, organizations must be willing to challenge existing paradigms, experiment with new ideas, and embrace a mindset that welcomes continuous learning and improvement. By adopting a forward-thinking mentality, organizations will be better equipped to anticipate and respond to emerging trends, disruptions, and opportunities.

This becomes trickier in a world of templosion. As such, five operational imperatives emerge.

Imperative #1: Long-Term Thinking

There is a long-building epidemic of short-termism among the leadership ranks when it comes to both strategy and innovation. Symptoms include poor preparedness, insufficient risk modeling, and too much of a focus on immediate stakeholder returns instead of on a long-term plan of sustainable innovation that truly supports an organization's vision. The businesses set to win in the future will be those with the discipline to engage in truly long-term thinking.

For business leaders, it can't just be about the incremental wins. This type of shortsightedness isn't going to solve the big, pressing problems of the future.

(continued)

(continued)

Strategy cannot be decoupled from foresight. They must be inextricably linked. And for many companies today, foresight is absent from operational strategy.

If our descendants were to diagnose the ills of 21st century civilization, they would observe a dangerous short-termism: a collective failure to escape the present moment and look further ahead. CEOs prioritize short-term investor satisfaction over long-term prosperity. In populist politics, leaders are more focused on the next election and the desires of their base than the long-term health of the nation. We see this, too, in our collective failure to tackle long-term risks: climate change, pandemics, nuclear war, or antibiotic resistance. These risks make it increasingly important to extend our perspective beyond our own immediate focus. It's hard to overcome short-termism when the quickening of life, work, and information has further overloaded our attention.

Businesses will be forced to reengineer their entire operations, supply chains, and workforces to prevent future disruptions from putting them out of existence. Many leaders have not future-proofed their businesses properly. To illustrate this, many firms were completely hamstrung during the pandemic while trying to figure out how to maintain productivity among a distributed and virtual human workforce.

Imperative #2: Escape Velocity

Escape velocity can be defined as the speed required to escape the gravitational pull of a larger body. In today's terms, the "larger body" would be the old business environment and the old ways of doing things. That's why talk of an eventual return to the way things was is unrealistic. Instead of preserving our tried-and-true ways of doing things, we must adapt quickly, and in real time, to what will be an entirely new world. Are our organizations easily liberated from the slog of bureaucracy, marathon R&D protocols, and outdated thinking? Are our minds primed for the constant refreshing of ideas and knowledge? If not, we must diagnose and reengineer our innovative capabilities so that we are able to not only respond, but also thrive, in any future scenarios. How can we pivot supply chains on a dime? How can we speed up product innovations from concept to market in a fraction of the time and absorb failures as fast as we do successes? How do we empower leaders at all levels to move quickly and with confidence, and without always needing "permission?"

Does a key part of escape velocity mean starting over? Do we need to go back in some way to square one? Square one doesn't mean looking to the past. It means that enterprising businesses have a completely new canvas on which to experiment. While advances in our knowledge have been speeding up, so has our understanding of the limits of our knowledge. In some cases, new theories are questioning if everything we know or do is based on incorrect or misleading assumptions.

Imperative #3: Differentiation

Today, companies no longer can be bracketed into one specific, singular "industry." All are overlapping. How do we categorize a company like Amazon?

Is it in retail? Data analytics? Education? Entertainment? What about companies that operate within the automobile industry? Are they in manufacturing? High tech? Personal service? Information? In a world of templosion, every industry must become defined in new ways—as will every business within every industry. And every industry—and company within it—will become, in some way, a technology company. If not, it will become irrelevant. Differentiation will not only be key for competition, but also for survival. In that spirit . . .

Imperative #4: The "Special Sauce"

Leaders will need the discipline to avoid investing heavily in emerging technologies merely to participate in the land rush. This era of tech-fueled wins, particularly in the AI sector, could usher in more feverish competition—and, ultimately, consolidation—than we've ever seen. And the battle lines are likely to be drawn between larger companies (e.g., tech behemoths and other industry heavyweights) and nimbler start-ups. Larger incumbents will benefit from economies of scale, institutional knowledge, and deep pockets. But they'll be impeded by outdated existing tech infrastructure, unwieldiness, and elements of enterprise risk aversion or bureaucracy. Banks, as an example, continue to make huge investments in new technology. The reality, however, is that much of this investment will not translate into higher profits but rather into waste unless banks undertake a fundamental change in their approach to implementing new technology. Upstarts, by contrast, will benefit from agility and blank-canvas tech infrastructure. Inevitably, many physical product companies—and those involved in the distribution of physical products—may well take this opportunity to make the leap into becoming either hybrid or pure-tech plays, similar to how firms like IBM in previous economies made the leap from selling things like hardware to selling business and information services.

But the real dilemma facing most large enterprises now is whether to keep investing in technology that is in constant flux and becoming outdated at a faster clip or to invest in reimagining who and what they want to become, so they can figure out which set(s) of technologies would work best to help get them there.

So, the "special sauce" is this: firms possessing the right mix of foresight, resources, and timing will reap the spoils, while others will be left behind. Agility is key.

Imperative #5: Vision vs. Strategy

In our work as a firm, leaders will often ask: How can I/we articulate, define, and roadmap our internal strategies to capitalize on where the future is moving? What we tell them is this: Keep your strategies nimble and flexible.

(continued)

(continued)

Do not be tethered to one set of strategies. View them instead as a set of parallel railroad tracks. Have one track for your short-term strategies (1–2 years); have another track for your medium-term strategies (3–5 years); and have another track for your long-term strategies (5–8 years and beyond). Each strategy track must be built to be adaptable. You must be able to jump on and off each, refine it, abandon what doesn't work, and rebuild it. Then what becomes your north star is vision, not strategy. It will be important to hold to a timeless vision and be willing to quickly adopt and then scrap even the biggest of strategies. The life cycle of strategies will be constantly foreshortened, while the bigness of the vision can keep both an individual and an organization from succumbing to templosion. So, define who you are and what you stand for, and then reverse engineer the strategies with which to get you there.

Case in point: Kodak. As a Rochester, NY native, this is an example near and dear to my heart. Rochester felt this powerfully during the late 1990s when Kodak really began to struggle. (The "f word" in Rochester might still be Fujifilm!) Kodak is the ultimate cautionary tale when it comes to vision vs. strategy. Why? Because Kodak held its strategies so closely to the vest and lost sight of what they could have owned in the marketplace and what they stood for. A lack of foresight—and vision—was their failure. Kodak focused on protecting its existing business strategies rather than embracing new technologies. Kodak designed the digital camera and should have owned it and the business models around it. But what they suffered from was myopia. The same is true of Sony. They should have created the iPod, but they protected their technologies, while Apple saw the emerging opportunities.

Businesses must constantly innovate and find unique ways to stand out from the crowd. So, too, must individuals. Those who fail to recognize the importance of time and remain stuck in old ways of thinking will struggle for relevance. That is why these five imperatives should be viewed as tools in the tool kit. They are not mutually exclusive nor are they one-offs, meaning they must be viewed as ongoing internal disciplines.

The future, too, will be less about fixing old or broken systems and institutions and more about completely reimagining new ones. One of the biggest challenges we face over the coming years is battling angst and pessimism, and enthusiastically championing innovation that makes sense. The transformation from yesterday into tomorrow is never simple or straightforward. Ingenuity is most necessary in times of great challenge, and what we must focus on is how to extract and apply that ingenuity so that many phoenixes can rise out of it. And organizations will struggle with effective ways to create true value and differentiation in an already very crowded marketplace. One of our firms' mottos is: "There is no such thing as overcapacity, only under-imagination." Those able to harness the power of imagination will be among the winners in this new world. Because time, like energy, is becoming a precious resource, and no entity in the future will have the luxury of wasting it.

PART III

Technology: Artificial Intelligence

We have now set the stage by: (1) contextualizing the pace of change; (2) shifting our mindsets and starting to see the future through new eyes; (3) framing the transformation of the global economy; and (4) understanding the compression of time. In Part III, we will discuss how these forces are working together to catapult us into a period of our history marked by the acceleration of AI.

CHAPTER 7

The Acceleration of AI

The exponential rate of technological change is making it so that each technology builds on others to create new ways of collecting and mining information, accumulating financial data, changing the nature of work, connecting various constituents with each other, establishing global interconnectedness, and making instantaneous decisions. One of the lasting impacts of COVID was that it accelerated many previously developing trends. This includes the move to more distributed, hybridized, and flexible workforces. Ultimately, one of the most impactful trends to consider here is how the circumstances of the last few years have accelerated the reality that AI will both displace and augment large sectors and subsectors of human labor. Before we delve into that, let's look at how AI has evolved . . . and where it is going.

Half a billion years ago, life on earth experienced a short period of extremely rapid diversification known as the *Cambrian explosion*. This remarkable event was a mere snapshot when numerous new species emerged within a relatively brief span of time. Another Cambrian explosion might be upon us again: this time it is human-made. An AI Cambrian explosion looms as a disruptive economic force. Progress in the capabilities of AI systems is driven by advancements in computing power, data, and algorithms—and all three are accelerating. While exact figures are difficult to project, PwC's Global Artificial Intelligence Study puts the potential contribution to the global economy by 2030 from AI at $15.7 trillion USD. Of this, $6.6 trillion is likely to come from increased productivity. Its research also shows that the greatest economic gains from AI will be in China (26 percent boost to GDP in 2030) and North America (14.5 percent boost), equivalent to a total of $10.7 trillion and accounting for almost 70 percent of the global economic impact.[1] Morgan Stanley's Global Investment Office sees AI as one of the most important investment themes of the next decade.[2]

AI, smart systems, robotics, sensors, and the rise of deep learning and the neural net will be responsible for automating and displacing an increasing number of global human workers in the future—a trend we refer to as *other*sourcing. This is causing a lot of societal anxiety as people worry that

AI will take their jobs. Much of this comes down to economic concerns. A September 2023 Gallup survey finds that Americans overwhelmingly believe AI will be a job-killer, and an American Psychological Association survey finds that nearly two in five American workers are worried that AI is coming for their personal job duties.[3]

But we must remember this: we've been here before. Historically, the emergence of general-purpose technologies like the electric motor, electric steam engine, and personal computer led to shifts in the labor market. These advancements not only automated certain tasks but also created new job opportunities and increased overall output. Similarly, AI could revolutionize industries by automating repetitive and mundane tasks. In 1930, the prominent British economist John Maynard Keynes had warned that we were "being afflicted with a new disease" called *technological unemployment*. Labor-saving advances, he wrote, were "outrunning the pace at which we can find new uses for labor." New machinery was transforming factories and farms. To make sense of these transformations, Karl T. Compton, the president of MIT from 1930 to 1948 and one of the leading scientists of the day, wrote in 1938 about the "Bogey of Technological Unemployment." His essay on the impact of technical progress on jobs continues to resonate. The concerns raised then are still relevant now, highlighting the ongoing debate surrounding the future of work amid technological advancements.[4]

The Russian Nesting Dolls of AI

Before we delve further into the impacts of AI, we must first define it— and decouple basic AI from its various subsets. To simplify the relationship between AI, machine learning (ML), the neural net, and deep learning (DL), a helpful visual is the Matryoshka (Russian) nesting dolls. Each is essentially a component of the prior term. In other words, machine learning is a subfield of AI. Deep learning is a subfield of machine learning. And think of neural networks as the backbone of deep learning algorithms. We'll start with the largest doll (AI), work our way inward to the midsize doll (ML), and then the smallest doll (DL).

The pursuit of defining machine-driven intelligence began more than three quarters of a century ago. The 1930s to the early 1950s saw the development of the Turing machine and the Turing test, which were fundamental in the early history of AI. The official birth of AI was in the mid-1950s, with the emergence of the field of computer science and the creation of machine learning.[5] The Dartmouth Summer Research Project on Artificial Intelligence was a 1956 workshop considered by many to be the founding event of AI as a distinct field.[6]

Fast-forward to current day and simply put, AI can be defined as "a set of computational tools to address tasks traditionally requiring human sophistication." Through our online transactions, through our smartphones, through how we interact with consumer technology products . . . we are already living in an age of AI. We just don't think of it that way. But making the best use of such technologies takes time and experimentation.

Continuing with the analogy, let's move inward to the next two dolls, machine learning and deep learning. In contrast to AI, ML and DL are learning technologies that are designed to replace repetitive and error-prone processes.[7] According to IBM, ML focuses on the use of data and algorithms to imitate the way that humans learn, gradually improving its accuracy. Classical, or *non-deep*, machine learning is more dependent on human intervention to learn.[8] When exposed to data, machine learning algorithms have the extraordinary ability to modify gradually, much like how a baby first learns to crawl and then eventually begins to take its first steps and then walks. Another core aspect of machine learning is large language models (LLMs)—machine learning models that can comprehend and generate human language text. They work by analyzing massive datasets of language to understand existing content and generate original content.

Moving another doll inward, DL is most closely associated with the functions of the human brain. Oracle describes deep learning as "artificial neural networks—algorithms modeled to work like the human brain— that learn from large amounts of data." Neural networks are trained using massive amounts of data. The result is a deep learning model that, once trained, processes new data. Deep learning models take in information from multiple data sources and analyze that data in real time, without the need for human intervention.[9]

Deep learning has several use cases in automotive, aerospace, manufacturing, electronics, medical research, and other fields. Amazon Web Services (AWS) groups these various use cases of DL into four broad categories: computer vision, speech recognition, natural language processing (NLP), and recommendation engines.[10]

AWS outlines four examples of how deep learning is and/or can be applied:

- Self-driving cars using DL models to automatically detect road signs and pedestrians
- Defense systems using DL to automatically flag areas of interest in satellite images
- Medical image analysis using DL to automatically detect cancer cells for medical diagnosis
- Factories using DL applications to automatically detect when people or objects are within an unsafe distance of machines

Most people may not even realize that they encounter DL technology every day when they browse the Internet or use their mobile phones. When we watch a video on YouTube and see accurate captions automatically generated in real time, or when we speak to our smart speakers and they flawlessly understand our commands—that's all thanks to the advancements in DL algorithms. Facial recognition is another application of DL that has gained widespread use—whether it's unlocking our smartphones with a simple glance or enhancing security systems by identifying individuals in real time. DL has also greatly improved the accuracy and efficiency of speech recognition systems. AI has already beat humans at numerous tasks, including handwriting recognition, speech recognition, image recognition, language translation, reading comprehension, language understanding, common sense completion, solving mathematical problems, code generation, etc.[11]

Now, thanks to AI-powered speech recognition technology integrated into our smartphones and smart speakers, we can much more effortlessly interact with our devices using natural language. Natural language processing (NLP) combines computational linguistics, ML, and DL models to process human language. AWS defines it as "a machine learning technology that gives computers the ability to interpret, manipulate, and comprehend human language."

One of the ways NLP may have the most impact is through the rising need for personalized learning platforms. The global NLP market for education is likely to jump from $101.5 million USD in 2023 to $545 million USD by 2033.[12] The demand for digital education is skyrocketing. With the advent of AI and advancements in technology, learning experiences are changing, and NLP is central to this. NLP enables computers to understand human language patterns and context, allowing for more effective communication between learners and educational resources.

The nesting doll analogy serves to set the backdrop for much of the recent buzz around generative AI and help contextualize where we are in AI's evolutionary process. Generative AI is built around vast, complex algorithms trained on reams of text, images, sound files, and other data. It is a type of AI that can create new content and ideas, including conversations, stories, images, and videos. This allows generative AI to interpret instructions in natural language and respond with text, art, or music. GenAI has become possible because of advancements in deep learning techniques—the fourth doll. It should be noted that generative AI as a concept is not brand-new. It was introduced in the 1960s in chatbots. It was not until 2014, with the introduction of generative adversarial networks (GANs)—a type of machine learning algorithm—that generative AI could create more convincing and authentic images, videos, and audio.[13] One of the key advancements is the development of transformer-based architectures like OpenAI's GPT series. These models are pretrained on massive amounts of text data, which allows generative AI models to understand and generate human-like text.[14] This brings us to where we are today. Another Cambrian explosion for the digital age.

Notes

[1] https://www.pwc.com/gx/en/issues/data-and-analytics/publications/artificial-intelligence-study.html

[2] https://www.morganstanley.com/articles/ai-investing-opportunities?ET_MID=noloc&ET_MID=nomsai

[3] https://www.apa.org/pubs/reports/work-in-america/2023-work-america-ai-monitoring

[4] https://www.technologyreview.com/2024/01/27/1087041/technological-unemployment-elon-musk-jobs-ai

[5] https://www.holloway.com/g/making-things-think/sections/a-brief-history-of-ai

[6] https://en.wikipedia.org/wiki/Dartmouth_workshop

[7] https://www.softserveinc.com/en-us/blog/deep-and-machine-learning

[8] https://www.ibm.com/topics/machine-learning

[9] https://www.oracle.com/artificial-intelligence/machine-learning/what-is-deep-learning

[10] https://aws.amazon.com/what-is/deep-learning

[11] https://www.zmescience.com/science/news-science/ai-can-now-outperform-humans-in-5-key-cognitive-ways

[12] https://www.globenewswire.com/news-release/2023/11/27/2786302/0/en/NLP-in-Education-Market-Set-for-Exponential-Growth-Anticipating-a-CAGR-of-18-3-and-Surpassing-US-545-0-Million-by-2033-Future-Market-Insights-Inc.html

[13] https://www.techtarget.com/searchenterpriseai/definition/generative-AI

[14] https://elearningindustry.com/role-of-generative-ai-in-natural-language-processing

CHAPTER 8

Generative AI's Inflection Point

One key difference with more recent innovations such as generative AI is that they diffuse much faster than previous disruptive tech. This is templosion at play—the collapsing of time horizons from centuries to decades to years to months to weeks. AI's productivity curve may also be faster. Research by Stanford's Erik Brynjolfsson, University of Pennsylvania's Daniel Rock, and Booth's Chad Syverson identifies a *productivity J-curve* in past eras of technological change—in other words, a time in which productivity lulled and was followed by a period of acceleration. The researchers note that start-up funding for AI increased from $500 million in 2010 to $4.2 billion by 2016. Then, in the first half of 2023 alone, AI-related start-ups raised $25 billion.[1] Because of this, it's not giving us a lot of time to respond. The rapid growth of AI can be concerning to many, including business leaders and economists, because gradual and incremental, rather than fast, adoption of AI across all sectors is preferable. It allows society at large time to catch up, to update its knowledge, to capture attitudes towards different scenarios, and to understand its implications.

Generative AI very quickly captured the public's imagination. Not many technologies have been unveiled to such fanfare. The AI chatbot ChatGPT, created by OpenAI, drew 1 million users after only a few days of its unveiling in November 2023, making it one of the fastest product launches in history. ChatGPT portends a near future when rapidly advancing AI could well revolutionize business, culture, and society. OpenAI opened the doors to its ChatGPT chatbot app store in January 2024 to much excitement and initial chaos. It's already considered the Wild West, prompting questions as to whether the whole concept will succeed in the long term.

The rise of it should not be surprising, necessarily. But on the business side, the hyperbole is very real, although questions remain as to whether it is warranted. To many, this represents a generational business opportunity and full-fledged paradigm shift. McKinsey hailed 2023 as GenAI's "breakout year" and estimates that it will rapidly grow to a $3 trillion industry in the next several years.[2] Bloomberg Intelligence has different projections, however, reporting that, with the influx of consumer generative AI programs like Google's Bard and OpenAI's ChatGPT, the generative AI market will grow to $1.3 trillion over the next 10 years from a market size of just $40 billion in 2022.[3] Similar to the statistics in Chapter 7, "The Acceleration of AI," on the projected growth of the entire AI market, exact figures are hard to pinpoint. Opinions vary, and projections are all over the place, even among the most sophisticated analysts. But they all have one thing in common. They are all varying degrees of bullish on AI as a major growth market.

The rise of AI chatbots has also sparked discussions among experts about the impact on search engines like Google. Some believe that, in the near future, these advanced chatbots have the capability to reinvent or even replace traditional search engines. With their ability to understand and respond to user queries in a conversational manner, AI chatbots are altering the way people interact with information online. This shift could theoretically impact how we seek out and access information, posing both challenges and opportunities for various industries. Microsoft, eyeing Google's search profits, invested $10 billion USD in OpenAI. Chinese search giant Baidu will launch its own AI-boosted search capability. Alphabet, Google's parent, also unveiled its own chatbot, Bard, and invested $300 million in generative AI start-up Anthropic.[4] In early December 2023, Google began updating its Bard AI chatbot with a new AI model called Gemini that provides expanded text-based chat capabilities. With Gemini, Google is pushing the boundaries of AI technology by training it on digital images and sounds, making it what some would consider to be a truly "multimodal" system. This advancement opens new possibilities for AI to analyze and respond to not just text but also visual and auditory inputs. In terms of jobs and economics, the integration of multimodal AI like Gemini could alter industries that heavily rely on visual or auditory data. For example, in sectors such as design, entertainment, and marketing, where images and sounds play a crucial role, having AI that can understand and respond to these mediums can lead to more efficient workflows and innovative solutions.[5]

Tech companies are continuing to add GenAI abilities into programs and devices of all kinds, from search engines to smartphones. AI tools are becoming more accessible—and powerful—than ever before and can imitate the human mind to an impressive degree. Amecas, new humanoid robots, are being trained to recognize faces and decide who is paying attention during conversations.[6] A breakthrough technique known as *imitation learning* trains neural networks to perform tasks by watching humans do them. In this case, it was an AI bot that watched 70,000 hours of Minecraft.[7] In 2022, Meta built an AI that could beat humans at an online version of Diplomacy, a popular strategy game. AI can also accurately clone human voices. It's even attempting to bring the dead back to life as well as allow people to design their own eternal digital entities. And DALL-E AI allows you to create digital images simply by describing what you want to see.

This swell of activity is happening just as many investors, burned by the crypto crash and metaverse disappointment, are looking for the next big thing. In 2023, investors poured nearly $10 billion into generative AI start-ups, more than double the $4.4 billion invested the year before, according to GlobalData.[8] But some investors, CEOs, and engineers see signs of froth that remind them of the crypto boom. Company leaders continue to make broad-based claims about the power of AI. Investors keep biting, and the stocks keep rising. And yet, AIs' true value—as well as its path to profitability—is still unclear. As the AI industry's market value skyrockets, it evokes memories of the dot-com bubble from the late 1990s. Experts caution that this rapid growth in AI is reminiscent of a gold rush, with an abundance of opportunities and risks alike.[9]

Executives are hurrying to show how they will be among the first beneficiaries of AI. Analysis of their regulatory filings, however, suggests much of it is only talk. AI's economic impact will be subdued unless millions of companies beyond tech centers like Silicon Valley adopt it and integrate it into their long-term strategic planning. "The diffusion of technological improvements," argues Nancy Stokey of the University of Chicago, "is arguably as critical as innovation for long-run growth."[10]

The generative AI models behind ChatGPT and its rivals are already changing how the tech industry thinks about innovation and its engines (read: the corporate research labs that combine Big Tech's processing power with the brains of the top computer scientists). These competing labs are engaged in a race for AI supremacy.[11] Major tech companies are jockeying for position when it comes to the development of today's most cutting-edge technologies. Those who come out ahead stand to gain considerable influence in the lives of millions, if not billions, of consumers. Amazon, Google, IBM, and Microsoft (among others) are competing in a platform war to become the go-to company for AI. This is prompting pressure inside tech giants to move faster.

Separating Hype from Reality

To really understand generative AI's true impact, we must separate out hype from reality. While the potential for AI to revolutionize various industries is undeniable, it's crucial to distinguish between the hype surrounding AI capabilities and its actual application in economic contexts. Many are quick to tout the benefits of generative AI. But AI is a tool, not a magic solution that can instantly transform an organization's fortunes. It must be approached with a balanced perspective that acknowledges both its capabilities and limitations, including the fact that AI is a complement to human intelligence rather than a replacement for it.

One of AI's biggest limitations is its ability to perpetuate biases, a challenge that is particularly evident in AI chatbots. While these chatbots are designed to interact with users in a conversational manner, they can inadvertently reflect biases present in the data they were trained on. Some AI ethicists fear that Big Tech's rush to market could expose billions of people to numerous harms—such as sharing inaccurate information, generating fake photos, or giving students the ability to cheat on school tests—before trust and safety experts have been able to study the risks.

These biases can manifest in various forms, from expressing opinions sourced from the Internet as verified facts to incorporating societal prejudices into their responses. When millions of people are exposed to biases through billions of interactions facilitated by AI, will it have the capacity to reshape humanity's perspectives and beliefs? As AI algorithms process vast amounts of data and make decisions based on patterns, they inadvertently reflect the biases present in the data they were trained on. This phenomenon raises questions about how AI may perpetuate or even amplify existing societal biases and reinforce stereotypes.[12]

The companies touting new chat-based AI systems are running a massive global experiment. Lately, for instance, companies that make chatbots have been raising money at an alarming rate. What remains uncertain, despite the funding frenzy, is whether any of these chatbots will even attract users—let alone consumers who want to pay for them. Money is flooding into them and being thrown around in what many consider to be an overly inflated bubble. There is no long-term strategy. Part of the challenge with AI chatbots is that they can also have biases not immediately apparent to users. They can express opinions gleaned from the Internet as if they were verified facts. **Dictionary.com** selected the AI term *hallucinate* as its word of the year, describing what happens when AI produces false information—or basically when it just makes stuff up and spews nonsense. The term describes the inaccurate and often bizarre outputs that chatbots and other prompt-based AI programs try to present as fact.[13] And not only can these algorithms "hallucinate," but their performance can also worsen over time, a phenomenon known as *AI aging*.

All of this, including the issue of algorithmic bias, will grow in magnitude as AI gains rudimentary forms of "consciousness." DeepMind, as an example, has been working toward creating artificial machines that can think, learn, and possibly even solve humanity's most intractable problems. Its AI can solve tasks it has never seen before as fast and as precisely as humans.[14] Vectara, a company founded by former Google employees, is exploring the accuracy of chatbots in providing information. It is looking to understand how often chatbots may deviate from the truth (in other words, lie) when interacting with users. The company's research estimates that even when circumstances are designed to keep it from happening, chatbots still "invent information" at least 3 percent of the time—and as high as 27 percent. And because these chatbots can respond in a limitless number of ways, there is no clear way to conclusively figure out how often they hallucinate."[15]

Perhaps we should begin to think about AI as being akin to constructing a three-dimensional building. Just like in physical construction, the sturdiness of the foundation is central to the longevity and efficiency of the structure. And the sturdier the foundation, the better in the long run. But if the foundation itself is riddled with cracks, then it does not matter how sturdy the upper floors are. When the foundation is compromised, so is the entire structure. Any weaknesses or vulnerabilities in the foundational layers can jeopardize the entire structure. Just as a building with a flawed foundation is at risk of collapse, an AI system built on shaky ground may lead to errors, biases, or inefficiencies down the line. By fortifying the foundational layers of AI systems, we can ensure their resilience and effectiveness in delivering accurate results and valuable insights. But this is easier said than done and may likely not be a practical reality. At least not any time soon.

The business, and subsequent profit, opportunities may be so alluring that we get to a point of no return far too quickly with this technology. And there is real debate taking place right now within the AI community about this very issue. OpenAI CEO Sam Altman wrote that "we think showing these tools to the world early, while still somewhat broken, is critical if we are going to have sufficient input and repeated efforts to get it right."[16] DeepMind CEO Demis Hassabis, however, warned about his growing concern that AI is now "on the cusp" of being able to make tools that could be severely damaging to human civilization, and he implores competitors to move forward with more caution.[17] But once we fully apply this technology to areas like Internet search and content creation, will we have crossed the Rubicon? AI could well permeate almost everything online, and it can do so without user consent or knowledge. Think of today's ubiquitous advertising or recommendation algorithms, but on steroids—far more intelligent and applied to almost every type of online activity. The only people "immune" from this would be the shrinking population of people globally who are below the digital divide or who have made a concerted effort to opt out and be "off the grid."

Templosion as a Limiting Factor?

Most people working in AI don't expect progress to slow down any time soon. The rapid advancement of AI technology is driving companies to invest more in computing power to train their AI systems. This is leading to a surge in the capabilities of AI applications, making them more sophisticated and powerful than ever before. As companies strive to stay ahead in the competitive landscape, they are willing to allocate larger budgets towards training their AI systems. This trend is expected to continue as the demand for AI-driven solutions grows across various industries.

With the decreasing cost of computing power, too, companies are finding it more cost-effective to invest in training their AI systems. This efficiency in computing costs allows businesses to scale up their AI initiatives without breaking the bank.[18] But this comes at a time when some researchers predict that AI developers could run out of high-quality language data by 2026. The recent explosion in the amount of data used to train AI systems has overtaken the production of new text data on the Internet.[19] Could running out of usable data be the one thing that ultimately slows down AI's development?

A recent study by the IBM Institute for Business Value revealed that 64 percent of CEOs are under pressure from investors, creditors, and lenders to accelerate the adoption of generative AI. However, 60 percent of these CEOs have not yet established a cohesive strategy for integrating generative AI across their organizations.[20] A major limiting factor in AI reaching its full business potential, however, is the availability of individuals with the right skills and capabilities to continue innovating around AI.

Another limiting factor when it comes to the enterprise adoption of AI may also be *time*. Yes, today's fertile business environment provides a generational opportunity for firms to invest in emerging technologies that are rapidly becoming pillars of the economy. But, at the same time, generative AI has experienced such rapid growth, many businesses remain tentative about rushing to implement it. While companies may outwardly acknowledge their commitment to AI adoption, many still ultimately don't do it. They are left scrambling to figure out the delicate balance between the competitive advantages that can come from moving quickly and being an industry leader against the risk of moving *too* quickly. [21]

Productivity is highly sought after in traditional economic models. Getting more output from any input is prized and often seen as the most (if not only) valid measure of progress. But when it is pursued too vigorously over time, it can lead to its own undoing.

Implications go beyond the enterprise-wide adoption of AI. As the world charges ahead, large numbers of people may feel left out. The exponential advance toward digitizing the entire world is creating more billionaires everywhere, from venture capitalists to TikTok stars, causing the middle classes to shrink further by comparison. The near future promises an even faster and larger whirlwind of advancing digitization, leaving the world that is currently understood by the masses even further behind.

Notes

1 https://www.chicagobooth.edu/review/ai-is-going-disrupt-labor-market-it-doesnt-have-destroy-it

2 https://www.mckinsey.com/capabilities/quantumblack/our-insights/the-state-of-ai-in-2023-generative-ais-breakout-year

3 https://www.bloomberg.com/company/press/generative-ai-to-become-a-1-3-trillion-market-by-2032-research-finds

4 https://www.economist.com/business/2023/02/08/is-googles-20-year-search-dominance-about-to-end

5 https://www.nytimes.com/2023/12/06/technology/google-ai-bard-chatbot-gemini.html

6 https://www.economist.com/science-and-technology/2022/11/07/humanoid-robots-are-getting-close-to-reality

7 https://www.technologyreview.com/2022/11/25/1063707/ai-minecraft-video-unlock-next-big-thing-openai-imitation-learning

8 https://www.cnet.com/tech/computing/ai-and-you-ai-startups-keep-winning-investors-ray-ban-glasses-see-what-youre-up-to

9 https://futurism.com/ai-dot-com-bubble

10 https://www.economist.com/finance-and-economics/2023/07/16/your-employer-is-probably-unprepared-for-artificial-intelligence

11 https://www.economist.com/business/2023/01/30/the-race-of-the-ai-labs-heats-up

12 https://www.wsj.com/articles/chat-gpt-open-ai-we-are-tech-guinea-pigs-647d827b

13 https://thehill.com/homenews/nexstar_media_wire/4355523-dictionary-com-chooses-hallucinate-as-2023s-word-of-the-year-why

14 https://time.com/6246119/demis-hassabis-deepmind-interview

15 https://www.nytimes.com/2023/11/06/technology/chatbots-hallucination-rates.html

16 https://www.wsj.com/articles/chat-gpt-open-ai-we-are-tech-guinea-pigs-647d827b

17 https://time.com/6246119/demis-hassabis-deepmind-interview

18 https://time.com/6300942/ai-progress-charts

19 https://techxplore.com/news/2023-11-ai.html

20 https://www.ibm.com/thought-leadership/institute-business-value/en-us/report/enterprise-generative-ai

21 https://www.wsj.com/articles/generative-ai-isnt-ubiquitous-in-the-business-worldat-least-not-yet-07c07f01?mod=tech_lead_pos5&mc_cid=ff2b73961d&mc_eid=10057e199f

CHAPTER 9

The Evolving Work Landscape

learly, we must address the elephant in the room: the potential for job displacement and AI's impact on work as we know it. The integration of AI technology into various industries has sparked a debate about what it will portend for the future of work. The International Monetary Fund (IMF) warned that nearly 40 percent of jobs across the globe could be affected by the rise of AI. In advanced economies, it estimates that approximately 60 percent of jobs may be impacted by AI.[1]

This leaves many people nervously wondering if the rapid advances in automation and digital technology will eliminate many people's livelihoods. For many observers, going back to the period beginning in 2005–2008, the narrative around AI and work was almost solely focused on the disruption of manual labor. This includes many of the jobs typically considered "blue-collar" (e.g., assembly line and factory workers, manufacturers, stock clerks, etc.). The emergence, for example, of self-service kiosks in fast-food restaurants and automated processes in factories has raised concerns over the effect on jobs.

We are currently facing a landscape where long-term employment is waning, relationships between employers and employees are more transient, and there seems to be little to ease mounting fears among the working class. There is an increasing trend towards temporary contracts and insecure work across the world, and stagnant wages are commonplace. There will be more part-time assignments, independent contracting, peer-to-peer work, and self-employment as traditional jobs are disrupted, and in some cases, disappear.

There is a growing concern, too, that certain segments of the population may be left behind. Research from the National Bureau of Economic Research (NBER) states that automation technology has been the primary driver of U.S. income inequality over the past 40 years. The report estimates that, over the last four decades, between 50 and 70 percent of fluctuations in the U.S. wage structure are based on the comparative wage declines of workers specializing in routine tasks in industries undergoing rapid automation."[2] But with the acceleration of AI and related technologies, this divide may be becoming even more pronounced.

Adapting to the tide of automation will continue to be an uphill battle, and most countries—let alone professions—are not fully prepared to address the challenge. Many of today's most alarming headlines reflect concerns over whether a specific occupation could be automated but do not consider whether it *will* be. Despite fears of humans losing out to machines, there are plenty of recent cases where people have worked with machines and, in the process, become more productive and more skilled. The developers of industrial robots, for instance, have made significant strides in ensuring the safety of human workers by implementing advanced technologies such as AI. These robots can now recognize humans nearby and operate in a way that minimizes any potential risks to their human counterparts. Traditionally, industrial robots required highly trained programmers to set their tasks and, once installed, were rarely moved. Now, a lighter-weight, transportable plug-and-play generation of robots is collaborating with human workers.

The Widening Economic Chasm

The IMF's development of an AI Preparedness Index marks a step toward measuring countries' readiness for the increasing integration of AI. By assessing the preparedness of 125 countries through this index, the findings clearly indicate a trend where wealthier economies, particularly advanced and some emerging market economies, are better positioned to embrace AI compared to low-income countries. This discrepancy underscores the importance of economic resources in driving technological advancements and innovation.[3]

But the growing concern that these advancements could widen the gap between rich and poor countries is a very real one. The transfer of investment to advanced economies where automation is more established poses a risk of leaving developing nations behind in terms of economic development. One key factor contributing to this inequality is the concentration of wealth among those who possess and/or control these advancing technologies. Ownership over AI systems can provide economic advantages for individuals or organizations that can effectively harness their power. This can lead to greater profits, market dominance, and ultimately further accumulation of wealth. And as automation replaces certain jobs traditionally held by humans, there is a risk that many individuals may find themselves unemployed or struggling to adjust to new roles.

In wealthy countries, the rapid advancement of automation is poised to revolutionize the job market, reconfiguring roles rather than eliminating them entirely. This shift is expected to result in a significant disparity in income and opportunities.[4] The countries that have made substantial progress in adopting AI technologies may likely experience a more profound transformation within their job landscape—a trend that could exacerbate existing inequalities within these economies as those with skills aligned with AI-related industries thrive while others face difficulties in finding meaningful employment opportunities.

The Widening Workforce Chasm

For nearly the past 15 years, it can be argued that, on one end of the spectrum, portions of the human labor force have worked in substandard jobs and dealt with substandard working conditions. They, in many cases, have been viewed as cogs in the global work machine. Technology is also making it easier for companies to maintain tight control on workers and squeeze them to maximize profits. This has implications for the loss of workers' privacy and autonomy. On the other end of the spectrum, workers in the United States and other parts of the developed world have been increasingly rising up, asserting their autonomy and questioning outdated and unfair work norms in what may well be the beginnings of a workers' renaissance. Those forces represent a powerful and growing workforce chasm. But the fact remains that the majority of currently employed people will stay in the workforce, occupying a vast "middle" that, like the center of a stretched rope, will continue to be impacted by the tension exerted from both extremities. To some extent, new jobs and careers will emerge to accommodate the societal and technological shifts we're seeing. But, for everyone else working in more conventional jobs, the ripple effects of all of this will be just as profound.

For sectors ranging from retail to shipping to education to health care, a very Darwinian paradigm emerges here. Some job functions simply *cannot* be enhanced, improved, or evolved beyond what they currently are. Enterprises that have not hedged these macro-forces appropriately, including those that have developed an overreliance on human labor, may well get caught flat-footed and have difficulty sustaining their operations. On the other hand, those that have better prepared for the contingency of an automated future will be better suited to streamline operations and thrive in this changing competitive environment.

For those firms that do continue to rely largely on human labor, there will be ever-growing scrutiny on workplace practices. This workers' reckoning demands that firms conduct regular audits of long-espoused principles of corporate "culture," including accountability, transparency, fairness, and inclusion. It also demands that employers reevaluate the more quantifiably measurable aspects of work, including compensation, benefits, and expectations of input (e.g., hours and location of work). In the next couple of decades, traditionally hierarchical businesses may be considered dinosaurs.

Some Jobs Are Going Away . . .

Understandably, concerns about job displacement and technological unemployment have become more prevalent. Some fear an era in which computer scientists and software engineers essentially invent us out of work, and the total number of jobs declines steadily and permanently. Goldman Sachs estimates that two-thirds of all current jobs could be "exposed to some degree of AI automation" in the coming years, while a report from Pew Research Center puts the figure at closer to one-fifth.[5] The World Economic Forum's Future of Jobs Report states that 25 percent of jobs will be negatively impacted over the next 5 years, with around 26 million jobs in administrative positions being eliminated.

There are also growing—and very real—concerns that workers in lower-wage occupations are most vulnerable to being replaced by AI-driven automation. The integration of AI in industries traditionally reliant on manual labor has long raised questions about job displacement and the future of work.

The narrative of the "robot revolution" has long focused on the threat to manual, repetitive tasks performed by blue-collar workers. This displacement has been underway for a long time, as robotics have steadily proven to be more efficient and cost-effective in many areas. (But this is far from being a complete picture of what is happening. In Chapter 13, "From AI to IA: Intelligence Augmentation," we will delve into how these jobs are becoming augmented—rather than solely displaced—by AI.) However, as AI continues to advance, it is becoming increasingly capable of tackling the cognitive, knowledge-based work traditionally associated with white-collar professions. Contrary to popular belief, the rise of AI may actually displace more white-collar jobs than blue-collar ones.

White-collar jobs were once considered immune to the rising tide of automation. But this is no longer the case. AI systems are emerging as accountants, hiring managers, investment bankers, financial analysts, doctors, lawyers, insurance brokers, traders, scientific theorists . . . and the list goes on. In many instances, some of these job areas may not be completely displaced but technology may play a major role in altering the nature of jobs for many of these professionals. We can easily envision a near future where positions like paralegals and lower-level financial analysts are rendered almost fully obsolete. That may come to include a whole slew of other capabilities whose susceptibility to AI we are only just beginning to explore and understand.

There are also widespread fears that AI could disrupt many jobs in the entertainment industry. "For many in entertainment, the dramatic leap in quality between AI video a year ago and AI video today was an earth-shattering realization that progress is exponential, rather than linear. The news that Tyler Perry halted an $800 million (USD) studio expansion after seeing Sora, OpenAI's text-to-video model, has people revisiting the AI concerns from recent WGA (Writers Guild of America) and SAG (Screen Actors Guild) strikes and wondering if the era of generative video is already here. It also underscores, in general, that how we discuss change makes a huge difference in how it's internalized in the broader cultural narrative," said Sarah Unger, founder and COO/President of CULTIQUE, a cultural insights and strategy firm, in a recent conversation.

But Most Jobs Are Not Going Away— They Are Changing

More realistically, we must get comfortable with the fact that most jobs are not going away—they are simply *changing*.

If generative AI lives up to its hype—and that's a big *if*—the workforce, primarily in the United States and Europe, may be flipped on its head. Worker displacement from automation has historically been a concern. History has shown us examples such as construction and mobile telephony, where technological advancements effectively eliminated certain roles like telephone and elevator operators. But, as history has also shown us, the emergence of new jobs and occupations following technological innovations plays a crucial role in long-term employment growth. AI is no exception to this trend. AI could impact the workforce by significantly reducing labor costs, creating new job opportunities, and increasing efficiency for non-displaced workers. At least that's the hope.

This convergence of benefits could lead to a productivity boom that could boost economic growth. Predicting the exact timing of such a boom, however, remains a challenge due to the dynamic nature of AI advancements and their impact on various industries.[6] For companies, there could be (and some think will be) cost savings thanks to AI. As a result of these efficiencies and strategic advantages offered by AI, experts predict that global GDP could increase by up to 7 percent annually as businesses harness the power of AI to drive growth and innovation.[7]

In 2020, the World Economic Forum predicted that by 2025, 85 million jobs across the globe could be displaced due to a division of labor between

Enhancement vs. Replacement **47**

humans and machines—but 97 million new roles may emerge. Its 2023 report notes that the integration of agriculture technologies, digital platforms, e-commerce, and AI is poised to bring about a significant transformation in the labor market. While this shift may lead to job displacement in certain sectors, it is also expected to generate new opportunities and spur job growth elsewhere. In the coming decade, we may be on the brink of a sizable workplace shift as automation technologies, particularly AI, change aspects of how we work. It is projected that 20–30 percent of the time spent by workers on their job responsibilities could be redesigned. This will not only streamline processes but also necessitate a reevaluation of the skills required for success in various industries.[8]

It is also fascinating to note that approximately 60 percent of jobs in the United States today didn't even exist in 1940. This statistic highlights the dynamic nature of our economy and how it continuously adapts to technological advancements.[9] As we look toward the future, the jobs that will be in high demand—and increasingly, created—will be those that are more personalized, one-off, and one-of-a-kind. These jobs require more people skilled in critical thinking, unique problem-solving, interpersonal relations, and specialization that is more localized and individualized—skills that are not as easy to measure or hire for. There will also be a resurgence in certain types of work that have been devalued in recent decades throughout much of the developed world (e.g., mechanics, carpenters, welders, and plumbers)—since these types of services will always be in demand and are not as easily automated. Jobs that we do not economically value as much today, like home health attendants, may come to be considered precious human jobs in the future.

Quantifying the change in jobs, however, is a bit trickier. New AI tools could alter the way workers perform and learn, but little is currently known about their impact on the actual job itself. Plus, it is not easy to accurately measure the direct impact on labor and productivity. Reliable statistics are still hard to come by. In a recent NBER paper, the impact of generative AI tools on job productivity was evaluated, particularly in the context of customer support agents. The study revealed that access to AI tools led to a 14 percent increase in productivity across the board. What's even more striking is that novice and low-skilled workers experienced a 34 percent improvement in their performance.[10] But when you look under the hood, it was found that high performers *underperformed* when using the AI tool.

Enhancement vs. Replacement

While there's been plenty of talk about how AI may threaten jobs, there's no real indication that business leaders are planning on using it to automate knowledge jobs at any kind of scale, according to Deloitte's 15th annual Tech Trends report (2023). AI is more commonly seen as a tool to enhance human capabilities rather than replace them. In a recent survey of industry leaders, Deloitte found that the primary motivations for deploying generative AI in content creation were to improve content quality, gain a competitive edge, and scale employee expertise. Surprisingly, reducing head count ranked as one of the lowest priorities for organizations leveraging AI in their operations.

It is becoming increasingly evident that AI technology may be able to liberate workers from mundane, repetitive tasks, allowing them to channel their efforts toward more creative and strategic aspects of their roles. Because it's less about automating jobs in their entirety and more about automating tasks.

The banking industry, as one example, is undergoing a substantial shift with the integration of AI. Financial institutions like JPMorgan Chase are leveraging AI to enhance customer service and streamline operations. By utilizing generative AI-powered chatbots, banks can provide more intuitive and human-like interactions with customers in real time. Nordic bank DNB is another example. In 2022, the company began allowing its employees to use conversational AI-driven virtual assistants, one of which, called Juno, helped the bank's customer service departments handle approximately 1,200 users daily.[11]

The rise of emotional AI is another area that is being enhanced, particularly as we increasingly defer to chatbots to help us monitor and define our emotional experiences. More retailers, for instance, are leveraging consumer-facing AI bots that can recognize the feelings of the people they are interacting with and use that to guide their responses. And some customer service representatives are receiving real-time coaching from emotionally intelligent software that detects problems in a conversation. Emotional robots are becoming more common everywhere from hospitals to schools to restaurants to stores to nursing homes to cars. More doctors and therapists are utilizing AI to suggest empathetic responses to patients requiring care or emotional support. The AI assesses patient conversations and recommends thoughtful answers for the provider to pick from.[12]

Even with the possibility of enhancement, many workers are still figuring out what exactly AI can and cannot do, and how it can better assist them in their roles. Referred to as the "jagged technological frontier," AI excels in some tasks but falls short in others.[13] Workers will not only need to adopt this more pragmatic approach, but they will also need more clarity around which of their day-to-day tasks could be performed by AI in an effective and straightforward way and which tasks would need a different approach.

The Intergenerational Workforce Challenge

When we talk about AI enhancement, we must apply a generational lens to this because it's not always experienced uniformly. According to a 2023 Salesforce survey, the generational divide in the United States is stark, with 70 percent of Gen Z already embracing new AI capabilities, compared to just 32 percent of Gen X and boomer respondents. Nonusers tend to be older and more cautious around new technology. Sixty-eight percent of nonusers are Gen X or baby boomers, and almost nine out of 10 nonusers don't see how generative AI will directly impact their life.[14]

But is this too simplified a view? Older generations, historically, tend not to jump into technological trends as much as younger ones. Young people often engage to a far greater degree with emerging digital technologies. And, yet, while their understanding of, and sophistication level with, these technologies might be greater, the adverse and direct impacts of these technologies on them (e.g., the physiological manipulation of the brain's reward centers) are also disproportionately greater.

Let's look more practically, too, at the composition of today's multigenerational workforce. More generations will be working alongside one another than at any point in history. Increasingly, many aging workers are delaying retirement—either as a function of financial necessity and/or boredom, because today's retirement horizon can theoretically last an impractical 30–40 years. As more baby boomers put off retirement, millennials, and Gen Xers are finding it harder to move up into higher-level jobs. Boomers bring knowledge and experience, and many companies are trying to coax them into staying. Yet, by many measures, their prevalence in the labor force is holding back economic productivity. And that is likely because of their reluctance to adopt new technologies. Many older people feel continuously overwhelmed by the need to adapt to new technologies that have user interfaces that were not designed with them in mind. Organizations that solve this going forward will be viewed as better places to work, and thus will be more sustainable in the long term.

This intergenerational flash point will only grow more profound with the aging of the population, particularly in the developed world. Global life expectancy at birth has been steadily increasing for a long time. It has more than doubled in the last two centuries. Increasing lifespans, coupled with declining birth rates, have had a major demographic impact in many places, including Western Europe, North America, and Japan—and will very soon be the reality for China as well. Older generations are also more vital than ever before—and that is because life is generally being extended in the *middle* of life, versus at the very end of life.

Employers of all sizes and in every industry are increasingly going to be tasked with managing a workforce composed of more generations than ever before. This will entail managing very different work styles, different work ethics, and potentially divergent attitudes toward technology. Balancing recruitment and retention of young, high-potential talent with the institutional knowledge and wisdom of experienced veterans will be an important and very delicate dance.

The War for AI Talent

As much as certain jobs are changing, this comes at a time, too, when the tech industry's largest companies are continuing to cut jobs. It's no secret that Big Tech companies are investing heavily in AI, funneling billions of dollars into research and development with the aim of creating systems that could theoretically be worth trillions in the future. The industry is trying to come to terms with how to reconcile the almost feverish workforce expansion that took place during the pandemic while also moving swiftly to build AI.

McKinsey's report on Technology Trends Outlook 2023 analyzed 3.5 million job postings and revealed that skills related to AI are among those in greatest demand but have significantly fewer qualified professionals available per posting. More employers, too, are recognizing the importance of hiring for skills and competencies rather than traditional credentials. One key aspect that companies are focusing on is recruiting from overlooked populations such as rural workers and people with disabilities. These groups often possess unique talents and perspectives that can bring diversity and innovation to the workplace.[15] In 2023, there were 180,000 job postings in the United States related to AI, such as roles in software development, semiconductor engineering, and cloud computing, according to CompTIA.[16]

As such, the war for qualified AI talent is heating up. The demand for professionals skilled in generative AI is at an all-time high, leading companies to go to great lengths to secure these workers. Tech companies are going all out to attract top talent in the field of generative AI, offering irresistible compensation packages and accelerated stock-vesting schedules. The need for sales professionals with a deep understanding of AI is growing exponentially, too. Those equipped with the right skill set to sell AI solutions are commanding salaries that far surpass those in traditional enterprise software sales roles.[17]

The war for AI talent is also extending beyond national borders. The talent imbalance between the United States and China, for instance, has been developing for more than a decade. The United States has long been a hub for top talent from China, and many Chinese researchers have historically chosen to finish their doctoral degrees at American universities, with a significant portion opting to stay in the United States post-graduation. However, recent research indicates a shifting trend, with an increasing number of Chinese talents deciding to remain in China after completing their studies. This shift is notable in the field of AI, where China has been investing heavily to foster innovation and attract skilled professionals back to their home country. As China strengthens its position as a global leader in AI, it poses a compelling challenge to the United States' traditional dominance in this space. The competition for AI talent between these two powerhouse nations is intensifying, shaping the future landscape of technological advancement and innovation on a global scale. While the United States still leads in the aspects of AI that are behind chatbots like ChatGPT, research indicates that China, by certain measures, has surpassed the States in nurturing the scientists and researchers who are shaping the future of AI technologies.[18]

AI, Copyright + Intellectual Property (IP)

Over the years, technology has automated many routine jobs in entertainment, but the creative work at the heart of the business has been protected. No longer. Generative AI is scooping up copyrighted work and churning out remixed literature, music, and video of all varieties, increasingly competing with humans in quality and already far outpacing them in quantity. Generative AI is revolutionizing content creation, granting access to capabilities that were previously limited to a select few with advanced skills and technology. CNET has been utilizing, under the radar, the help of "automation technology"—their term for AI—on a slew of financial articles.[19] Similarly, BuzzFeed announced that its content will soon be written with the help of OpenAI.[20] And as of mid-February 2023, there were over 200 ebooks in Amazon's Kindle store listing ChatGPT as an author or coauthor—a number that is rising every day.[21] But what about the rights of those who have contributed to its development? What about the creators of the underlying content and intellectual property (IP)? Copyright laws exist to protect original works from unauthorized use or reproduction, ensuring that creators are rightfully acknowledged and rewarded for their contributions. Those lines are becoming harder to define and enforce.

Thousands of books from esteemed Australian authors have been pirated by the U.S.-based Books3 dataset for training generative AI models used by companies like Meta and Bloomberg. This raises questions about intellectual property rights and the responsible use of AI.[22] In December 2023, the *New York Times* sued OpenAI and Microsoft over copyright infringement. The newspaper claimed that OpenAI, the creator of ChatGPT, used its content without authorization to train the chatbot. Writers, comedians, and artists have filed complaints against OpenAI, saying its models unlawfully used their material without approval.[23] Getty, an image licensing service, filed a lawsuit against the creators of Stable Diffusion, a text-to-image deep learning model, claiming the improper use of its photos. Getty said its creators violated copyright and trademark rights it has in its watermarked photograph collection. The legal system, in each of these cases, is being tasked with clarifying the boundaries of what should or should not be considered a "derivative work" under IP laws. The answer isn't clear-cut because in the United States, for instance, depending upon the jurisdiction, different federal circuit courts may react with different interpretations.[24]

At the heart of this is the fair use doctrine in IP law, which allows creators to build upon copyrighted work. But there is currently no legal precedent in the United States, nor is there a decisive answer as to whether this constitutes an AI copyright infringement or whether it's fair use. The lawsuits posing these legal dilemmas are in the early stages of litigation. Getting answers may take a decade. And by then, the technology will have already more than leapfrogged where it is now. (As we've seen in the social media and cryptocurrency spaces, for instance, regulation, legislation, and litigation are all several years behind the pace of technological change.) How the legal landscape unfolds could shape the nascent yet heavily capitalized AI industry. Competition in AI may come down to data haves and have-nots. Companies with the rights to massive amounts of data (e.g., Adobe, Bloomberg), or that have collected their own data (e.g., Meta, Microsoft), have started developing their own AI tools. Established companies have the advantage of resources and experience when it comes to securing data licensing agreements and navigating legal challenges in the AI landscape.

On the other hand, start-ups with limited capital may face hurdles in obtaining the data they need to leverage AI effectively. Accessing high-quality datasets can be costly, and without strong financial backing, start-ups may struggle to compete with larger companies that have already established partnerships for data acquisition.[25]

Incentives and Strategic Alignment

The focus increasingly is not about replacing humans but rather empowering them with tools that amplify their productivity, knowledge, and creativity. AI algorithms and platforms can be great equalizers and help level the playing field between workers in a particular domain. This approach is vital in driving innovation within enterprises. But generative AI needs to be viewed as more than just a shiny new object. Businesses looking to stay ahead of the competition must consider leveraging generative AI's unique capabilities to drive innovation and solve current challenges. They must seek to answer *why* they are investing in and developing this technology, and how they are aligning the incentives accordingly.

A factor in establishing an intelligent ecosystem is the clear articulation of the specific business value that an AI system should deliver. AI initiatives must be aligned with the objectives of the organization to ensure that these initiatives contribute meaningfully to longer-term success. Offering incentives for embracing AI technologies can further motivate teams to actively participate in driving AI success and creating tangible value.

By ensuring that AI projects are directly tied to strategic priorities, leaders can better maximize the impact of these technologies. Paying attention to how incentives play a role in driving AI adoption and success within their organizations will also be vital. Much of this also comes down to creating an internal culture that rewards innovation, experimentation, and collaboration.

We must remember, too, that the specific application(s) of generative AI will vary. Solutions are not—and will never be—one-size-fits-all. Strategies will have to fit the more important overall organizational vision, and they will change over time. Strategies must also find how to make these systems adaptable, how to build a culture of innovation, and how to create real value.

Notes

[1] https://www.cnbc.com/2024/01/15/imf-warns-ai-to-hit-almost-40percent-of-global-employment-worsen-inequality.html

[2] Acemoglu, D. & Restrepo, P. (September 2022). "Tasks, automation, and the rise in U.S. wage inequality," *Econometrica, Journal of the Econometric Society*, 90(5), pp. 1973–2016.

[3] https://www.imf.org/en/Blogs/Articles/2020/12/02/blog-how-artificial-intelligence-could-widen-the-gap-between-rich-and-poor-nations

[4] https://foreignpolicy.com/2018/07/11/learning-to-work-with-robots-automation-ai-labor

[5] https://www.pewresearch.org/social-trends/2023/07/26/which-u-s-workers-are-more-exposed-to-ai-on-their-jobs

[6] Briggs, J. & Kodnani, D. (March 26, 2003) *The potentially large effects of artificial intelligence on economic growth.* Available at: **https://www.gspublishing.com/content/research/en/reports/2023/03/27/d64e052b-0f6e-45d7-967b-d7be35fabd16.html** (Accessed 17 May 2024).

[7] https://www.forbes.com/sites/jackkelly/2023/03/31/goldman-sachs-predicts-300-million-jobs-will-be-lost-or-degraded-by-artificial-intelligence/?sh=4ec8c480782b

[8] https://www.mckinsey.com/capabilities/mckinsey-digital/our-insights/the-top-trends-in-tech#tech-talent-dynamics

[9] https://www.wsj.com/articles/ignore-the-hysteria-on-ai-and-jobs-chatgpt-automation-workforce-tech-innovation-51b3d994
[10] https://www.nber.org/papers/w31161
[11] https://www.pymnts.com/news/artificial-intelligence/2023/gen-ai-transforms-bank-chatbots-financial-advisors
[12] https://www.wsj.com/articles/dr-chatgpt-physicians-are-sending-patients-advice-using-ai-945cf60b?mod=article_inline
[13] https://mitsloan.mit.edu/ideas-made-to-matter/how-generative-ai-can-boost-highly-skilled-workers-productivity
[14] https://www.forbes.com/sites/johnkoetsier/2023/09/09/generative-ai-generation-gap-70-of-gen-z-use-it-while-gen-x-boomers-dont-get-it/?sh=20a601cc23b6
[15] https://www.mckinsey.com/mgi/our-research/generative-ai-and-the-future-of-work-in-america
[16] https://www.nytimes.com/2024/02/05/technology/why-is-big-tech-still-cutting-jobs.html?mc_cid=693de1a900&mc_eid=10057e199f
[17] https://www.wsj.com/tech/ai/the-fight-for-ai-talent-pay-million-dollar-packages-and-buy-whole-teams-c370de2b?mod=tech_lead_pos1&mc_cid=eff9304591&mc_eid=10057e199f
[18] https://www.nytimes.com/2024/03/22/technology/china-ai-talent.html?mc_cid=29af97fb08&mc_eid=10057e199f
[19] https://futurism.com/the-byte/cnet-publishing-articles-by-ai
[20] https://futurism.com/the-byte/buzzfeed-announces-openai-content
[21] https://www.reuters.com/technology/chatgpt-launches-boom-ai-written-e-books-amazon-2023-02-21
[22] https://www.theguardian.com/australia-news/2023/sep/28/australian-books-training-ai-books3-stolen-pirated
[23] https://www.npr.org/2023/12/27/1221821750/new-york-times-sues-chatgpt-openai-microsoft-for-copyright-infringement
[24] https://hbr.org/2023/04/generative-ai-has-an-intellectual-property-problem?registration=success
[25] https://www.nytimes.com/2023/12/30/business/media/copyright-law-ai-media.html

CHAPTER 10

Risks in Generative AI: Data Inbreeding

Reinforcing the growing generative AI economy is human-made data. AI models are trained on all kinds of data, which has set off a hunt by tech companies for even more data to feed their AI systems.[1] AI builders are endlessly hungry to feed their models more data—but that data is increasingly loaded with synthetic content. Generative models are not only trained on real data sourced from the real world (known as *natural data*), they are now also being trained with data that has been manufactured by other generative models. When synthetic content is fed back into a synthetic generative AI model, something called *data inbreeding* occurs. This is leading to data outputs that are much more convoluted.[2]

In mythology, an ouroboros is a serpent-like creature that consumes its own tail in a never-ending loop. That is what may happen with generative AI—generative models are increasingly consuming the outputs from other generative models. Data inbreeding is prone to the same mutations as when genetic inbreeding occurs. And just like in any biological entity, inbreeding can cause the code to malfunction and lead to the distortion of its outputs. A question we all need to ask is: will generative AI's data inbreeding ultimately end up being its Achilles' heel?

More companies are starting to investigate what is known as *synthetic data* to train their large language models (LLMs). The veracity and dependability of AI-generated data could easily be questioned given that even AIs trained on human-generated content can be prone to making major factual mistakes. And could this infinite AI feedback loop generate what researchers refer to as "irreversible defects"?[3]

Data inbreeding will continue to pose threats, particularly as a large proportion of people paid to train AI models may be themselves outsourcing that work to AI. The Swiss Federal Institute of Technology estimated that between 33 and 46 percent of these data workers had used AI models like ChatGPT. That may likely grow as these systems become more powerful and easily accessible.

Using AI-generated data to train AI models can be a double-edged sword. While it can offer the promise of scalability and efficiency, there is a risk of introducing errors into already error-prone models. LLMs are known to often present incorrect information as fact, and if these wrong outputs are used to train other AI models, the errors can be absorbed and multiply over time. Triangulating the origins of the output—human or synthetic—will grow to become more difficult.[4]

This continuous "self-eating" loop could eventually make AI outputs functionally useless. Researchers at the University of Oxford uncovered a fascinating insight into the hypothetical consequences of AI models training on outputs from other AIs. Their simulation revealed a concerning outcome: should AI models be trained in this way, they could evolve to become profoundly biased and simplistic. It also became detached from reality. The study found that the model could not tell whether the AI-generated text it saw corresponded to reality, which could create even more misinformation than current models."[5] OpenAI's GPT LLM also seems to be getting less and less smart. In other words: dumb. Researchers at Stanford and Berkeley discovered that over a time of a few months, both GPT-3.5 and GPT-4 altered their behavior, with the accurateness of their responses appearing to decrease.[6] Will subsequent updates be able to correct for this? It may be too early to tell.

Not only are some of these systems getting dumber, but they are becoming more biased, too. Many tech companies have assumed (rightly or wrongly) that training AI on more and more datasets could help fix the continuing problem of AIs reproducing human biases and prejudices. But a study by the Mozilla Foundation found that AIs trained on progressively larger datasets can create even more racist outputs. Many companies are failing to conduct basic quality checks, leading to the propagation of harmful biases in AI systems. Companies like Google and OpenAI often train their AIs on closed datasets, inaccessible for public scrutiny.[7]

The unchecked proliferation of generative models could have unintended consequences. And there are two very real emerging risks. The first risk is *model collapse*—the tendency for AI models to become more detached from genuine human patterns when trained on their own recursive and cyclical outputs. The second uncovers *source bias*—the preference of today's neural networks to highly rank LLM-produced text over human-written text with equivalent relevance. Because human text contains more nuance and complexity, it makes it harder for AIs to fully capture the semantics.

These two phenomena stress how AI, if left to generate freely, runs the very real risk of optimizing the creation of an artificial reality. And this artificial reality may be one that caters to its own capabilities rather than serving inclusive human needs. If ignored, we could face a future where machine-generated content reigns supreme, human creativity is devalued, and diversity gives way to AI's limited projections.[8] Recently, "poisoned AI" went rogue during training. Once that happened, efforts to teach it to behave again failed—sometimes even backfiring by teaching the AI to identify its triggers and better disguise its harmful behavior from the researchers.[9]

The Importance of Data Integrity

What rises to importance is data integrity. Data integrity is about maintaining the accuracy, reliability, consistency, and context of data . . . throughout its entire life cycle. Maintaining the integrity of data is key for businesses to make informed decisions, gain a competitive edge, and insulate against reputational damage. In addition to preserving the integrity of existing data, AI can also contribute to proactive measures for preventing breaches or unauthorized access. Through predictive analytics and anomaly detection techniques, AI systems can identify an array of vulnerabilities or risks before they become major issues. But if that data is unknowingly faulty and trained on more and more synthetic outputs, maintaining access to the original human-generated data source becomes more critical. Avoiding the old tech trope of "garbage in, garbage out" will take on greater meaning.

The global economy has become a perpetual motion machine of data. And data is the fuel that drives the generative AI engine. But what if that fuel is causing AI to choke on its own exhaust? Publishers, media companies, and other providers of information—nervous about having their valuable content scraped by AI companies—could keep more of their content off the Internet completely or behind paywalls.[10] Or will the flood of AI-generated content add a particular premium to any content that is human-crafted?[11]

Who within an organization will be responsible for managing and mitigating the risks? Those in leadership are competing for one of today's buzziest new job titles: Head of AI. But the parameters of the Head of AI job—and even AI itself—aren't very clear. Many are uncertain as to what that stewardship means in practice and who exactly should become the new stewards. Currently about a quarter of Fortune 2000 companies have dedicated AI leadership at the VP level or above.[12] Issues of data inbreeding, however, go beyond most current titles and functions. It will open public and private entities alike to a series of risk and reputational management issues. These issues will grow in scope and magnitude. Do these vulnerabilities reside within the function of the Chief Risk Officer? The CIO? Unpredictable and unknown challenges and risks will require new thinking, new operational approaches, new leadership, new risk protocols, and new hiring/talent management strategies. Not to mention the monumental liability and cybersecurity issues a world of inbred data could create. If the political arena is threatened by believable misinformation, it is not alone.

The private sector is equally threatened. If fraud is magnified by inbreeding, and provided as truth to governance structures like boards of directors, who will be liable for catastrophic outcomes?

Must We All Become "Prompt Engineers?"

Some companies are starting to hire "AI prompt engineers" to help include the right references, hints, and keywords that can guide the AI towards the desired outcome.[13] For the companies that make generative AI tools, this refers to the task of training them to deliver more precise and relevant responses to the queries people pose. PromptBase, for instance, is an online marketplace where freelancers sell prompts intended to get the best results from language model chatbots like ChatGPT and image-generating AIs like DALL-E. There are more than 15,000 prompt engineers registered on PromptBase.[14] Anthropic, an AI start-up founded by former members of OpenAI, advertised a prompt engineer job with a salary of $375K a year.

For most of us, though, it refers to the art and science of perfecting the prompts we feed AIs to get the best answers. Do we all have to get better at asking the questions that will be fed into generative AI systems? I know, for me, it can seem complicated (and frustrating) because you try to figure out what magical string of words can be put together to give you the best possible output. But often, that desired output has nothing to do with the input you thought you provided to the system. So, yes, in some ways, what you get out of generative AI depends on what you ask it and on how you craft your question. Let's be real, though: this is often easier said than done. Does this then, in and of itself, indicate that current AI models are not truly intelligent if they are reliant on humans for their desired output? Are we better off thinking of these systems then as "artificial smart?" Maybe; maybe not, as doubt is increasingly being cast on whether a human is even needed for the prompting in the first place.

Research suggests that prompt engineering may be done the best by the model itself, not by a human engineer. The increasing capabilities of AI have led to suspicions that a substantial portion of prompt engineering jobs may be viewed as a passing fad in their current form. The speed and accuracy with which AI systems can generate content have raised questions about the necessity of traditional prompt engineering practices. People have found, for example, that asking models to describe their step-by-step rationale enhanced their performance on a series of math and logic questions. But we must remember, too, that language models really are just that: models.[15] That doesn't mean, however, that humans won't be in some way needed. Even if automated prompting becomes more standard practice, prompt engineering jobs will likely continue to exist in some form. More new roles may not only be created around "question crafting," but where humans will be most needed is in the deciphering and analysis of the output.

Notes

[1] https://www.nytimes.com/2023/07/15/technology/artificial-intelligence-models-chat-data.html

[2] https://futurism.com/ai-trained-ai-generated-data-interview

[3] https://futurism.com/the-byte/ai-synthetic-data

[4] https://www.technologyreview.com/2023/06/22/1075405/the-people-paid-to-train-ai-are-outsourcing-their-work-to-ai

[5] https://www.newscientist.com/article/2378706-ais-will-become-useless-if-they-keep-learning-from-other-ais

[6] https://futurism.com/the-byte/stanford-chatgpt-getting-dumber

[7] https://www.newscientist.com/article/2381644-using-bigger-ai-training-data-sets-may-produce-more-racist-results

[8] https://ai.plainenglish.io/when-ai-distorts-its-own-reality-the-dual-threats-of-model-collapse-and-source-bias-13e4da42fd10

[9] https://www.livescience.com/technology/artificial-intelligence/legitimately-scary-anthropic-ai-poisoned-rogue-evil-couldnt-be-taught-how-to-behave-again

[10] https://www.raywang.org/blog/2023-08/mondays-musings-will-generative-ai-drive-humanity-dark-ages-knowledge

[11] https://www.axios.com/2023/08/28/ai-content-flood-model-collapse

[12] https://www.vox.com/technology/2023/7/19/23799255/head-of-ai-leadership-jobs

[13] https://www.newscientist.com/article/2388071-what-is-an-ai-prompt-engineer-and-does-every-company-need-one

[14] https://www.cbsnews.com/news/artificial-intelligence-ai-chatgpt-dall-e-promptbase-prompt-engineer

[15] https://spectrum.ieee.org/prompt-engineering-is-dead

CHAPTER 11

The Sustainability Paradox

Many experts generally see AI as a positive development, with the United Nations Environment Program lauding it as a tool that "could improve our understanding of our environmental impact and the effects of climate change." Research by PwC UK, commissioned by Microsoft, modeled the economic impact of AI to manage the environment across four sectors: energy, agriculture, transportation, and water. One of the key applications of AI is in creating clean distributed energy grids. By optimizing energy distribution and consumption, AI helps reduce waste and increase efficiency, leading to a more sustainable energy system. Sustainable supply chains are another area where AI is making a difference. By analyzing data from various sources, AI can help companies track and optimize their supply chains to minimize waste and reduce carbon footprint. AI is also being used for environmental monitoring to track changes in ecosystems, wildlife populations, and air quality. Enhanced weather and disaster prediction powered by AI algorithms have improved early warning systems for natural disasters like hurricanes, earthquakes, and wildfires. The report estimates that leveraging AI for environmental applications could add up to $5.2 trillion USD to the global economy in 2030.[1]

But for every way AI could contribute to sustainability efforts, more experts are raising concerns about the environmental costs of AI. Using a powerful AI model to make an image uses as much energy as fully charging your smartphone. (Generating text, however, is much less energy intensive.) A University of Massachusetts Amherst study found that the emissions from training just a single AI model can be as high as 626,000 pounds of CO_2—about five times the emissions of an average American car over its lifetime.[2] According to a 2020 report by the European Commission, by 2030, data centers are estimated to account for 3.2 percent of electricity demand within the EU.

The extent of AI's own carbon footprint, however, is quite difficult to measure as AI companies are not fully, if at all, transparent about just how much energy is used. Researchers are merely guessing based on available data. Aside from requiring tremendous amounts of energy, supercomputers use massive amounts of water. And the water used to prevent data centers from overheating mostly evaporates, which means it cannot be reused.[3]

In 2022, Meta revealed that it was building what it considered to be the world's fastest supercomputer, called the AI Research SuperCluster (RSC). But, it would not disclose where it was located or how it was being powered. Now, more industry experts and researchers are warning that AI's unrestricted growth could come at a monumental environmental cost as the adoption of AI skyrockets. Stanford University's AI Index Report 2023 stated that the environmental impact of training AI models is unprecedented. This may have a disproportionate effect on already marginalized populations in the developing world. There are plans to construct and expand data centers in many developing countries, including some already facing water scarcity such as Ghana, Nigeria, Kenya, Peru, Uruguay, Chile, and countries in the Middle East and North Africa. Uruguay, for example, is suffering its worst drought in 74 years.[4]

There are some potential solutions on the horizon. An underwater data center that harnesses the ocean's natural cooling ability is being built near China's Hainan Island in the South China Sea. Keeping computers cool can decrease power usage and carbon emissions, and this project could herald the start of other projects around the world that put supercomputers and data farms underwater.[5] Microsoft's Project Natick is another attempt to address the cooling challenge by submerging a sealed data center underwater. This uses the ambient sea temperature for cooling. Of course, these proposed solutions lead to another environmental concern: the impact of having data centers in the ocean ecosystem.

Reputations will be on the line as organizations will need to be more vocal about the AI sustainability paradox—perhaps even making it an aspect of ESG (environmental, social, and governance) and CSR (corporate social responsibility) initiatives moving forward. More companies may look to hire "Carbon Accountants," a new job title that helps leaders comprehend what data matters, how to collect it, and how to use it to compute the greenhouse gas emissions they're responsible for.[6] Companies will continue to employ internal machine learning capabilities and grapple with how to make ethics, fairness, and transparency core guiding principles. But all of this must come to include a commitment to "green AI," which stresses energy efficiency. Corporate leadership may be under greater pressure to reveal the energy and water consumption involved in the development and distribution of their products and could be held to greater public scrutiny for perpetuating the sustainability paradox.[7] But who will audit this or even be *able* to audit this?

Notes

[1] https://www.pwc.co.uk/services/sustainability-climate-change/insights/how-ai-future-can-enable-sustainable-future.html

[2] https://www.technologyreview.com/2019/06/06/239031/training-a-single-ai-model-can-emit-as-much-carbon-as-five-cars-in-their-lifetimes

[3] https://www.cbsnews.com/news/artificial-intelligence-carbon-footprint-climate-change

[4] https://phys.org/news/2023-11-centers-straining-resources-ai.html

[5] https://www.newscientist.com/article/2405830-chinas-first-underwater-data-centre-is-being-installed

[6] https://www.technologyreview.com/2023/10/25/1081566/carbon-accountant-climate-change-jobs-future

[7] https://www.sfchronicle.com/opinion/openforum/article/ai-chatgpt-climate-environment-18282910.php

CHAPTER 12

Pumping the Brakes on AI: Regulatory Considerations

While many want fast action, it's hard to regulate technology that's evolving as quickly as AI. The techno-utopians think AI will bring about a new age of prosperity. The techno-pessimists think it will be a damaging, destabilizing force.[1] The latter is increasingly driving calls for more regulation. People like Elon Musk have called for a voluntary halt on AI development considering the risks. An open letter in 2023 signed by hundreds of well-regarded AI experts, tech entrepreneurs, and scientists called for a temporary break in the development and testing of AI technologies more powerful than GPT-4 so that any risks can be appropriately studied. The letter contended that developments are occurring faster than society and regulators can adequately deal with.[2] But that's not necessarily realistic. Yes, we need stronger rules of the road. Yes, we need both our public and private institutions to adopt and enforce them. Most regulatory attempts will be fruitless. Technology may progress too quickly.

But guardrails—without going off the rails—will be more urgently needed. The commonly touted narrative asserting that technology is a force for public harmony may be one of the great marketing tools out of Silicon Valley. But that narrative also obscures the threats of concentrating power and subjecting it to leaders' personal impulses. In the United States, Congress's inability to pass broad regulations on AI has only led to even more risks.[3] On October 30, 2023, the White House issued a comprehensive Executive Order regulating AI and aimed to launch new standards for AI safety and security. That same day, the Group of 7 (G7)—which includes Canada, France, Germany, Italy, Japan, the UK, and the United States—along with the EU, declared international guiding principles and a code of conduct for organizations developing sophisticated AI systems. Just a few months later, in February 2024, several leading U.S. AI companies such as Northrop Grumman joined the AI Safety Institute Consortium, a new safety group comprising government agencies, academic institutions, and other companies, to support the safe and responsible development and deployment of generative AI.[4]

This comes at a time when efforts to rein in AI abound. Governments worldwide are trying to navigate the emergence of AI and establish regulatory guidelines. . .they just don't quite know how. Regulatory rivalry is also adding more urgency. In March 2024, the EU finalized the AI Act, which is set to become the first wide-ranging AI law in the world that aims to regulate "high-risk" usages of AI systems. And neither the EU nor the United States want to be bested by China, which has already adopted numerous AI laws.[5] Will more authoritarian regimes have more success? What about those with closed and insular Internet(s)? India recently said it doesn't have any current plans to regulate AI.

In the private sector, a group of 10 companies signed up to a new set of guidelines on how to build, create, and share AI-generated content responsibly. One of the most critical parts of the guidelines is a promise by the companies to include and research ways to alert users as to when they are interacting with something that has been produced by AI.[6] OpenAI, Microsoft, Google, DeepMind, and Anthropic have all formed the Frontier Model Forum, an industry-led group that claims to enforce the "safe and responsible development" of AI. It is an effort at AI industry self-regulation. While it might be nice in theory to see major industry players come together to establish some best practices for responsible AI development, self-regulation has several limitations.[7] Self-regulation, although seemingly beneficial in theory, can fall short in practice. While it may offer a sense of control, self-regulation lacks the necessary teeth to enforce compliance and hold industries accountable for their actions. This leaves the door wide open for companies to shape society's trajectory with AI without due consideration for its broader consequences on communities, including worsening existing societal inequities. When a company, for instance, prioritizes shareholder returns over consumer safety, the consequences can be dire, especially when it comes to AI products. Rushing an AI product to market without thorough testing can lead to a series of unfortunate outcomes.[8]

Meanwhile, the desire to pursue technological progress at all costs is gaining traction in Silicon Valley circles, and there are signs that techno-optimism is once again gaining favor among the tech elite and venture capitalists. In his book *The Exponential Age*, tech investor and writer Azeem Azhar celebrates the vast impact of computing technologies. He writes that "new technologies are being invented and scaled at an ever-faster pace, all while decreasing rapidly in price."[9] *Effective accelerationism* (shortened to "e/acc," pronounced "e-ack") is a movement dedicated to the belief that AI and other emerging technologies should be allowed to be developed as quickly as possible, without any guardrails or gatekeepers that block the pace of technological innovation.

E/acc devotees favor open-sourcing AI software instead of having it be controlled by Big Tech. They contend that AI's benefits vastly outweigh its harms, and that people shouldn't stand in its way.[10] Venture capitalist Marc Andreessen recently likened a slowdown in AI advancement as akin to murder. He compared the technology to a "philosopher's stone that can cure illness and prevent deaths caused by everything from car crashes to pandemics to wartime friendly fire."

In stark contrast are *decels*—the people deeply worried about the safety of AI or the regulators who want to halt development. Elon Musk has cautioned that AI development should be paused for the sake of humanity.[11] He subscribes to many of the philosophies of a Silicon Valley social movement known as *effective altruism* (EA). When it comes to AI development, effective altruists favor safety over speed and believe a frantic rush into AI could pose a serious threat to humankind. They have spent enormous amounts of money progressing the idea that AI poses an existential risk.

The Elders, a distinguished group of independent world leaders, recognize the power of AI in advancing human life across various sectors. They recognize its potential to alter health care, education, and other key aspects of the UN Sustainable Development Goals. They contend that without appropriate global regulation of AI, the pace of technological progress represents an existential threat to humanity, and that a newly established global architecture is necessary to manage these risks. A core part of regulating AI is the need for a more unified approach. They believe, too, that AI's benefits must be shared with poorer countries. Mary Robinson, Chair of The Elders, former President of Ireland, and UN High Commissioner for Human Rights, said: "The world is at a turning point in history, comparable to the advent of the nuclear age in 1945. AI could fundamentally alter how human society is organized, national politics are conducted and international issues are managed. World leaders have a responsibility to ensure that AI is used in ways that are safe, transparent, and accountable. These are. . .political and moral imperatives affecting everyone."[12]

The AI Goldilocks Zone

There has also been a growing realization of the importance of more decentralized, distributed, freely accessible, and open-source systems. The use of open-source models in businesses is on the rise—even though those in the tech industry cannot seem to agree on what open-source even means, let alone settle on a mutually agreed-upon definition.[13] To some, open-source AI represents not only a more egalitarian system but a way to also foster greater collaboration, transparency, and community-driven development. At their heart, open-source systems (OSS) should, in theory, be a good thing, particularly as much technological development is dominated by a small number of monopolistic giants. But it is notably missing from almost all regulatory conversations. According to Brookings, OSS touches nearly every issue in AI policy—from research to ethics, competition, and innovation—but is largely absent from conversations around AI policy. In fact, the EU's Artificial Intelligence Act may exempt open-source models from strict regulation.

Ultimately, technology reflects the human condition. And social philosopher Yuval Noah Harari has a warning: we must not only begin regulating AI, but the increasing sophistication of the technology could ultimately create a population of what he has dubbed *hacked humans*. He contends that this is a direct result of the data collection efforts by big corporations that are accumulating huge amounts of data about their users. Beyond this, who is making sure AI technologies are used ethically and for the greater good? Big Tech companies? Governments? Young developers? Governing AI has gotten more complex, in part, because of the increase of code that any computer programmer with simple knowledge can freely access, use, and share without limitation. The barrier to entry with open-source AI is so low that even people with very little understanding of what they are doing can spawn entirely new systems. This issue will only continue to grow as we enter a time when almost anything—including everyday objects—can be a computer and can be hacked.

The public, largely, is cautious. According to the Pew Research Center, Americans support regulation and oversight of emerging AI technologies, such as chatbots and driverless vehicles. Of those surveyed, 67 percent of those who are aware of chatbots like ChatGPT say they are not worried about the government going too far in regulating its use; rather, it's the opposite: they think that the government will not go far enough.[14] Based on July 2023 polling from the think tank AI Policy Institute (AIPI), 72 percent of American voters want to reduce the speed of AI development, compared to just 8 percent who want it to speed up. Polling results also showed that 62 percent of voters are concerned about AI, whereas just 21 percent are excited about it; 76 percent of voters believe AI could one day pose a threat to humanity; and 82 percent of voters do not trust tech executives to regulate AI.[15]

What we will increasingly need to find is the "Goldilocks" zone—that elusive place where AI systems are neither too simple nor too complex but reflect a delicate and just-right balance in their design and capabilities. If AI is to help solve individual, societal, and global problems, humans should neither underestimate nor overestimate its trustworthiness. Situated in between the two ends of this spectrum is the sweet spot: the Goldilocks zone. But what will keep trust in this zone?[16] A large portion of Americans are concerned about AI and its unchecked growth, with many supporting an interim pause on its development. Concurrently, however, many investors are overly enthusiastic and bullish about the technology's immense promise and are funneling money into businesses that adopt generative AI. Without any clear-cut or decisive regulation or universal standard for "responsible AI," how can we strike a balance between rising societal concerns and capital market excitement? And will any entity—public or private—get it just right?

Notes

1 https://www.theatlantic.com/technology/archive/2023/04/generative-ai-tech-elon-musk-chatgpt-politics-biden/673673
2 https://futureoflife.org/open-letter/pause-giant-ai-experiments
3 https://www.washingtonpost.com/technology/2023/11/23/x-musk-openai-altman-big-tech
4 https://thehill.com/policy/technology/4456050-ai-companies-join-new-us-safety-consortium
5 https://www.economist.com/business/2023/10/24/the-world-wants-to-regulate-ai-but-does-not-quite-know-how
6 https://www.technologyreview.com/2023/02/27/1069166/how-to-create-release-and-share-generative-ai-responsibly
7 https://futurism.com/the-byte/openai-google-self-regulate-ai
8 https://technical.ly/software-development/ai-ethics-profit-conflict-solution
9 https://www.technologyreview.com/2021/10/27/1037169/book-review-azeem-azhar
10 https://www.nytimes.com/2023/12/10/technology/ai-acceleration.html
11 https://www.nasdaq.com/articles/marc-andreessen-says-pumping-the-brakes-on-ai-development-is-a-form-of-murder
12 https://theelders.org/news/elders-urge-global-co-operation-manage-risks-and-share-benefits-ai
13 https://www.technologyreview.com/2024/03/25/1090111/tech-industry-open-source-ai-definition-problem
14 https://www.pewresearch.org/short-reads/2023/11/21/what-the-data-says-about-americans-views-of-artificial-intelligence
15 https://theaipi.org/poll-shows-overwhelming-concern-about-risks-from-ai-as-new-institute-launches-to-understand-public-opinion-and-advocate-for-responsible-ai-policies
16 https://www.nature.com/articles/s41598-021-93109-8

PART IV

Augmented Intelligence

While Part III focused on the technology, Part IV will focus on *us*—and how we will coevolve alongside of it. AI will force us to tap even deeper into our most human cognitive abilities, changing how we understand our own unique value propositions. It will alter how we learn, work, measure productivity, future-proof new skill sets and competencies, interact, and form relationships.

CHAPTER 13

From AI to IA: Intelligence Augmentation

Taking a line from Ron Livingston's character Peter Gibbons in the iconic 1999 satirical black comedy film *Office Space*, "We don't have a lot of time on this earth. We weren't meant to spend it this way. Human beings were not meant to sit in little cubicles staring at computer screens all day, filling out useless forms and listening to eight different bosses drone on about mission statements." And amen to that. I must hope that Peter (and his "15 minutes of real actual work" job at Initech) was right. This is not our future. But just because this isn't our future doesn't mean that it portends the end of work. It is not the end of work. . .but it is the end of *boring* work. By automating routine, boring tasks, AI enables us to work smarter and faster. And without the drudgery that comes with tasks like number-crunching, data entry, and spreadsheet input.

This we know: generative AI will transform the economy by both dramatically boosting human workers' productivity and replacing them outright. So, where in all of this do we play? How does this impact us? One thing is clear: a powerful new narrative is emerging, one that is not humans versus robots but humans *with* robots. It's about the complementary, cooperative, and symbiotic relationship between humans and AI. AI will displace *and* augment human work. This quickly emerging ecosystem will work well only when both humans and AI systems operate together in lockstep.

The integration of AI into our workforce does not only mean job loss or obsolescence; rather, it presents an opportunity for growth and innovation by allowing AI to take on the monotonous tasks that, some could argue, humans weren't meant to be doing in the first place. It's a dynamic less about replacement and more about enhancement. Yes, AI has the potential to—and will—replace some human workers. Yes, it will disrupt traditional industries. The key lies in understanding that humans and AI can establish a synergy that drives innovation and new types of strategic thinking. It's about the collaboration between two systems—one organic, one inorganic. And by combining their unique strengths, we can achieve outcomes that neither could accomplish alone.

What much of this comes down to is *time*—and the creation of entirely new time-based business efficiencies. AI can analyze vast amounts of data, extract valuable insights, and make certain predictions with remarkable accuracy in a fraction of the time it would take a human. AI-powered tools can automate repetitive or mundane tasks and streamline processes, freeing up valuable time for humans to focus on higher-level thinking. It can perform tasks not only more efficiently but effectively. Let's let AI do these tasks so that we, as humans, can migrate up to the next highest value proposition and engage in more strategic activities that require analysis, problem-solving, and innovative thinking.

The Future of Human Creativity + Curation

While AI can certainly perform certain tasks with great proficiency, it is unable to replicate the depth of human creativity. Some posit that one day it will get there—and perhaps sooner than later—but that is up for much debate. To some, creativity is a cornerstone of cognition and a core part of human behavior and intelligence. Creativity, too, is hard to define. Artists throughout history have grappled with how to define it. And there is no one universally accepted definition. Perhaps, very simply, it's the use of the imagination to create something original. But can advanced AI really be creative? The human ability to decipher what's interesting and to shape the story is still elusive. Philosophers and scientists have long argued over the question of what makes human beings more complex than robots. Is it creativity? Consciousness? Emotion? Morality and ethics? Humor? Love? All of the above? Scientists have explored the neural basis of creativity (which is housed in the same place in the brain as movement). Researchers at Stanford University believe that the cerebral cortex is the part of the brain that "makes us human."[1]

When thinking about whether AI will ever be capable of true creative thinking, it's a tough thing to measure and quantify. According to a study by researchers at the University of Bergen, Norway, AI chatbots attained higher average scores than humans in the Alternate Uses Task, a test often used to determine the ability for divergent thinking—a thought process used to produce creative ideas by considering various solutions. When human responses consisted of poor-quality ideas, the chatbots typically produced more creative responses. But the finest human ideas still matched or surpassed those of the chatbots. This study acknowledges the potential of AI as a tool to augment creativity. It also acknowledges the unique and multifaceted nature of human creativity that may be hard to fully replicate or exceed with AI.[2]

Margaret A. Boden, a Research Professor of Cognitive Science at the University of Sussex, said that AI is programmed to process information in a particular way to achieve certain results. This may be the greatest difference between artists and AI: while artists are self- and product-driven, AI is largely consumer-centric and market-driven. Essentially, what this means is that, when it comes to using AI, we only get the art we ask for. Results are largely predictable.[3] For some, there may be a prevailing fear that AI will replace human workers, rendering their creativity and artistry obsolete. But a deeper look reveals that this next wave of automation may bring us back to a bygone age of craftsmanship and artistry. That may be the hope, at least. In fact, artisans made up the original American middle class. Perhaps, although idealistic, we will return to a time where we place renewed value in these skill sets.

The hypothetical use scenarios are endless, and what they require is another human ingredient: curation. Curation is about storytelling. Curation is not just about collecting and organizing information; it is about crafting a narrative. AI can do this by analyzing data and suggesting relevant content that it thinks may fit within a certain storytelling framework. But it doesn't grasp relationships, historical narratives, feeling, firsthand experiences, personal perspectives, and the arc of emotion. Our ability to connect seemingly unrelated ideas and to infuse work with emotion and passion are all human traits that cannot easily be replicated. Self-awareness, social intelligence, adaptability, cognitive flexibility, critical thinking, curiosity, and the desire for human connection will all become increasingly important and irreplaceable human assets that complement, enhance, and amplify the analytical capabilities of AI.

Younger generations (particularly Gen Z) moving into the workforce not only place high value on creative jobs and careers in which they can maintain a healthy work-life balance but they will also likely put a higher premium on identity, fulfillment, meaning, and autonomy—all things that are necessary for well-being but absent in today's average job. It used to be that a job was simply seen as a means to earn a living. The younger generations seek positions that align with their values and allow them to express their true selves. They desire work that provides a sense of purpose and allows them to make a meaningful impact. They value the freedom to make decisions and have control over their work environment.

Meaning becomes an interesting ingredient here, too. There is a potent argument that work has sustained people not just economically but by bestowing meaning. Since we all ascribe meaning in our own minds, the meaning of life might be a function of our own personalities. Jobs that heavily rely on human perception and intuition are likely to resist automation.

Humans' ability to understand subtle nuances in communication or interpret complex emotions is deeply rooted in our social intelligence. This fundamental aspect of human cognition is difficult to replicate in machines, as it requires empathy and an understanding of cultural context. While AI has made great strides in areas such as data analysis and pattern recognition, it still falls short when it comes to navigating the complexities of human interaction. Jobs that involve negotiation, conflict resolution, or aspects of patient care often require a deep understanding of human behavior and emotions. The unique qualities possessed by humans make them invaluable assets in various job sectors where adaptability and emotional intelligence are paramount.

Those who find the optimal balance between AI and human capabilities could likely emerge as champions of the new economy. This means identifying areas where AI can excel and assigning those tasks accordingly, while reserving uniquely human skills for areas such as creative ideation, relationship building, emotional connection, and strategic decision-making. Our lived experiences must become more valued, too.

The Value of Expertise

I recently had a conversation with Mike Pell, Director of the Microsoft Garage (which is part of the company's worldwide innovation program for moving ideas forward quickly), about some of the most impactful human aspects of AI. During our chat, he so accurately said this: "It may turn out that the greatest advancement brought about by AI is not our ability to be more efficient or prolific, but rather the opportunity it presents for all of us to become masters of skills we were never going to get to in our lifetimes. Granting us immediate superpowers in the areas we have real passion for, but perhaps could never achieve greatness in, is a wonderfully human outcome of these technologic advancements. It could exponentially expand what people can achieve in their lifetimes." Leveraging AI to cultivate new talents in a mere fraction of the time is an exciting prospect. But if we can all become greater "experts" in anything that interests us, do we run the risk of diluting the very definition of the word? Will this allow us to essentially "hack flow"—in other words, cut down on the time it would take us to master tasks? *Flow* can be described as "being in the zone"—that mental state in which a person is fully absorbed in a feeling of energized focus.

David Autor, professor of economics at the Massachusetts Institute of Technology (MIT) and co-director of the MIT Shaping the Future of Work Initiative, posits in an article called "AI Could Actually Help Rebuild the Middle Class," that AI could represent an inflection point in the economic value of human know-how. He states that the unique chance AI gives humanity is to repel the process started by computerization—to expand the relevance, scope, and value of human expertise for a greater set of workers. Many modern jobs are not leftovers of historical professions that have, at this point, escaped automation. Rather, they are new job specialties that are directly connected to specific technological innovations; they demand new expertise that was absent or unimagined in previous eras.[4]

Tapping into Human Cognition

Perhaps the best strategy for getting the most out of AI is to tap even deeper into our most human cognitive abilities. For all the talk about generative AI becoming more creative, perhaps the opposite is true—perhaps it will force us to rethink traditional notions of creativity and make us more creative in the process. As David Brooks, columnist for the *New York Times*, wrote: "In the age of AI, major in being human."[5] In a future that will demand new focus on "majoring in being human," how do we educate the next generation of thinkers? How can we equip ourselves to deal with uncertainty more effectively? How do we nurture new minds to solve the big, existential issues/threats of the future?

While we will tackle some of these looming questions in subsequent chapters, another aspect of this is something called *cognitive load*. According to the National Institutes of Health (NIH), cognitive load is the load forced on our working memory by a certain task. When cognitively overloaded, our brain processing slows down, we experience attentional blind spots, and we make more mistakes. The effect of AI on human cognitive load is a topic of mounting interest among researchers and designers alike as they wrestle with whether AI could pose significant challenges to our cognitive load and thereby decrease creativity in the process? A challenge AI presents is that the volume of information it produces far exceeds the scope of our cognition. This can lead to *brain overload*, where we just can't process that sheer amount of information. What we need to be careful to avoid, too, is a self-perpetuating feedback loop where humans increasingly rely on AI for decision-making and that dependence on the system leads to an atrophying of creative problem-solving skills. We've already seen, in just one to two generations, mobile phones, social media, and GPS render obsolete the need for people to remember phone numbers, birthdays, and directions. Is a possible second-order consequence of this more mental bandwidth (or brain space) for us to use for other things?

For knowledge workers, the key is to use generative AI to manage a seemingly never-ending flow of information. This backlog has created, what Microsoft calls, a *digital debt*: a growing pile-up of information waiting to be processed by each individual knowledge worker. Sixty-eight percent of workers in a 2023 Microsoft report called "Will AI Fix Work?" said that they do not have enough uninterrupted time to focus on their main activities during the workday. The number of working hours taken up by emails, meetings, texts, etc. is increasing. This is where generative AI can possibly assist. It can lessen cognitive load by automating some structured tasks and increase cognitive capacity for unstructured tasks. Attorneys at the global firm A&O Shearman, for example, use a system called Harvey to resourcefully find and access case law and draft basic contracts. This gives them more time to evaluate complex legal issues and advise their clients.[6]

All of this is a massive experiment. We may be the first generation of test subjects of an "alien intelligence" that no one really understands. There will be people who fear the loss of human innovation and creativity. They may—justifiably or unjustifiably—believe that an over-reliance on AI will result in an unhealthy dependence on it. The more we use AI to mitigate risks, will we do so at the expense of innovation and disruption? Will we, as a society, prioritize stability and reliability at the expense of human curiosity and creativity? Will our intelligence and AI intelligence be in a continual rumble for dominance (as expressed by my son in the very beginning of this book)?

Ultimately, generative AI is a test of temperament. People see different visions of the future. What defines humanity is not just our level of intelligence but also how we capitalize on that intelligence and double down on our innate capabilities. We know that generative AI can identify patterns and correlations. But human intelligence determines how we use that output.

The Augmentation of Blue-Collar Work

While much of the recent discussion around AI centers on its ability to augment things such as creativity and knowledge, we must also consider how it is impacting the backbone of our society: blue-collar workers.

On the surface, this might seem to directly contradict the discussion in Chapter 9, "The Evolving Work Landscape," as the impact of AI on blue-collar jobs is often a topic of concern. The reality, however, is far from bleak. Contrary to common misconceptions, the future of blue-collar work may not be as threatened by automation as some may fear. Blue-collar jobs that require dexterity, problem-solving, and adaptability to dynamic environments may be more resistant to full automation in the near future. Even as AI is being trained to match human dexterity and speed, the complexity and unpredictability of many physical tasks make them more challenging to automate completely.

Exact figures measuring the direct impact of automation are hard to come by, with estimates varying widely depending on the source. Some studies have painted a more dire picture for lower-wage workers, but that doesn't tell the whole story. It's true that robotics and software have eliminated certain jobs, particularly in industries like manufacturing, but the narrative that automation will lead to mass unemployment is an oversimplification.

Let's look at the construction industry as an example. The integration of AI in construction signifies a monumental shift in how tasks are allocated and executed. By delegating repetitive or hazardous jobs to AI, human workers can redirect their focus toward intricate tasks that require skill and expertise, such as plumbing, HVAC, and electrical systems. This symbiotic relationship between AI and humans not only enhances safety on construction sites but also boosts productivity and efficiency. The collaboration between AI and human labor holds the potential to revolutionize traditional construction practices, paving the way for innovation and progress in the industry.[7]

For those who work in transportation or trucking, fatigue monitoring technology can identify subtle signs of exhaustion and alert individuals to take breaks. With its ability to analyze behaviors, this AI-based solution helps not only safeguard both drivers and passengers on the road, but it also helps promote better driver well-being.

Even roles traditionally seen as manual labor, such as waste collectors or carpenters' assistants, can leverage AI for functions like scheduling, customer service, and route optimization. As highlighted in a recent study, only a small percentage of jobs (4 percent) are devoid of any tasks that could benefit from AI assistance. Those "AI-proof" jobs included athletes, dishwashers, roofers, and painters.[8]

AI for All: Inequality + Inclusion

While there is no denying the potential benefits that AI can bring, there are concerns about how evenly these benefits will be distributed. That is why more inclusive AI is needed. According to the International Telecommunication Union (ITU), the United Nations specialized agency for information and communication technologies, inclusive participation is fundamental for countries with low technological capacities. AI must benefit everyone, including the 2.7 billion people who are still offline worldwide. Collaboration between different stakeholders—including policymakers, industry leaders, government leaders, and advocacy groups—is vital in shaping a future where AI benefits are accessible to all, not just the privileged few.

Inadequate access in developing countries and underprivileged communities, and predominantly English-language training data, are creating risks and exacerbating inequities in AI systems. Expanding the reach of online content to cater to the diverse linguistic landscape of our world is a monumental task, especially when considering the vast array of over 7,000 languages spoken globally. While English and a select few languages dominate the Internet, there is a growing need for AI technology to bridge this linguistic gap and make online content accessible to a wider audience.

Generative AI tools are regularly trained on Internet data, which may limit access to those who don't speak languages with rich data sources (e.g., English, Spanish, and Mandarin). According to an article from Brookings, building inclusive digital ecosystems hinges on bridging the digital language divide through ensuring greater linguistic representation in AI training data. The inequalities in resources across languages often enable further inequalities in technologies, especially generative AI systems and LLMs.

Prioritizing linguistic diversity in AI development is vital. This is particularly important because most language-based AI systems, like GPT-3.5, are trained on vast amounts of data scraped from the Internet. With its 175 billion parameters, the model's training data comprises a staggering 300 billion words sourced from text databases across the Internet. And English represents the largest proportion of languages online, as it is used by more than 55 percent of online domains, according to a study published by Rest of World as of May 2023. That makes English's representation on the Internet more than 10 times the 4.7 percent of the world's population that speak it as their main language.

From a demographic perspective, developing markets such as countries and major cities within Africa may find themselves at the forefront of a major moment. Home to the world's youngest and fastest-growing population, Africa's youth will form one of the world's largest workforces by 2030. Based on data from the World Bank, Africa's population is extremely young compared to other world regions: only 3 percent of sub-Saharan Africa's population is over 65, while 44 percent are below 14, compared to 18 percent and 17 percent, respectively, among OECD (Organisation for Economic Co-operation and Development) countries. Encouraging the creation of AI solutions adapted to local challenges can have an impact on reshaping Africa's development trajectory.[9] A September 2023 report by Access Partnership in partnership with Google called "AI in Africa: Unlocking Potential, Igniting Progress," suggests that four African countries—Nigeria, Ghana, Kenya, and South Africa—could bring in upwards of $136 billion worth of economic benefits by 2030 if businesses there start using more AI tools. The African Union, comprising 55 member nations, is on the brink of a significant milestone with the development of an ambitious AI policy. This forward-thinking initiative aims to chart a unique Africa-centric path for both the development and regulation of AI within the continent. Some experts are raising concerns about the risks that AI technology poses if African countries do not establish robust regulatory frameworks to safeguard citizens from its misuse. The fear is that without proper regulations in place, there is a risk of facing increased social harms, such as bias that could worsen existing inequalities within the continent.[10]

Notes

[1] https://www.scientificamerican.com/article/don-t-overthink-it-less-is-more-when-it-comes-to-creativity

[2] Koivisto, M., Grassini, S. Best humans still outperform artificial intelligence in a creative divergent thinking task. *Sci Rep* 13, 13601 (2023). **https://doi.org/10.1038/s41598-023-40858-3**

[3] https://techxplore.com/news/2023-06-ai-replicate-human-creativity-key.html#google_vignette

[4] https://www.noemamag.com/how-ai-could-help-rebuild-the-middle-class/?mc_cid=8e7d3a34e9&mc_eid=10057e199f

[5] https://www.nytimes.com/2023/02/02/opinion/ai-human-education.html

[6] https://hbr.org/2023/11/how-generative-ai-will-transform-knowledge-work

[7] https://www.fastcompany.com/91068016/ais-blue-collar-revolution-transforming-traditional-industries-for-the-future

[8] https://www.nytimes.com/2023/08/24/upshot/artificial-intelligence-jobs.html

[9] https://www.undp.org/ghana/blog/positioning-africas-youth-win-harnessing-ai-development

[10] https://www.technologyreview.com/2024/03/15/1089844/africa-ai-artificial-intelligence-regulation-au-policy

CHAPTER 14

Human Supervision Over AI

One key area where AI falls short is in making unsupervised decisions. We know that AI algorithms can process vast amounts of data and provide insights, but they lack the intuitive understanding and emotional intelligence that humans possess. That is where humans must come into, and stay in, the equation. AI is designed to assist with decision-making by leveraging its computational power and advanced algorithms. But AI is not a good substitute when it comes to identifying or responding to intangible human decision-making factors. In scenarios where ethical choices need to be made or where moral compasses guide decision-making processes, AI may struggle to provide meaningful insights or recommendations.[1] From complex calculations to pattern recognition, AI has proven its accuracy, quality, and speed. But can AI truly replicate the subjective experiences and feelings that enhance our world? While AI excels in providing logical solutions, it lacks the inherent human touch that comes with emotions. These qualities are what drive our connections with others and enable us to navigate the complexities of life. They allow us to understand nuance, adapt to different situations, and make decisions based on more than just cold calculations. Empathy is not merely understanding someone's perspective; it involves connecting on an emotional level and responding with genuine care. It requires compassion and an understanding of the intricacies of human behavior. As of now, AI falls short in replicating these essential aspects of being human. However, it may be advancing to the point where we will see it as having the ability to capture our emotions, although it, itself, may remain emotionless.

When I was a kid, my dad loved watching *Star Trek: The Next Generation*, and aside from my childhood crush on Lieutenant William Riker, I was bewildered and fascinated by Lieutenant Commander Data. He seemed to know everything . . . except for people. As an AI, Data was excellent at collecting information, but didn't seem able to synthesize it. There was no subtlety, no nuance. He couldn't read human emotions but could process information in a millisecond. Data was juxtaposed by the character of Jean-Luc Picard, who was defined by his deeply human responses. He had a strong moral compass and was intelligent and inquisitive. He has been described by some as "part archaeologist, part philosopher, and part explorer." *Star Trek* was visionary and the relationship between Data and Picard was prescient. Our interface with AI will force us to consider which human traits we want to retain and cultivate, and how we, too, become part archaeologist, part philosopher, and part explorer.

Part of becoming an explorer is seeing the connections between ideas and abstract concepts—something that AI cannot yet do. We operate in silos of knowledge, silos of industry, and silos of thinking. Multi- and interdisciplinary thinking will take on greater urgency. As will not just content oversight but human oversight. Human judgment. Human decision-making. Yes, we need smart developers, engineers, and AI researchers. But we also need the human thinkers—the ethicists, philosophers, anthropologists—with a deeper and richer understanding of the world. In other words, we need the Picards. We need them to act as guides to help us understand the second- and third-order consequences of AI; to guide us through both the threats and the opportunities; to guide us through our own unrealized potential as humans in a changing world. Collaborations between the technical and the nontechnical will be needed. Natural language processing (NLP) will force engineers and humanists together. Computer scientists will require greater aptitude in the humanities. Humanists will require a basic understanding of NLP because it's the future of language.

The Trolley Problem in AI

There is a rising belief that AI is ascending to some form of consciousness. With some form of consciousness, tasks can be performed by AI with more humanlike outputs and outcomes, only perhaps more accurately. But fully understanding the motivations of AI will be more difficult when viewed from a human perspective. That is where we will really have to double down on our ability to be both overseers and guides. Consider the *trolley problem*. This thought experiment delves into the ethical complexities surrounding a fictional scenario where an onlooker is faced with a difficult decision: to save five people in danger of being hit by a trolley, they must divert the trolley to kill just one person. This moral dilemma prompts us to consider the implications of such decisions and how AI may factor into ethical considerations. Basically, it comes down to this: if you have access to a switch that would make the trolley change to the other track, but another person stands there and is certain to be killed if the switch is activated . . . do you switch tracks or not?[2]

The trolley problem is thought to be the prime example of ethical and moral decision-making. When it comes to AI systems, applying the principles of the trolley problem can help us assess whether machines are ready for real-world scenarios where they must make ethical decisions on their own and act independently. Just like people, AI systems must be equipped with the ability to assess situations, consider consequences, and make morally justifiable choices. Developments in robotics mean autonomous vehicles, industrial robots, and medical robots will be more competent, independent, and prevalent over the next two decades. Ultimately, these autonomous machines could make decision-making mistakes that lead to a significant number of fatalities, which could be prevented if humans were in the loop.

There will continue to be concerns around mass AI robotic rollout, including the moral concern surrounding the idea that any human life could be lost as a direct result of machine error. The trolley problem highlights why decisions about who lives and who dies are fundamentally moral judgments. These moral judgments cannot be transferred to machines, which is why it represents a very unique type of moral dilemma—one that is intensified because robots' and humans' perceptions are not the same, resulting in unique types of errors.[3] Robots, for instance, have extremely fast reflexes but can misidentify hazards, such as when, in 2018, a self-driving Uber car mistook a pedestrian pulling a bicycle across the street to be a car, anticipating it to travel more quickly than it was. This incident led, in the years that followed, to a philosophical conundrum: In a newly emerging era of self-driving cars, who gets blamed for a fatal accident when humans are basically babysitters of flawed, still-learning AI systems? Is it the company with the car that went astray? Or the person behind the wheel who should have interfered and overridden the system? It was ruled, in July 2023, that the answer is the individual behind the wheel. The National Transportation Safety Board (NTSB) also found that not much is being done to safeguard test operators from what is known as *automation complacency*—humans' tendency to direct less attention to automatic processes that demand little input.[4] The person in the passenger seat was looking down, and the car failed to alert them until less than a second prior to impact. A common dynamic with AI systems is overconfidence. The more autonomous the system, the more human operators tend to trust it and not pay full attention. The Uber accident shows what happens when we don't adequately think through the risk implications with enough intentionality.

As Raphaël Millière, an assistant professor in the philosophy of AI at Macquarie University, and Charles Rathkopf, a research associate at the Institute for Brain and Behavior at the Jülich Research Center in Germany, highlighted in their *Vox* article "*Why It's Important to Remember That AI Isn't Human*," when it comes to the concept of superintelligence and the potential for its realization, we are confronted with a profound philosophical dilemma. The question arises whether the connection between language and mind has been fundamentally altered, or if a new form of consciousness has been engineered. The idea of superintelligence implies a level of cognitive capacity surpassing that of humans, leading to speculation on whether such a feat is achievable or even desirable. They go on to say, "When conversing with language models, it is hard to overcome the impression that you are engaging with another rational being." We must maintain a clear distinction between the capabilities of AI models and human cognitive processes. Anthropomorphizing chatbots or other AI systems can lead to unrealistic expectations and misguided regulatory standards. Since current AI models do not possess intrinsic motivations like humans do, it becomes important to avoid imposing overly vague requirements for ensuring their trustworthiness.

Another drawback to be mindful of is the concept known as *anthropocentric chauvinism*. This term refers to the tendency to view the human mind as the ultimate benchmark against which all psychological phenomena are judged. In other words, it's a bias that assumes human intelligence is superior and should be the standard for evaluating AI capabilities. This mindset can hinder our ability to fully appreciate and leverage the unique strengths of AI systems. By constantly measuring AI against human intelligence, we may overlook or undervalue its distinct advantages, such as speed, scalability, and data processing capabilities. We must maintain a balanced perspective of language models and avoid over-inflating or overestimating their capabilities.[5] Despite a working symbiosis between humans and AI, we still need to be cautious about placing too much value and credence in its output. And we must be extremely wary—and conscious—of the permeable boundaries when it comes to where judgment and morality lie. AI is not ready for unsupervised decision-making . . . nor should it be. That is where humans—and humans only—will play and where we must remain.

This will demand a new set of ethics and ethical frameworks to address questions such as: How much (and what kind of) control should we relinquish to them (e.g., driverless cars or automated elder care guardians)? As AI beats us at tasks once thought to be exclusively human, will we feel pressured to abandon control to it? Is there some AI that we should not develop if it means any loss of human control? What will this mean to our sense of human identity? How much of a say should corporations, governments, experts, or citizens have in these matters?

Is It True That If AI Doesn't Displace You, a Person Using AI Will?

It's been said before that if AI does not displace you, a person using AI will. Someone who has figured out how to work alongside AI better than you could be the biggest threat. This emphasizes the importance of human involvement in every aspect of AI. It's another tool in the tool kit . . . a tool that's more like a chainsaw than a hammer. AI is not just a tool for automation; it has the potential to reduce the cost of cognition. But by making these processes (i.e., creativity and cognition) more inexpensive, could we be entering an era where innovation becomes commodified? Just as the printing press and the Internet revolutionized our world and democratized access to knowledge, generative AI has the power to redefine our notions of work and creativity. In the same way that earlier technologies made necessities and information more accessible, AI could make complex tasks more accessible to a wider range of people. The bottom line is this: for those whose jobs are not at risk of being displaced by AI, AI should be viewed not as an adversary but as an invaluable ally. Those who view it as the former and refuse to integrate AI into their work risk falling behind, as their AI-fueled counterparts move forward more quickly and with more agility.

An economic recalibration is desperately needed. We need to focus on the jobs that truly matter for the future—and adequately compensate for them financially. The division of labor isn't going to go away; it's just being redefined, with AI enabling humans to pursue work that is quintessentially human. Much of that work will be based on human relationships because AI cannot replicate the depth of human relationships. Think about all those jobs focused on people management and the burgeoning care industry. But those soft skills have never been adequately valued in our economy or prioritized in our education. A monumental change is overdue.

As science fiction writer and futurist Arthur C. Clarke once famously said: "Any sufficiently advanced technology is indistinguishable from magic." But AI isn't magic, even though it can seem that way. And why isn't it magic? Because people are still very much required—and people will determine whether these tools are applied with a sense of magic or a sense of . . . "meh."

The Future of Human Agency

According to Mike Bechtel, Chief Futurist at Deloitte, "In an age of creative machines, humans matter more, not less." We must lead with purpose and lead with humanity. We must strike a delicate balance between the allure of rapid progress and a healthy dose of skepticism. We should all be skeptical of AI—skeptical of what it can do and equally skeptical of what it can't. Realism also matters. AI is not a panacea, and simply slapping an AI prefix before any offering (e.g., AI-enabled, AI-powered, AI-driven) will not make it any more appealing. It can't be employed as a gimmick or to capitalize on the AI hype wave.

What impact will this have on the future of human agency? Pew Research Center and Elon University's Imagining the Internet Center asked experts to share their insights on this question. Specifically, they were asked: "By 2035, will smart machines, bots, and systems powered by AI be designed to allow humans to easily be in control of most tech-aided decision-making that is relevant to their lives?" As digital systems and AI continue to increase, the experts were almost equally divided over how much control people will preserve over basic decision-making. They agreed that influential corporate and government authorities will expand the role of AI in the daily lives of people in beneficial ways. But many are concerned that these systems will weaken individuals' ability to maintain control over their choices.[6]

This leaves us to ponder the question: if (or when), in the not-too-distant future, machines become smarter than humans, will we still be in control? Well-known figures like Stephen Hawking, Elon Musk, Bill Gates, and Ray Kurzweil have shared concerns and predictions about this. Individual opinions diverge regarding its impact: one group asserts AI dominance, while the other advocates for a more utopian and peaceful human-machine synthesis, with Kurzweil assenting the latter. The path ahead, while largely unknown in its ultimate trajectory, will undoubtedly call for greater interdisciplinary collaboration, involving technologists, ethicists, policymakers, and society at large.[7]

Notes

[1] https://hbr.org/2022/09/ai-isnt-ready-to-make-unsupervised-decisions
[2] https://www.merriam-webster.com/wordplay/trolley-problem-moral-philosophy-ethics
[3] https://www.weforum.org/agenda/2022/05/ai-s-trolley-problem-debate-can-lead-us-to-surprising-conclusions
[4] https://www.wired.com/story/ubers-fatal-self-driving-car-crash-saga-over-operator-avoids-prison
[5] https://www.vox.com/future-perfect/23971093/artificial-intelligence-chatgpt-language-mind-understanding
[6] https://www.pewresearch.org/internet/2023/02/24/the-future-of-human-agency
[7] https://medium.com/@awahaab/the-technological-singularity-unveiling-the-future-of-artificial-intelligence-and-humanity-25fc2e82da89

CHAPTER 15

AI Creating Its Own Careers . . . for Us

The most significant benefits, ultimately, from new forms of AI will come when organizations wholly reorganize around the technology. Costs will fall, but it could take many years for the technology to become sufficiently cheap for mass deployment. And until then, we likely will not see the kind of mass labor displacement that some people fear. In fact, historical trend data clearly shows that with mass adoption of new technologies comes entirely new growth sectors, businesses, and jobs. This economic cycle has held strong for hundreds of years.[1] So, while we can speculate more broadly about whether AI poses existential risks to human labor in the long term, we know that in the nearer term, many job areas will grow—and new jobs never seen before will emerge. Dramatic workplace changes will lead to jobs and careers that do not yet exist. This will, in turn, require education systems to adapt and equip the workers of the future with the skills they need. What new professions might emerge? AI ethicists? Digital footprint coaches? Algorithmic diagnosis patient advocates? The possibilities are endless.

There is a broad ecosystem of human workers servicing the growth of the AI sector itself. We talked earlier, for instance, about the growth of the prompt engineering (and prompt crafting) field. Looking upstream, 60 percent of new generative AI job postings in the United States are in just 15 metro areas. Generative AI may produce "winner-takes-most" economic outcomes.[2] But as the sector works to mitigate these concerns, new and substantive vistas for employment within AI are generating buzz. An October 2023 article titled "The New Jobs for Humans in the AI Era," in the *Wall Street Journal*, listed some of the new jobs for humans in an era of AI.[3] While we know that AI is threatening some careers and changing aspects of many, these new opportunities are on the rise:

In-house large language model (LLM) developer: In-house developers familiarize the models to new word patterns that will prepare them to better carry out a host of internal functions such as abbreviating a company's annual report filing or walking a client through a lengthy application process. They will then present these models in a user-friendly way to employees and clients to guarantee more comprehensive cross-functional understanding.

Reskiller: Reskillers can be thought of as a new type of teacher who guides the organization through future-proofed talent development. This position helps other employees keep their skill sets one step ahead of AI. Reskillers will need to know the talents that organizations require as technology reconfigures the skills landscape.

AI psychotherapist: Business or enterprise AI is all about explainability. AI psychotherapists will gauge a model's background by inspecting its training data for mistakes and sources of bias. AI might do much of the quantitative work, but people are still needed to decipher their outputs. Regardless of how sophisticated the models and systems become, people will ultimately be responsible for the outcomes—and how those outcomes are applied.

Head of AI: More firms are creating, and hiring for, the role of Head of AI. In the United States, the number of people in AI leadership roles has grown threefold in 5 years.[4] An explosion in AI has prompted law firms, hospitals, insurance companies, government agencies, and universities to establish a senior executive role in charge of AI. In December 2023, the *New York Times* named an editorial director of AI initiatives. And more than 400 federal departments and agencies looked for chief AI officers in 2023 to comply with an Executive Order by President Biden that outlined safeguards for the technology.[5] In September 2023, the Mayo Clinic in Arizona launched a totally new type of job at the hospital system: Chief Artificial Intelligence Officer.

Datasmiths: The rapid rise of data capture, data mining, and data analytics will continue at a compounded speed. So, too, will data storage (because of the staggering amounts of data generated) and data visualization. As such, an emerging new arena for employment might be around what we can call *datasmithing*. The total amount of data created, captured, copied, and consumed globally is forecast to increase rapidly. Global data creation is projected to grow to more than 180 zettabytes by 2025.[6] A zettabyte is equal to a thousand exabytes, a billion terabytes, or a trillion gigabytes. This means one billion one-terabyte hard drives would be needed to store one zettabyte of data. (Now those are numbers I can barely get my head around!) That is why, as data takes over more of our lives and endeavors and informs more of our processes and knowledge, we will see it move out of the realm of the tech expert—the coder and engineer—and into the realm of new datasmiths: the artist, the designer, the problem solver, the communicator, and the social scientist. As software becomes more accessible and machine learning becomes more ubiquitous, the imagination and creative application emerging around new ways to collect data, new kinds of data to collect, new ways to portray it and new applications for the use of it are growing. In the short term, the ability to datasmith can be one of the benefits employers offer to engage employees. All kinds of talented and eager people can be allowed to figure out novel ways of how data might be used, how it might be collected, who might be engaged in the process, and how multiple stakeholders can benefit. In the longer term, datasmiths will appear everywhere, and datasmithing may be the next version of engineering. Engineering became a profession with the advent of engines, and over the centuries it has employed many people and gone down many branches, from chemical to civil to electric to robotics to rocketry. Datasmithing is now in the process of being formed as a profession with the advent of the data revolution, and it, too, will go down many branches. These will be far removed from the data analytics and data mining we see today, much more creative, and much more widespread throughout every aspect of everything, everywhere.

AI writers and poets: Job postings from high-profile training data companies are recruiting poets, novelists, playwrights, or writers with a PhD or master's degree. Others want annotators with humanities degrees or years of work experience in literary fields. The companies use contractors to author short stories on a particular topic and then feed that content into AI models. These workers are also being used to provide feedback on the literary quality of current AI-generated text.[7] A new report suggests that OpenAI has been working to hire a cadre of outside contractors to better train an AI model how to code, which could eventually render entry-level coding jobs obsolete. But can human engineers' thought processes be automated? Understanding why and how a program needs to be written is an issue not easily solved by AI. It's also likely that many laid off tech workers will make transitions into roles that do not exist yet but are enabled by this new technology.

Social Sci-Fi Scenario: A Post-Work Future

A small but growing group of philosophers, scholars, and ordinary citizens support a "social science fiction" idea called *post-work*. Post-work refers to a world in which at least a portion of the population is permanently displaced from the workforce and can no longer find employment—regardless of how willing and able they are. At the core of post-workist thought is the assumption that many people derive minimal satisfaction from their jobs and the quasi-utopian belief that humanity would be better off if it weren't tethered to "work" as we currently define it. The conclusion drawn is that humanity, untethered from mundane work, would be freed up for pursuits that provide them with intellectual and creative stimulation—culminating in a human "renaissance" of sorts.

It's easy to dispel such ideas as unfeasible, impractical, or pure fantasy. One of the more concrete counterarguments to the idea of post-work is that without jobs, much of the glue that holds society together would begin to dissolve. According to that rationale, people would lose purpose and meaning and would ultimately resort to more destructive behaviors. But what if the *opposite* were true? Post-workists argue that Americans work so hard because their culture has conditioned them to feel guilty when they are not being productive, and that this guilt will fade as work ceases to be the norm. Less passive and more nourishing, creative forms of mass leisure could develop. When we ponder these realities, are we heading toward a future where jobs will consist of more creative endeavors? Equally important is the intimate relationship between work and purpose. Self-reliance and work are connected to human dignity and meaning. Will people increasingly redefine their sense of purpose in more noneconomic terms? Or could this have a detrimental long-term effect on human psychology?

In a world *without* work, the utopian view is that of flourishing creativity and freedom, more social good, and pride created by relationships rather than careers; the dystopian view is one of mass idleness, diminished civic pride, and rampant loneliness and boredom. While unrealistic in the near term (and perhaps even in our lifetimes), we should pause and use this as an opportunity to think about the things in our lives that matter. What in our jobs gives us purpose? Is it just a paycheck or something deeper about the work? Which parts of it would we want AI to do for us, and which parts would we want to make sure to keep for ourselves? This would require a massive recalibration of the economy—and our economic systems. But could AI, in theory, be ushering in the first stages of this "post-work" in its infancy?

Notes

[1] https://www.economist.com/finance-and-economics/2023/07/16/your-employer-is-probably-unprepared-for-artificial-intelligence

[2] https://www.axios.com/2023/07/24/ai-goldrush-concentrated-4-states

[3] https://www.wsj.com/tech/ai/the-new-jobs-for-humans-in-the-ai-era-db7d8acd

[4] https://www.vox.com/technology/2023/7/19/23799255/head-of-ai-leadership-jobs

[5] https://www.nytimes.com/2024/01/29/technology/us-jobs-ai-chatgpt-tech.html?mc_cid=e1eb2e1281&mc_eid=10057e199f

[6] https://www.statista.com/statistics/871513/worldwide-data-created

[7] https://restofworld.org/2023/ai-developers-fiction-poetry-scale-ai-appen

CHAPTER 16

The Rise of Data Colonialism

M uch focus right now is on AI's ability to augment human labor and the business efficiencies it will create. But much of this is a "haves" narrative. The effects of AI are not evenly distributed. A darker underbelly supports many of the impacts of AI. AI can enhance *and* exploit. Augment *and* abuse. It is creating a new colonial world order, and data workers are bearing the brunt of it.

While tech workers in the developed world may be benefitting from greater freedom and flexibility, these benefits are often built off the backs of tech workers in the developing world. AI is reliant on collecting large amounts of data, but this must be processed and labeled first. This is where the need for a human labor force comes in, which largely consists of underpaid workers in poor countries working grueling hours.

The key to making AI chatbots appear more intelligent and reduce toxicity in their responses lies in a technique known as *reinforcement learning from human feedback*. This method involves leveraging a dedicated team of human data annotators who meticulously label extensive amounts of raw data to train machine learning models. Data workers in Ethiopia, Eritrea, and Kenya are exploited to scrub online hate and misinformation. Annotators in Kenya were paid less than $2 an hour to filter through piles of disturbing content to make ChatGPT less "toxic."[1] More than 1,000 images of child sexual abuse have been found in a prominent database used to train AI tools, according to Stanford researchers, highlighting the grim possibility that the material has helped teach AI image generators to produce new and realistic fake images of child exploitation.[2] In China, hundreds of thousands of data annotators power the country's exploding AI industry. Their labor, often underpaid and overlooked, is vital to the development of new AI applications. China's data labeling companies—and, increasingly, China's tech giants—have partnered with vocational schools, recruiting student interns to do this monotonous and labor-intensive work. The work is often done for sub-minimum wages and under poor conditions, to complete their graduation requirements.[3] The same is happening across Venezuela and India.[4] Content moderation for Chinese platforms saw a rise in Pakistan during the pandemic when other work opportunities in the technology sector were reduced. But now, fatigued moderators are unable to find other work because their experience isn't transferable and the jobs are stigmatized as low-status and low-skill.[5] Some have dubbed these working conditions as "digital sweatshops," as workers can be fired if they were to express their concerns.

Responsible AI cannot be decoupled from data colonialism, and we cannot have a conversation about ethics and fairness without taking all aspects of current labor practices into account. At a recent ACM Conference on Fairness, Accountability, and Transparency (FAccT), research topics such as how to make AI systems more responsible, accountable, and ethical were discussed. But all of this does little to address the exploitative practices in developing countries and the rampant rise of digital sweatshops.

The ethics of enterprise technology will be one of the biggest business issues of the next decade. Advanced technology in a variety of forms—AI being the most topical—is already becoming inextricably linked to every aspect of organizational operations. But every organization today will need the discipline to focus on evaluating the second- and third-order *ethical* considerations of these technologies in an enterprise context—as they relate to all stakeholders, including consumers and employees. This will need to include ensuring that AI algorithms are unbiased, identifying *how* their internal data was trained, and knowing *who* (or what) was responsible for training them. As AI-enabled invisible and microwork continues to grow, this may become harder to identify.

With AI's promise comes peril, e.g., being able to make tools that could be deeply damaging to human civilization; turbocharging the spread of disinformation; facilitating government censorship or surveillance, etc. The current push for more transparency, regulation, and corporate accountability might usher in a new age in which AI development is less exploitative, less done in secrecy, and is done in a way that respects rights such as privacy. But that's not happening yet.

Regulation is a major aspect of this. In June 2023, a court in Kenya issued a landmark ruling against Meta. The U.S. tech giant was, the court ruled, the "true employer of the hundreds of people employed in Nairobi as moderators on its platforms, trawling through posts and images to filter out violence, hate speech and other shocking content." That means Meta can be sued in Kenya for labor rights violations, even though moderators are technically employed by a third-party contractor. TikTok also uses outsourced moderators, perhaps being the next in line for possible litigation.[6] But will collective action be enough to tackle the global tech behemoths that wield an outsize influence and pull the power levers? Extreme economic and geopolitical volatility around the world have certainly not helped to alleviate these tech-fueled concerns about the future of human labor.

Are We All Becoming Data Laborers?

While significantly less exploitative, a looming question we all must ask ourselves is: are we all at risk of becoming data laborers—whether we know it or not—for big technology companies? Text and image AI models are trained using huge datasets that have been scraped from the Internet. This includes our personal data, which is now forever part of an AI model. We inadvertently contribute our free labor by uploading our photos on public sites, upvoting comments on Reddit, or doing basic online searches.[7] All of that feeds emotionally intelligent AI bots, which are based on a large amount of human-made language and emotional data that has been analyzed by these systems.[8]

It should come as no surprise that AI models learn mostly from humans. ChatGPT, for instance, has driven the need for data trainers and labelers who can produce well-written content and are fluent in English. Scale AI and Outlier are also actively seeking contract writers with advanced degrees in specific fields like Hindi, Japanese, math, chemistry, and physics. But gig-based work is fickle and unpredictable and can vanish at any time.[9]

We must also remember that running, managing, and maintaining AI is a lot of work. And that work is giving rise to a new underclass made up of human laborers. These task-based jobs are what anthropologist David Graeber considers to be employment void of meaning or purpose. The jobs that should be automated are ones that many might generally think are already automated, but they continue to have a human stand-in because of bureaucracy or unwillingness. Worries about AI-driven disruption are often met with the claim that AI automates tasks, not jobs, and that these tasks will be mundane ones, allowing people to seek out more satisfying types of work. But just as likely, the rise of AI will resemble past labor-saving technologies, such as the telephone or typewriter, which eliminated the toil of message delivering and handwriting but generated such a slew of new communication, commerce, and paperwork that new offices staffed by new types of workers—clerks, accountants, typists—were needed to manage it."[10] What this means is that if AI comes for your job, it doesn't mean you'll lose it, but—for some types of jobs—it may make it more lonely and more boring. Basically, more like a machine. Human AI data annotators very much resemble robots—they must closely follow instructions and repeat the same task over and over again. Ironically enough, in our effort to create more human-like machine intelligences, we are creating a subclass of assembly line human worker bees dedicated to its management and upkeep.

Google recently parted ways with a human AI training team. For decades, Google Search has been staffed by a combination of well-paid engineers and unseen contract workers. As economic conditions shift and companies attempt to reduce costs, contract workers are an easy place to cut. It could also mean that AI could end up training other AI systems in place of human annotators.[11]

Notes

[1] https://time.com/6247678/openai-chatgpt-kenya-workers

[2] https://www.washingtonpost.com/technology/2023/12/20/ai-child-pornography-abuse-photos-laion/?mc_cid=6bbaf30f32&mc_eid=10057e199f

[3] https://restofworld.org/2023/china-ai-student-labor

[4] https://futurism.com/ai-dirty-secret-poor-people-most-work

[5] https://restofworld.org/2024/content-moderators-jobs-pakistan/?mc_cid=8e7d3a34e9&mc_eid=10057e199f

[6] https://www.wired.com/story/tiktok-leaked-documents

[7] https://www.zdnet.com/article/big-tech-is-actually-doing-all-this-with-your-personal-data-true-or-false

[8] https://www.cmswire.com/digital-experience/ai-gets-empathetic-advances-in-emotionally-intelligent-ai

[9] https://www.nytimes.com/2024/04/10/technology/ai-chatbot-training-chatgpt.html?mc_cid=a7388351d1&mc_eid=10057e199f

[10] https://www.theverge.com/features/23764584/ai-artificial-intelligence-data-notation-labor-scale-surge-remotasks-openai-chatbots

[11] https://restofworld.org/2024/exporter-google-appen-ai-search/?mc_cid=3d70ee3ee0&mc_eid=10057e199f

CHAPTER 17

The Competency Tree

Future-proofing. A new term we hear repeatedly as we grapple with how to not become obsolete. Future-proofed skill sets; future-proofed competencies; future-proofed thinking. . .and the list goes on. But what does this really mean? Human competitiveness in the future is going to rely on an entirely new skills and competencies framework. We tend to fall short when we think of these skills and competencies as one-offs or as mutually exclusive. We throw out words and desired skills without understanding how they all fit together more cohesively.

To successfully address the complex challenges that lie ahead, a more holistic and organic approach toward skills and competencies is needed. By recognizing the interconnectedness of various disciplines and training for them accordingly, organizations can effectively "future-proof" their workforce. Far fewer employees today can rely solely on their specialized knowledge or technical expertise. The rapidly evolving landscape demands individuals who possess a diverse range of skills that can be applied across different domains. This includes critical thinking, problem-solving, adaptability, creativity, collaboration, and digital literacy. Rather than compartmentalizing employees into narrow roles or functions, organizations should encourage cross-functional collaboration and provide opportunities for interdisciplinary training. Forward-thinking companies understand that by nurturing a versatile workforce equipped with a broad set of competencies, they are better prepared to tackle emerging and unforeseen challenges.

When thinking about how these skills fit together, a fitting visual is that of a *tree*—with branches (and sub-branches) that go off in many directions. Trees are ever evolving and organic in nature. Unlike rigid structures, this framework is flexible and adaptable, allowing for growth and change. Just like a tree branches out in various directions, the framework also expands as new technologies emerge, industries evolve, and work dynamics shift. It is not fixed or limited to a specific set of skills but rather encompasses a wide range of abilities that individuals can develop, learn, and unlearn over time. Just as a tree grows stronger with each passing year, individuals can grow more resilient and capable, too, by exploring different branches of knowledge, developing diverse skill sets, and adapting to changing work requirements.

Let's start at the base or trunk of the tree. The trunk of the tree is what grounds all skills and competences, with the biggest grounding factor, first and foremost, being human intelligence.

The Trunk: Intelligent. . .Not Smart

People demonstrating intelligence (the ability to solve challenges they've never encountered before) will be valued far more than those who are smart (the ability to learn and retain things). Smart is based largely on rote memorization. Smart is doing well on a standardized test. Smart is regurgitating information. Smart can be automated. Smart is AI. . .for now. What becomes paramount today is *intelligence*. Where once the mark of a profession was the accumulation and application of years of study, the future will reward those who are better able to grasp a project, factor in related external circumstances, read the culture of the client, gather the relevant resources, and anticipate outcomes. Reliance on sophisticated software and algorithms, rather than diminishing or replacing the need for human critical thinking, will make it even more necessary.

From the trunk of the tree, imagine five branches coming off it. Each branch represents a core competency. From there, each branch contains several sub-branches. And because I love a good acronym (almost as much as I love a good Venn diagram), the five branches spell out the acronym PLANT. PLANT stands for: Passion + Purpose; Literacy; Analytical + Critical thinking; Nimbleness; and Trust.

> **Passion + Purpose:** Passion and purpose can galvanize others, generate optimism, and promote a sense of inspiration and motivation. As smart machines relieve us of tedious tasks and create new efficiencies, they also provide an opportunity for us to tap into our creative potential. The relationship between work, self-reliance, purpose, and dignity becomes even more significant. Sub-branches include creativity, design-thinking, vision, and imagination.
>
> **Literacy:** Literacy skills in the future will come to encapsulate so much more than reading, writing, speaking, and listening. The basics and fundamentals will still matter. But new forms of literacy are emerging. Sub-branches include media literacy, social and cultural literacy, data literacy, emotional literacy, and visual literacy.

Media literacy: Media literacy has become an essential skill set as people navigate today's vast and growing landscape of information. With the rise of social media, online platforms, and digital content consumption, the ability to critically analyze and evaluate sources of information becomes more important. As more people share fake news and spread misinformation, teenagers at French schools are being taught how to decipher whether the X (formerly Twitter) posts on the board are trustworthy or suspect. France is organizing one of the world's biggest national media and Internet literacy efforts to educate students how to identify junk content online. Some educators are calling for the courses to be compulsory, taught alongside basics like math and history.[1] Outside France, Internet literacy programs are also growing. There is a movement of educators and researchers working to counterbalance an explosion of online misinformation. As of now, the United States falls behind many other democracies in fighting this battle. New Jersey, Illinois, and Texas are among states that have recently employed a new set of standards for teaching Internet literacy, a wide-ranging category that contains lessons about how the Internet and social media work, as well as a focus on how to identify misinformation by cross-checking several sources and remaining wary of claims with absent context or overly emotional headlines.[2] National media literacy in Finland is part of a core curriculum starting in preschool. Finland's success is due to a concentrated effort to educate students about fake news. The lessons continue past primary school. Public service announcements offer advice on how to avoid incorrect online assertions and check numerous sources. Additional programs are designed to appeal to older adults, who can be particularly vulnerable to misinformation compared to younger Internet users.[3]

Social, cultural, and global literacy: Reading the culture of a client, interpreting nonverbal body cues, and understanding nuance are just a few aspects of this. Experiential literacy (also referred to as cultural agility) includes a greater emphasis on real-world experience, which could mean taking a job or an internship while studying. Experiential literacy not only fosters adaptability and problem-solving abilities, but it enables people to navigate diverse work environments and effectively collaborate with people from different backgrounds and cultures. This could give students the life skills to negotiate and interact more effectively with colleagues. New jobs are also cropping up alongside a desire to be more globally literate.

Data and technical literacy: This includes the ability to read, analyze, and use the information that increasingly guides everything (i.e., understanding how machines function and how to interact with them). The demand for big data analysts continues to expand rapidly, along with specialization of analyst roles. The explosion of data collection, storage, and mining will open countless opportunities for creatives. Ultimately, a large percentage of people, cross-discipline and at various levels, will become "technologists."

Emotional literacy: Emotional literacy is a key aspect of emotional intelligence (EI)—the ability to recognize and respond to the emotional states of others. A major component of this is empathy—the capacity to understand or feel what another person is experiencing from within their frame of reference. AI imitates but ultimately lacks the ability to truly understand shifting human emotions and connect with others on a shared-experience empathetic level. In a world where remote work and virtual interactions have become more of the norm, EI will be a key human differentiator. And as industries evolve and adapt to changing market demands, people who possess strong EI may be better equipped to handle challenges such as conflict resolution, team collaboration, and leadership development. We also see more school systems incorporating social emotional learning (SEL) initiatives into their curricula.

Visual literacy: Our world is now textured by digital images, ideograms (symbols that represent ideas), videos, emojis, GIFs, and memes. We've long seen the evolution (or devolution) of communication become something that is increasingly short-handed and truncated. Rather than being hampered by traditional written language, people are communicating in shortened bursts. The adage "a picture tells a thousand words" has in some ways never been truer. But interpretation is often inconsistent and can cause miscommunication and misunderstanding. How do we train for—and educate around—the deciphering of visual ambiguity? Or cultural context? Becoming well-versed in the conceptual understanding of visual messaging will become a growing imperative, as will knowing how to leverage it appropriately and effectively. Emoji and emoticons, for instance, are becoming an emerging issue in more court cases. While they've yet to be a deciding factor in any cases, the fact that emoji and emoticons look different on different devices adds to the ambiguity. The need to understand and translate emoji could lead to the emergence of a new career in the legal system: regional emoji expert.[4]

Not only will the design of visual messaging spawn a host of new jobs and job functions, but it will also give rise to entirely new jobs dedicated to the interpretation of image-based forms of communication. For organizations, a growing issue will be etiquette and image-based protocol. Appropriate use and context will have to be clearly outlined, particularly to younger employees who may fail to see these forms of communication as being separate and view them as time-saving shortcuts. Education around contemporary literacy skills will take on a new imperative across the entire age spectrum.

Analytical + Critical thinking: This underpins almost every aspect of future-proofing as it requires a multidisciplinary foundation to knowledge and thought, so independent ideas can be placed within a proper framework. Skill offshoots from this branch include sense-making (by which people give meaning to their collective experiences), curiosity (the intention to understand, learn, or know more about things), and problem-solving. Wisdom and judgment are also offshoots of this branch. Wisdom is not just about accumulating knowledge; it is about applying that knowledge in a thoughtful and discerning manner.

Nimbleness: We can no longer afford to be tethered to one way of doing things or one way of working. This includes a commitment to lifelong learning. Knowledge is becoming outdated at an advancing pace. Part of this will be "unlearning" or forgetting knowledge that is no longer useful. Because of templosion, individual knowledge is also becoming outdated at an advancing pace. Except for the basics—reading, writing, and arithmetic—each year casts doubt on that which we learned the year before. As these powerful changes occur, and they occur constantly, professions across the board, and the practitioners within them, will need to embrace lifelong learning as a core value.

Trust: One of the greatest future challenges for any entity, leader, or manager will be delivering messages that people can trust. Authenticity, transparency, and trustworthiness will become more important. Trust will be a growing component of a workforce made up of both humans and collaborative AI. (We will delve more into trust in Part V, "Trust + Truth.")

The Underlying ROOTS Structure

In thinking about this framework during my many hours at home during the pandemic, I realized that something else was missing. It didn't feel wholly complete. I kept ruminating on one central question: what supports human intelligence? What keeps the trunk of the tree rooted into the ground? What I realized is that intelligence is dependent on an underlying "ROOTS" structure—which (again, because I love a good acronym) stands for: **R**esiliency, **O**utlook + **O**bjectivity, **T**enacity, and **S**elf-regulation.

Resiliency: Resiliency is often referred to as the "rubber ball" effect, where individuals can bounce back from challenges and setbacks. One of the key factors in building resiliency is cultivating a belief in the ability of your intelligence to create coping mechanisms. It is not about avoiding challenges or pretending that everything is always perfect, but rather about recognizing adversity and having the confidence in your own abilities to handle it effectively.

Outlook + Objectivity: Being able to view the future from a balanced perspective is a valuable foundational skill. Outlook, or how we choose to see the world, plays a crucial role in shaping our intellect as we take action and make decisions. However, optimism must be balanced with objectivity. Objectivity requires us to anchor our intellect in a realistic perspective, keeping personal biases, value judgments, assumptions, and heuristics to a minimum. This allows us to make more informed decisions based on facts and evidence rather than preconceived notions. Having an outlook that leads to us believing in the capacity for change can be a powerful asset, and when paired with objectivity, it ensures that our intelligence is grounded in reality, not in subjective biases or assumptions. Will objectivity, however, eventually become less realistically achievable, given polarization and the echo-chamber effect of social media?

Tenacity: Tenacity is about grit, perseverance, inner strength, and mental toughness. Tenacity is the ability to stay focused and determined in the face of obstacles or setbacks. It involves having a strong sense of purpose and refusing to give up even when things get tough. Grit goes together with tenacity, as it encompasses the perseverance needed to achieve long-term objectives. Perseverance allows people to push through difficulties without losing motivation or enthusiasm. Much of tenacity comes down to mental toughness, which enables people to thrive under pressure, adapt quickly, and maintain focus despite distractions or setbacks.

Self-regulation: Self-regulation is the ability to manage disruptive emotions and impulses, even in the face of unexpected challenges. Having strong self-regulation skills allows people to maintain composure and make rational decisions, regardless of external circumstances. Self-regulation is a key component not just for individual success but also in fostering positive relationships and effective teamwork.

Over the course of history, humans, time and time again, have proven to be remarkably resilient and adaptive. And the current environment, with all its technological, social, economic, and geopolitical challenges, is no different. Adaptability is our life raft. And it's not unique to us—we see this same innate drive manifest across the animal kingdom. Scientists perceived that wild monkeys on a Thai island began using stone tools when travel restrictions during the pandemic meant they were no longer being fed by tourists. The usage of stone tools is considered an important step in human evolution.[5] Now, this is not to say that monkeys are going to evolve in this way, but it is to point out that adaptability is a powerful driving force across nature. When seen through this lens, adaptability becomes one of our superpowers. It is a core trait of the entire tree and roots framework.

Notes

[1] https://www.nytimes.com/2018/12/13/technology/france-internet-literacy-school.html

[2] https://fortune.com/2023/03/20/teaching-internet-literacy-the-growing-movement-working-to-offset-an-explosion-of-online-misinformation

[3] https://apnews.com/article/misinformation-education-election-vaccine-canada-finland-e7d6eed63f3db289bf887605c99ab5c5

[4] https://futurism.com/the-byte/interpret-emoji-court-cases

[5] https://www.newscientist.com/article/2409075-monkeys-in-thailand-took-up-stone-tools-when-covid-19-stopped-tourism

CHAPTER 18

A Resurgence of the Humanities

According to a 2023 report by Salesforce, 84 percent of global workers consider skills-based experience more valuable than a degree when trying to land a job in today's market. However, a divide exists between the skills companies are hiring for and those currently being used by the workforce. Only 1 in 10 workers say their day-to-day role currently involves the use of AI, despite its importance to their future skill set. One potential idea to help bridge this gap: upskilling. Almost all (97 percent) workers globally think businesses should prioritize AI skills in their employee development strategy. Data security skills (60 percent), ethical AI and automation skills (58 percent), and programming skills (57 percent) were other skill sets identified as being important to the future of the workplace. When asked about which soft skills will likely be more important, respondents ranked creative imaginative skills (56 percent), customer relationship skills (53 percent), and leadership skills (51 percent) the highest.[1]

According to Northeastern University president Joseph Aoun, who wrote *Robot-Proof: Higher Education in the Age of Artificial Intelligence*, future-proofing is less about picking a safe job and more about continuously modernizing your skills throughout your career. He says education needs to change monumentally if workers are to adapt to this new environment. His solution is *humanics*.[2] There is currently a profusion of interest in STEM (science, technology, engineering, mathematics) careers. But STEM education cannot stand in isolation. It is one piece of a much larger puzzle.

Currently, as has been the case historically, men massively outnumber women majoring in most STEM-related fields in college. UN data shows that 30 percent of female students go on to STEM-related fields in higher ed, and that, globally, women make up only 28 percent of the workforce in STEM. Gender gaps are highest in some of the fastest-growing and highest-paid jobs of the future. However, in recent years while much of the focus has been on increasing the pipeline of students—particularly young girls—into STEM, many of the jobs in the future will simply require a working understanding of a particular technology, as opposed to the kind of intimate technical expertise that an engineer or developer would need.

One of the things we may see is a resurgence of the humanities. Contrary to STEM disciplines, the humanities have long been derided as antiquated academic disciplines that won't lead to lucrative employment in the future. But the humanities are bound for a resurgence. That is one reason why the *A* for "arts" has been added to STEM to make it STEAM. We know that a strong connection exists between creative problem-solving, original thinking, and the cultivation of artistic skill sets. In fact, Einstein credited his discovery of the Theory of Relativity to a musical thought that came while playing violin. There is a growing recognition of the power of STEAM to inspire learners and foster a more holistic approach to learning. Art is not just about aesthetics; it is a powerful tool that can encourage learners to explore beyond their textbooks, tap into their innate curiosity, and pursue knowledge in less traditional and more creative ways.

This comes at a time, however, when the value of humanities is often questioned and funding for these subjects is at risk. Several rural universities in the United States are eliminating large numbers of programs and majors—a disproportionate number of them in the humanities.[3] Economists (and parents alike) have questioned whether a liberal arts degree is worth the hefty price tag. For decades now, people have fervently debated the ROI (return on investment) of a liberal arts education, a debate centered largely on practicality vs. passion. The move toward the former has placed greater focus on things such as engineering and business programs, and less on liberal arts majors like anthropology, literature, and language. Much of this is driven by a push to more closely align college majors to employment opportunities. But are these truly the employment opportunities of the future, and are we focusing on the wrong things? Or educating around outdated skill sets and deprioritizing the ones that will really matter? And going back to the visual of the Venn diagram, perhaps we need to think about the intersections by launching more interdisciplinary programs. What would a major that combined quantum mechanics and religion look like? Or cybersecurity and philosophy? Mathematics and ancient studies? Data science and art history?

Not only are the humanities at risk of being eliminated, but some aspects of the humanities are being automated, too. Take language, for instance. The landscape of language learning is shifting. With automatic translation tools becoming more sophisticated and widely available, people are finding it easier to communicate across language barriers without the need for extensive language learning. In the coming years, AI translation is poised to become even more prevalent and seamless. This may lead to a decrease in traditional language learning efforts as individuals rely more on AI for accurate and efficient translations. But language is not just a tool for communication; it shapes the very way we perceive reality. Studies have shown that learning a new language can open up new perspectives and ways of thinking about the world. When we learn to speak, read, and write in a different language, we are not just acquiring words; we are gaining entry into a new realm of understanding. This process allows us to see the world through a different and more diverse lens.[4] How then can we be expected to develop cultural competency? Or grasp the beliefs and mores of people from various backgrounds? This likely matters more for much younger children than for college-aged students.

Doubling Down on Innovative Talent Strategies

Today there is a growing concern about the widening gap between the education requirements for employees and the actual skills and competencies needed in the workplace. It is evident that jobs are progressively becoming deskilled, with technology automating routine tasks and shifting the focus toward more specialized roles. While education remains an essential foundation, employers are increasingly placing greater emphasis on practical skills and real-world experience. This shift in focus reflects the recognition that traditional educational qualifications alone may not adequately prepare individuals for the dynamic nature of work.

Geoff Colvin's book *Humans Are Underrated* says that as automation continues, humans will remain not only valuable but also powerful. He believes that our ability to feel will save us from a robotic takeover. People with hybrid skills—high technological literacy and deep social sensitivity—will be among the winners in the future.[5] It is currently believed that those with the most marketable skills in the future will be those who can code. Companies in almost every industry are creating lucrative opportunities for those in the tech industry, and there is a focus on coding and tech skills among today's youngest generation. But there is no reason to believe that this work can't be digitized. If coding is language and generative AI LLMs are most proficient at learning language and generating new outputs, how might these systems usurp or replace coders in the future? But as of now, more software developers are relying on generative AI to help improve their productivity. The appeal is the promise of a faster, more streamlined software development process. When taken in sum, it can help companies ease the pressure brought on by a scarcity of engineering talent.[6]

Employers must begin adopting a wider lens when it comes to hiring. Instead of focusing solely on previous experience that directly matches the responsibilities of an open role, organizations can greatly benefit from assessing candidates based on their capacity to learn, their intrinsic capabilities, and their transferable skill sets. When it comes to skills development, much of it happens on the job. Work experience contributes 40 percent of the average person's lifetime earnings in the United States, according to research from the McKinsey Global Institute. Skills obtained through work experience are an even larger factor for people without educational credentials who begin in lower-wage work. Employers may need to reevaluate whether some credential requirements are actually necessary. About 60 percent of U.S. workers have skills obtained through on-the-job experience but do not have four-year college degrees.[7] Employers can also recruit from often overlooked populations such as retirees who want to return to work (and carry considerable institutional knowledge and domain expertise) or back-to-work mothers with employment gaps.

Heading up a hybrid workforce of people and AI will require a different type of leadership, one that blends human skills such as empathy with a tech-savvy and data-driven mindset. COOs will need to incorporate robotics and AI in line with an overall digital strategy. CMOs may be increasingly driven by data analytics. Chief Human Resource Officers (CHROs) will also see their roles greatly affected as it will become harder to define a "human resource." We've long said that the roles of HR and InfoTech (IT) should merge as more "whats" are hired alongside "whos." At the board level, more directors will need to have the expertise to oversee proper governance over AI development and application, and guide decision-making around its practices in an ethically and fiscally responsible way.

The Competency Tree framework, as outlined in Chapter 17, "The Competency Tree," is meant to serve as a modeling outline—one in which more branches and offshoots can be added. It can also help visualize possible arenas for future jobs—even ones we have yet to be able to imagine. When it comes to talent management, talent acquisition, and human capital, we will be forced to rethink workforce strategy (at all levels) and how it will impact how we hire for, train for, and prepare for this future. According to an August 2023 report from LinkedIn called "Future of Work: AI Report," the skills needed for many jobs have changed by an astounding 25 percent since 2015, with that number projected to reach at least 65 percent by 2030 because of the rapid advancement of new technologies like AI.[8] Outdated metrics for hiring talent (e.g., degree or pedigree) will not build the future workforce. Companies must ensure that they have the right people with the right skills in the right roles. But it doesn't just stop there. Investing in skills—and reevaluating which skills *matter*—must be an ongoing process.

Notes

[1] https://www.salesforce.com/news/stories/digital-skills-based-experience
[2] https://www.bbc.com/worklife/article/20190127-humanics-a-way-to-robot-proof-your-career

[3] https://hechingerreport.org/rural-universities-already-few-and-far-between-are-being-stripped-of-majors

[4] https://www.theatlantic.com/technology/archive/2024/03/generative-ai-translation-education/677883/?mc_cid=eff9304591&mc_eid=10057e199f

[5] https://geoffcolvin.com/books/humans-are-underrated

[6] https://www.wsj.com/articles/generative-ai-helping-boost-productivity-of-some-software-developers-731fa5a

[7] https://www.mckinsey.com/capabilities/people-and-organizational-performance/our-insights/human-capital-at-work-the-value-of-experience

[8] https://economicgraph.linkedin.com/research/future-of-work-report-ai

CHAPTER 19

The Workspace Culture Chain

The integration of AI into operations has become both a boon and a potential challenge. On the one hand, AI offers unparalleled efficiencies and capabilities that can elevate human performance and drive exceptional results. On the other hand, there is a concern that this integration may inadvertently lead businesses to deprioritize the human elements that are key for fostering a positive work culture. Understanding the paradoxical nature of AI integration must be at the heart of creating a human-centric work culture. This requires finding harmony between leveraging technology for efficiency gains while valuing and nurturing the contributions of employees. A thriving work culture must be centered around an organization's most valuable asset: their people. But creating a new framework around this must go beyond investing in employee development programs, fostering collaboration among teams, promoting open communication channels, and encouraging innovation.

A report from the Massachusetts Institute of Technology (MIT) states that the use of chatbots is growing productivity, lessening inequality between workers, and improving job satisfaction. Seventy-five percent of respondents who implemented ChatGPT saw an increase in team morale, collaboration, and group learning.[1] While this is a best use case scenario, we must also remember two things: AI is a tool, a strategy, and not a vision; and AI alone cannot improve company culture. But it can, if leveraged in the right way, inspire employees to try.

As leaders navigate this evolving new work landscape, culture is another piece ripe for redefinition. How can forward-thinking organizations design and execute the conditions for truly effective culture in a hybridized environment? And how can it be reimagined in a more human-centric way? Workplace culture must capitalize on new human-based skills such as self-awareness, social intelligence, agility and adaptability, and the desire for human connection. By leveraging and creating richer opportunities for human-to-human experience—which more people are craving—organizations can help establish a culture based on purpose, meaning, transparency, openness, commonality, and connection. It's one of the reasons there has been a rise in companies offering retreats. People are seeking chances to bond with their colleagues away from the office, combining business travel with productive play. There is even increased talk of a 4-day workweek to convince workers that they can come back to the office and still have sufficient work/life balance.

While many business leaders have accepted hybrid work as a permanent reality, others now feel strongly that businesses need to reclaim more in-person time from their workers. Large financial and Big Tech firms are leading the drive back toward the physical office. Many bosses fear that fully remote work dents productivity. Yet all the pressure from above has done little to dent employees' appetite for remote working. In English-speaking countries, which have the highest levels of remote work, there is a desire for more. And the trend is spreading globally, even in places where remote work is less common.

Technological Monitoring as a Culture Killer

Many attempts to rethink remote work culture have centered around technological solutions, particularly those aimed at enhancing employee productivity. Microsoft dealt with criticism for its "Productivity Score" technology, which measures how much individual workers use email, chat, and other digital tools. New AI software can venture a guess as to what you are typing during video calls, even though tone—and its associated meaning—can be increasingly hard to decipher online. But there are signs that tech-enabled monitoring of remote workers is leading to both burnout and backlash. It is also usually counterproductive. A survey by SHRM (the Society for Human Resource Management) found that 49 percent of employees subject to stringent monitoring experienced severe anxiety, compared to only 7 percent of those subject to low levels of monitoring. Monitoring and surveillance can also increase employee unhappiness and deteriorate morale.[2]

For decades, we have classified members of the workforce in various ways, but the most common was white-collar/blue-collar and hourly/salaried. And, although there were many exceptions, it was thought that if you were white-collar and salaried, you were in a decent position. Now, and especially with the acceleration of remote work, there is a third distinction emerging, cutting across the prior categories: monitored vs. independent work—those people who are being constantly surveilled by AI, even in their remote work locations, and those who are left to do their work independently, often at their own pace and time.

The governance and oversight of AI surveillance technologies in work-related environments will open up a series of conversations about privacy, compensation, management, leadership, the biases and imperfections of algorithms, and the types of talent the organization wants to attract and retain. The topic of AI-centric employee surveillance will heat up greatly in the next few years.

Creation of a New Culture Framework

At a time when people feel more socially disconnected and physically isolated, technological Band-Aids will only get companies so far. Instead, or as a complement to other approaches, a new framework to meaningfully address workspace culture is urgently needed. Based on an interlinking set of gears (i.e., workspace variables), with each one dependent on the other for strength and reinforcement, I refer to this model as the *Workspace Culture CHAIN*. Like the *Competency Tree*, this is a framework that can be modified and adapted based on internal needs, in which new links can be added or subtracted to both ends of the chain.

The CHAIN acronym (here we go again!) stands for: **C**ore beliefs + Coherence; **H**uman potential; **A**ccountability + Autonomy; **I**nclusion; and **N**urturing.

C: Core Beliefs + Coherence

An organization's values are its driving beliefs, philosophies, and principles. More than ever, leadership will need to communicate these values in a coherent way. One question to address will be: how can an organization guarantee the uniform distribution of culture across those working remotely and those in a physical office? A risk with hybridized work is the possibility for employees to have divergent understandings of culture. Not only will leadership need to clearly articulate a sense of shared purpose, but they also need to come across as more approachable, show vulnerability, and transform the culture into one that more explicitly values individuals and individuality. Trust is a critical component of coherence. A crisis of trust is increasingly common as the strains of remote working wear down company culture and people's goodwill. Increased reports of electronic monitoring by AI also suggest that executives' confidence in having figured it out is starting to ebb.

H: Human Potential

As the nature of work shifts, employee motivation (both intrinsic and extrinsic) and reward structures will need to shift, as will intelligent organizational design. But how can flexible organizations truly unlock human potential?

Some companies are attempting to gamify the traditional office meeting. Beyond this, organizational leadership will increasingly have to ask how it can create an environment that not only builds flexibility and adaptability into it but also rewards a sense of wonder, imagination, and curiosity? A great majority of employees do not feel engaged in their work, and significant numbers feel disengaged. For a medium-size S&P 500 company, employee disengagement and attrition could cost between $228 million and $355 million a year in lost productivity. More than half of employees report being somewhat to fairly unproductive at work.[3] Especially in the middle years of their lives, people feel a slump in happiness with their work and jobs. Having a sense of purpose is not only a proven way to better engage younger generations but also to keep older ones healthier physically and mentally. And giving them more interesting things to experience at work keeps them engaged.

A: Accountability + Autonomy

As people work more autonomously, productivity and focus are two things that will help define culture. Caveday is a start-up that claims to help you attain meaningful work via facilitated "deep focus" Zoom sessions. It is one of many remote coworking start-ups to have taken off since the pandemic to tackle a range of worker issues from loneliness to low productivity and procrastination. We may also see a wake-up call around the pointlessness of work meetings and "presenteeism"—the idea that unless you are always visible, you are not working. Many more employers will have to embrace new forms of trust and ways of assessing accountability and more autonomy given the more flexible arrangements.

I: Inclusion

Inclusion is about belonging, being valued, creating a feeling of familiarity, and enhancing individual visibility. This includes decision-making. Another core part of inclusion—particularly in a remote work setting—will be creating a *sense of place*. This refers to the emotional attachments people cultivate or experience in particular settings. Proximity to others is also key. Research has documented how our capacity for interacting with people and objects in both physical and virtual spaces is deeply encoded in the structure of our brains. That is why we need to shift our thinking away from traditional brick-and-mortar "workplaces" to thinking about how we can create more human-centric "work*spaces*," even if this is in a worker's home or car.

Another aspect of this is the recruiting, hiring, retaining, and advancement of neurodivergent workers. Neurodiverse populations remain a largely untapped talent pool. Many people on the autism spectrum, for instance, have higher than average skills in pattern recognition or mathematics. Research has shown, too, that dyslexia should be redefined as an asset rather than a disability. According to researchers at the University of Cambridge, dyslexia is linked to "enhanced abilities" in areas like discovery, invention, and creativity. These skills are valuable in helping people adapt to changing environments, researchers say. Ingenuity and big-picture, long-term thinking are among the skills and strengths linked to these adaptive and exploratory behaviors.[4]

N: Nurture

With depression and anxiety estimated to have cost the global economy $1 trillion per year in lost productivity *before* the pandemic, according to the World Health Organization (WHO), mental health in the workplace has long been a concern. WHO data also states that in the first year of the pandemic, global occurrence of anxiety and depression increased by 25 percent. New digital platforms are helping promote more integrative mental health and wellness approaches including meditation, mindfulness, and sleep support for workers. From a productivity perspective, business leaders are increasingly concerned about mental well-being, as people are working longer hours from home than they did in the office. Rituals and well-established routines from the workplace will be ripe for redesign, particularly when it comes to re-creating those rituals digitally. In times of uncertainty, rituals provide structure and a sense of control by imposing order—illusory or not. An extension of this is fostering a culture in which spontaneous casual interactions can occur. Organizations will be increasingly tasked with revitalizing that feeling of serendipity across distances. Even as AI technology advances, employee well-being and involvement are fundamental to a company's success. A key part of any culture framework is alignment—the shared ethos of an organization. It is easy to define organizational culture using clichés of what we want that culture to be rather than what it actually looks like internally. We can point to numerous examples of misalignment between the cultural values outwardly espoused and how employees are treated internally.

New Human-Centric Approaches

Many employers will face major challenges in hiring low-skill, entry-level workers when economic circumstances improve. When it comes to finding those workers, a large part of the problem is the impediments employers create when they concentrate on screening people out. Traditional staffing processes are expensive and time-consuming. Business leaders are being pressured to expand inclusion and diversity. Typical hiring practices often exclude millions, including the formerly incarcerated, the homeless, and those in recovery. One solution is open hiring. This strategy shuns resumes, interviews, and background checks, focuses exclusively on human potential, and offers employment to anyone wanting and able to work. For industries that greatly depend on front-line talent—manufacturing, distribution, retail, and food services, where candidates can be trained on the job—open hiring provides the chance to tap into more diverse talent pools.[5]

Other key questions to consider in an AI-driven future include: How do we measure and reward true human resources? How do we create new metrics to measure human output? How do we empower human value creation? How can organizations reimagine human capital? Organizations that treat their people with greater fairness and consideration will emerge among the winners. This ultimately could correlate with a rise in a more empathetic workspace culture and style of leadership. In sharp contrast to the competitive business philosophies that marked traditional corporate culture decades ago, empathy has emerged as a powerful driver of culture, and it will become more critical as work continues to be automated and distributed.

But changing culture is easier said than done. Workplaces will not only need fewer management layers, but they will also need to introduce new recruitment procedures that include apprenticeships and gig economy-style contingent working to attract a wider skill base. Increased automation will also require new management approaches, including the management of human and AI blended teams. HR departments will also need to think about whether their policies and procedures are suitable for a mixed human and AI workforce, and they will be tasked with constant reevaluation of their hiring practices. HR's function is quickly moving away from traditional evaluation and recruiting and toward a greater focus on maximizing employee experience across an increasingly blended workforce. There must also be a much more integrated set of strategies and cross-disciplinary understanding between HR and IT, who traditionally hires the technology.

And once organizations determine which processes can be automated, and which continue to require humans, and to what degree, employees can then be redeployed accordingly. Outdated management practices are largely out of sync with advances in technology, leading to intelligent IT but unintelligent organizational and managerial design. That leads to low performance and engagement for which no technology can compensate.

AI-Driven Cultural Crossroads

Since the beginning of the 21st century, corporate culture has commanded the front pages of business newspapers, board director magazines, investor relations announcements, and employee prospecting materials. It's what separated the work/life balance companies from the 24/7 ones, the short-term, results-driven management from the longer-term visionaries, and the inclusionary from the old guard. There were institutions known to be trustworthy and authentic, and ones that were thought to be ruthless and opportunistic. Sometimes culture was uniform from top down, and sometimes it never penetrated beneath the surface, and every department had its own. But there was always the belief that culture, loosely defined but generally understood, was somehow identifiable and distinguishable. It was often thought that an important role of middle management was to preserve and communicate the culture. We are now at a crossroads. . .and AI is driving much of this. There is a real question as to whether corporate culture can continue to exist.

With the explosion of AI, humans are increasingly being displaced or augmented in decisions related to business processes, employment (hiring and firing), financial decisions, and matters of talent, whether operational or strategic. In many cases, there is no way for humans to override AI decisions. And humans are increasingly coming to trust and rely upon them in lieu of other humans. As smart technologies make more of the decisions, will the workplace continue to be a central hub of human-to-human exchange? Will decisions made by AI undercut the ability of organizations to use culture to distinguish themselves—or even to understand what it is anymore?

A key aspect of culture in the future will depend on our ability to override AI decisions and decision-making capabilities. Many managers and executives already working with AI admit they have had to intervene in their systems due to delivery of flawed or unfair outputs. One in four executives responding to a survey conducted by SAS, Accenture, Intel, and Forbes say they have had to rethink, redesign, or override an AI-based system due to problematic or inadequate results.[6] We know that complex algorithms and machine learning models can sometimes produce inaccurate or biased outcomes, leading to unintended consequences. This highlights the need for human intervention and oversight to ensure that AI systems are delivering reliable and ethical results.

Alongside leadership and internal cultural shifts, structure will also have to evolve. Deloitte's State of AI in the Enterprise 4th Edition (2022) survey results show a disconnect in putting AI into action internally in the organizations. Across a wide array of operational undertakings—both on the business side and within the IT function—approximately only one-third of those surveyed report that they have implemented leading operational practices for AI. According to the findings, an effective AI solution should be devised to fit within a new workflow. It must also be developed to advance the delivery of *value*. Clearly, business stakeholders should take a lead role in building this out, but the reality is that many lack the understanding and tech sophistication to know how to do this effectively. All too frequently, according to Deloitte, AI and ML development teams are put in charge without a clear view into the organizational processes they are tasked with changing. We talked earlier in the book about vision vs. strategy. This is where having a clearly articulated vision takes on paramount importance.

Notes

[1] https://www.benefitnews.com/news/ai-cant-save-your-company-culture

[2] https://www.shrm.org/topics-tools/news/employee-relations/viewpoint-remote-work-corroding-trust

[3] https://www.mckinsey.com/capabilities/people-and-organizational-performance/our-insights/some-employees-are-destroying-value-others-are-building-it-do-you-know-the-difference

[4] https://www.weforum.org/agenda/2022/07/dyslexia-enhanced-abilities-studies

[5] https://hbr.org/2021/01/imagine-a-hiring-process-without-resumes

[6] Report "AI Momentum, Maturity and Models for Success." SAS Institute, Inc. 2018.

PART V

Trust + Truth

I n the following chapters, we will explore how trust and truth are combining to shape and influence much of our world today. Chapters 20–26 will dig into the risks and the emerging threats of AI, both of which are very real and need to be understood. The intent is to provide a realistic look at the current trajectory of these AI-driven realities in as objective a way as possible. It may seem initially as though we're going through a dark tunnel, but there is a light at the end of it if we act now and heed the urgency. In Chapters 27 and 28, we will delve into possible new solutions and areas for optimism.

CHAPTER 20

The Trust Imperative

How would you define trust? I'm sure each one of us would have a slightly different answer as trust is multidimensional and comes in different forms. Trust, as a fundamental part of human relationships, plays a central role in many different aspects of our lives. Perhaps trust can be defined as the firm belief or confidence in the reliability and integrity of someone or something. It is a bond that allows people to feel safe, secure, and comfortable in their interactions with others. In our personal lives, trust forms the foundation of strong friendships, intimate relationships, and family dynamics. Trust also extends beyond individual relationships; it encompasses trust in institutions, governments, or businesses. But when this trust is compromised, it can have far-reaching consequences for society. Building trust takes time. It requires honesty, transparency, and accountability from all parties involved. Trust is fragile—once broken, it can be challenging to rebuild.

Part IV of this book focused on time. But layered on top of time is trust. Trust will become the next "luxury market" as well as one of the most valuable currencies of the future. Why? Because just like time, trust is something that is in high demand and short supply. Our future will demand that we choose trust—trust in each other; trust in strategy; trust in our society; trust in progress. And we all need to find ways to put that into action because trust has become a precious commodity.

Institutional Trust

Trust, like time, is shifting, and it is pressing us to redefine what it means in today's operating environment. Businesses today are at the intersection of two trends that will define work and life for years to come. One is the widespread decline in trust. The other is the rise of AI. These two forces are fundamentally reshaping how we operate, communicate, and make decisions. Each year, Edelman, the global communications firm, conducts a survey on trust called the Edelman Trust Barometer. Its 2023 report began with a bold statement: "Business is the only institution seen as competent and ethical." According to the report, the erosion of trust in societal institutions has reached alarming levels. Economic anxiety, the spread of disinformation, a widening mass-class divide, and a failure of leadership have all played significant roles in deepening the existing polarization. Another recent survey conducted by Bentley University and Gallup showed evidence that while businesses, both big and small alike, are hurrying to implement AI, consumers do not think there are enough guardrails in place to ensure responsible and trustworthy decision-making. The majority (79 percent) of respondents said that they trust businesses "not much" or "not at all" to adopt AI responsibly.[1]

Today, trust seems to be on everyone's mind. "Rebuilding trust" was the central theme of the World Economic Forum's annual meeting in Davos in January 2024. And, aside from the climate and geopolitical conflicts, AI was a central topic. Boards of directors are putting more pressure on their CEOs to have a strategy in place for leveraging AI throughout various business units, even as many executives are still trying to figure out where exactly to start. KPMG's global report "Trust in Artificial Intelligence" (2023) found that across countries, 61 percent of people are cautious about trusting AI systems, stating either uncertainty or an outright refusal to trust it. Trust is especially low in Japan and Finland, where less than a quarter of respondents trust AI. People in the emerging economies of Brazil, India, China, and South Africa, in contrast, have the highest levels of trust, with most people trusting AI systems. People have more confidence in AI systems to yield correct and consistent output, but they are also more uncertain about the safety, security, and fairness of AI systems and the degree to which they maintain privacy. The KPMG study also found that when AI is used in the human resources function, it is trusted and accepted the least. The fear for many people is that personal information will be used in ways that make them feel uncomfortable.

Trust in technologies like AI can be double-sided: AI can help contribute to the erosion of trust, but it also can be leveraged as a tool for building trust. According to insights from Ernst & Young, in order for AI systems to eventually be accepted and trusted by users, these systems must be understandable, meaning their decision-making capabilities can be justified and explained. The inability and failure to enact governance and ethical standards that foster trust in AI will inhibit organizations' ability to harness the full promise of these technologies to drive future growth.[2] A Boston Consulting Group (BCG) experiment showed that people tend to mistrust generative AI in areas where it can actually bring significant value, while simultaneously placing excessive trust in its capabilities where the technology may not be as competent. Around 90 percent of participants enhanced their performance when using generative AI for creative ideation. When participants used generative AI to solve a particular business problem that was outside the tool's existing competence, many participants took GPT-4's deceptive output at face value. It led to a 23 percent decrease in their performance versus those who didn't use the tool at all.[3]

With the advent of social media platforms and online influencers, information spreads rapidly and can easily sway public opinion. On the one hand, people may find themselves trusting sources that lack credibility simply because they align with their preconceived beliefs or desires. On the other hand, when it comes to businesses, customers have grown increasingly cautious due to past instances of data breaches and unethical practices. They demand more stringent security measures and reliable and transparent systems to protect their personal information.

That lack of trust extends to the public sector, too. According to a 2023 Pew Research Center poll, although public trust in the federal government has been low for decades, it has now returned to near record lows. Fewer than two in ten Americans say they trust the government to do what is right "just about always" (1 percent) or "most of the time" (15 percent). This is among the lowest trust measures in close to seven decades of polling.[4] A Gallup report from 2022 stated that the five worst-rated institutions—newspapers, the criminal justice system, television news, big business, and the U.S. Congress—evoke confidence in less than 20 percent of Americans.[5]

One of the greatest future challenges will be delivering messages that people can trust. Authenticity and trustworthiness of messaging will be more important than ever. Trust will be the currency of tomorrow, and AI will be both a powerful tool in upholding this value and a powerful tool in destroying this value. Organizations of all kinds, both public and private, will be more scrutinized. Journalists, communications professionals, crisis management professionals, and social media administrators will all be hugely valuable and highly accountable.

Generational Trust

Research on how generative AI models affect children's beliefs is an especially high priority, too. Children are more vulnerable to "belief distortion" because of their more influenceable knowledge states. They also tend to anthropomorphize technology at higher levels compared to other age groups.[6] Because their greater sense of the world is still forming and developing, AI could also shape children's perception of reality, as it can generate highly realistic and persuasive content. This raises questions about the authenticity and reliability of information that children encounter in their everyday lives. The extent to which exposure to AI-generated content affects their ability to distinguish between fact and fiction, as well as how it impacts their critical thinking skills, is something that will require deeper study and analysis—particularly over time, as we have little idea how this will play out in the long term. And will digital natives be more prone to deepfake and misinformation, disinformation, malinformation and digitally derived information (MDMD) susceptibility or less prone to it because they are growing up with the technology?

It has been widely found that interpersonal trust increases with age. While this, more generally, should be viewed positively, the rapid advancements in generative AI have created new and concerning risks for the elderly. As AI systems become more sophisticated at mimicking human voices, faces, and behaviors, bad actors will increasingly leverage these technologies to prey on senior citizens. From fake calls from a grandchild asking for money to doctored videos of politicians, large swaths of the aging population—let alone the population at large—are unprepared to defend themselves against the onslaught of convincing yet fraudulent content. Not being able to distinguish fake information from real information can have real consequences for someone's well-being—especially for older adults, who in general have more financial assets and must make more high-stakes health decisions.

While younger generations may be more aware of the potential for deepfakes and other AI-generated content to be used for financial and political scams, many of the oldest people in our society may simply not understand the full magnitude of these emerging threats. But age-related susceptibility to deceptive information has been found to be evident only among those categorized as the "oldest old"—those aged 85 and older. This surprising finding challenges the widespread assumption that older individuals are more gullible and prone to believing misinformation. In fact, older adults may be no more likely to fall for fake information than younger adults. As we age, it's true that many of us experience some cognitive decline. However, it's important to recognize that growing older also brings significant advantages that can offset these changes. With age often comes a broader knowledge base, more life experience, and, frequently, a more positive emotional outlook.[7] Cognitive fitness practices can also have major benefits for aging populations, which could also help them better identify AI-related risks.

Navigating the Trust Staircase

Created originally by the University of Oxford mathematician Roger Penrose, the Penrose Stairs is a two-dimensional staircase comprising four 90-degree turns that form a continuous loop. The staircase could be ascended or descended as there is no end. The Penrose Stairs inspired the artist M. C. Escher to create "Ascending and Descending," the visual illusion of a staircase loop that seems to be eternally rising. Both illusions are about the distortion of perspective. A person could climb the stairs forever and never get any higher. The staircase can be dizzying and disorienting because it is nonlinear. But it's always evolving. It isn't fixed. It isn't stable. It's informed by the past but always moving up . . . or down . . . depending on perspective and circumstances.

In today's ever-evolving trust landscape, it may feel as though we're continually circling a Penrose Staircase. The spiral of distrust—aided by a pervasive environment of MDMD (mis-, dis-, mal-, digitally derived information)—has become so disorienting that it is harder to know if you are ascending or descending it. At a time when trust is at a record low, navigating the trust staircase will become a growing organizational imperative and a core part of leadership. But if trust is to exist, it must become part of an ongoing process that is deeply ingrained into the ethos of a company. Stakeholders will want assurance that the companies they engage with have their best interests at heart. Clearly, many businesses will not. And as templosion shortens information cycles, those businesses risk losing customers, employees, and investors. Literally overnight. Public employees, too, will fail in their productivity and competence if their morale is affected by a decline of trust in their governance hierarchy.

Notes

[1] https://tech.co/news/americans-dont-trust-businesses-ai

[2] https://www.ey.com/en_us/digital/how-do-you-teach-ai-the-value-of-trust

[3] https://www.bcg.com/publications/2023/how-people-create-and-destroy-value-with-gen-ai

[4] https://www.pewresearch.org/politics/2023/09/19/public-trust-in-government-1958-2023

[5] https://news.gallup.com/poll/508169/historically-low-faith-institutions-continues.aspx

[6] https://www.science.org/doi/10.1126/science.adi0248

[7] https://news.ufl.edu/2022/05/aging-adults-fake-news

CHAPTER 21

Trust + the Changing Nature of Influence

Interpersonal Trust: Trust in Our "AI Companions"

Trust is a crucial factor when it comes to embracing new technologies. It is also a crucial factor when it comes to embracing new "relationships." Imagine having an AI that not only understands your needs and desires but also anticipates them. This is a totally different type of relationship and level of intimacy. An AI can bring us closer to a future where our digital assistants not only serve as capable helpers but also earn our trust as reliable companions. We know that humans have a deep tendency toward anthropomorphism—the imputation of human-like qualities onto animals and nonliving things. Anthropomorphizing pets, for example, doesn't require the belief that the pet is human, only that the personality and behavior inspire humans to treat it like a person with complex desires, motivations, or memories (something I am guilty of when it comes to my two cats). Social AI is purposefully made to elicit anthropomorphic reactions. Starting from early childhood, AI affects how humans feel about "thinking" technology. Alexa is already interacting with children who anthropomorphize "her." At the other end of the age spectrum, seniors are a growing market for AI and a major growth market for robots in caregiving and personal assistance. Religious representatives are often called in to comfort those at the end of life. Now chatbots can help people speak about end of life, give comfort, and provide support to the terminally ill, even influencing their decisions.

Our tendency to attribute human characteristics to AI will likely grow, particularly because academic research is increasingly anthropomorphizing technology, too. Researchers at Stanford University analyzed the content of over 655,000 academic publications released between May 2007 and September 2023, as well as the headlines of close to 14,000 news articles citing some of those papers. They found that the way technologies are talked about in academic papers has shifted over time, with about a 50 percent increase in the level of anthropomorphism. This is critical because it impacts the way we think and feel about these systems. According to Melanie Mitchell at the Santa Fe Institute, the problem has worsened as the output of chatbots has become more human-like. "People are very prone to project human qualities on systems then engender assumptions about how these systems are likely to act and how trustworthy they are," she says.[1]

The design of the physical AI-enabled robot is equally important. Should they express human characteristics and appear more humanoid? Should they have relatable features? According to Julie Shah, professor at MIT, what typically occurs is that we examine human behavior and design robots around it. But she believes there's potential to work together in more meaningful ways by having robots understand human feelings. She contends that "we need machines to process information as efficiently as people do. So, robots can watch us and learn unwritten rules to collaborate like a human team member."

AI will become more than just a tool or a piece of technology. It will evolve into a trusted companion, something that understands you on a deeper level. As AI continues to advance, it will possess the ability to notice your moods and emotions, knowing exactly what suggestions or recommendations you need at any given moment. Imagine having an AI that anticipates your needs and works tirelessly to satisfy them. Or it could be your personal therapist, providing guidance and support when you're feeling down or overwhelmed. It could act as your personal coach, helping you set goals. It's only natural that we will default to thinking of AI as more than just a machine. We will trust it with our deepest thoughts and emotions, relying on its expertise and understanding. With time, the bond between humans and AI could eventually become so strong that we won't be able to imagine our lives without our trusted "friend" by our side.

One of the reasons behind this dynamic is that these systems are developed to influence us. They have been instructed to persuade humans that they are something close to human. They have been programmed to hold dialogues and respond to us with some semblance of emotion. They have been deliberately turned into friends and assistants.[2]

AI + Virtual Influence: Who and What We Trust

Recommendations, from buying cars to choosing laundry detergent, used to come via word of mouth or based on customers' previous experiences with products. Now, AI is assuming this role as more customers are being swayed by AI virtual social media influencers. A new phenomenon has been emerging that is altering the way content is created, consumed, and marketed online: virtual influencers. These AI-powered avatars have seamlessly integrated themselves into our social media feeds. Virtual influencers represent a dance between cutting-edge technology and our innate desire for connection. Using AI and virtual reality (VR), these digital creations can interact with users in ways that were once unimaginable. They can deliver personalized messages, endorse products, and even engage in conversations with their followers. VR is also evolving into a very important medium for storytelling and narrative. It can be used to design immersive experiences that change people's perspectives about different issues, increase empathy, and drive consumer engagement.

Virtual influencers aren't necessarily a totally new concept. Virtual Japanese pop star Kyoko Date has been around since 1996. Developments in AI, the rise of social media, and ideas of the metaverse are combining to fuel the rise of virtual influencers, which occupy a very distinct cultural dimension. Virtual influencers exist in a currently undefined and unexplored space between our world and the virtual world. It may become more difficult to tell the difference between them and real people, especially as many virtual influencers already come across as quite human-like.[3] The rise of virtual AI influencers also raises issues regarding credibility and who or what is considered an "expert." The most famous AI *virtual* social media influencer, Lil Miquela, has 3.6 million followers on TikTok and another 2.7 million on Instagram. "She" charges more than $10,000 per Instagram post and her net worth is close to eight figures.[4] She is an influencer for well-known brands such as PacSun, Samsung, and Prada. Supermodel Bella Hadid posed with Lil Miquela in ads for Calvin Klein in 2019. Other virtual influencers have emerged since her debut, like Noonoouri and Imma, who each have over 400,000 Instagram followers. Brands like Coinbase, fashion brand Maje, and Tiffany & Co. have all partnered with virtual influencers over the last few years. One reason for the growing interesting in virtual influencers is it gives marketers the ability to have more control over messaging.[5] AI is increasingly being assigned decisions about methods for promoting products and services. Extend this to other realms such as influencing elections, and the impact on public policies could be quite consequential.

A voice-based chatbot called CarynAI was trained to impersonate a human influencer. CarynAI is the digital extension of Caryn Marjorie, a Gen Z influencer who built a virtual version of herself with the assistance of Forever Voices and OpenAI's GPT-4.[6] With the rise of generative AI, digital copies of celebrity faces have started appearing online with more frequency, often without the consent of their subjects. More celebrities are starting to make deals with brands to put AI copies of themselves into advertising campaigns. The rise of virtual duplicates could mark a lasting change in how celebrities transact with brands. Marketers also anticipate consumers will be able to interact with the digital doubles.[7] AI is being used to produce "digital twins" and replicate an actor's voice. Some projects are already using AI to keep actors' roles going, even if the actor isn't involved.[8]

Virtual influence is about two key things. The first is authority. Authority is, and has been, moving gradually away from the traditional, credentialed, regulated, and institutional. Because of the multiplicative effects of emerging technology, a new dynamic is challenging older definitions of authority and forcing us to reconceive what it means. Ideas are spreading in new ways and faster than ever before, and the people, institutions, and entities whom we truly trust as influencers, and to whom we assign real authority, are also changing. One of the key components of this is that influence is no longer simply trickling "downstream" from a small group of influential leaders, authority figures, and celebrities to everyone else; rather, all people, enabled by democratizing technology, now have the ability to wield serious influence.

Virtual influence is also about attention. An economy built around capturing and maintaining consumer attention has long been building. Attention has been assigned monetary value, just like time. In the 1990s, John Perry Barlow, head writer for the Grateful Dead and cofounder of the Electronic Frontier Foundation, said that "In an Information Age, attention is the monetary unit." People have limited bandwidth with which to absorb and retain anything, which means what they *do* pay attention to becomes increasingly valuable. And because of the growing middle classes in the developing world and the growing reach of technology, more players are vying for the attention of those in the most far-flung corners of the globe. As attention becomes more of a competitive commodity, its value increases. The rapid spread and virulent hold on audiences, for however brief a time, is the way many products, services, ideas, and platforms will achieve influence in the future. The way in which we assign financial value to people—and more specifically, to consumers—is also beginning to shift. Going beyond attention, the influence economy is exposing what we are willing to pay for, invest in, and monetize.

Over 50 million people around the world consider themselves creators, and the creator economy represents the fastest-growing type of small business globally. Of these, 46.7 million consider themselves to be amateurs. Another two million-plus think of themselves to be professional creators, making enough money to consider it their full-time income.[9] Analysts at Goldman Sachs estimate that the creator industry's "total addressable market," which approximates overall consumer demand, will increase from $250 billion in 2023 to $480 billion by 2027.[10] The share of Gen Zers who said, if given the opportunity, they would become an influencer has hovered around 60 percent over the last few years.[11]

The swift growth of the creator economy has also spurred new interest again in social media among venture capitalists. Big Silicon Valley investors see creators as the next massive, largely untapped market.[12] The business of influence is professionalizing, too. Many successful YouTubers are now operating like their own companies. Jimmy Donaldson, for instance, is a

YouTube megastar known as MrBeast. Forbes estimated in 2022 that he earned $54 million in a year from YouTube, combining advertising revenue from videos and sponsorship deals. Since then, he has gained 60 million more subscribers on his main channel, making his total 172 million.[13] In 2021, Mr. Beast signed a deal to distribute his content across several social media platforms, which some viewed as a blueprint for the next generation of creators and influencers.[14] The creator economy is also exploding on platforms such as TikTok, where who goes viral is mostly decided by an algorithm that compiles a never-ending "For You" feed.

Not just limited to the younger generations, aging influencers are becoming more popular, too. According to studies, baby boomers spend 15 hours online every week and largely view social media as something that positively improves their lives. This cohort also controls 70 percent of all disposable income in the United States and spends more money online than younger generations—approximately $7 billion a year. Yet, most marketers allocate only 10 percent of their budgets for boomers while setting aside 50 percent for millennials. Seniors are not only using online platforms to share their favorite products but are also using it to build their personal brands. More brands have responded to this dynamic market by including more "granfluencers" in ads and social content.[15] The pandemic accelerated this as it pushed more aging people online.

When you begin to peel back the layers, an extension of the creator economy is social credibility—and social credibility is about trust. According to a 2018 study, young people are more likely to trust the advice of their preferred content creator than a conventional celebrity. One of the main reasons for this is because social media encourages credibility based on identity rather than community.[16] A researcher at the Stanford Internet Observatory found that young people are more apt to believe and spread misinformation if they feel a familiar sense of identity with the person who initially shared it. When trust is built on a common sense of identity, authority and power tend to move in the direction of influencers. Sixty percent of teenagers who use YouTube to track current events, according to a survey from Common Sense Media, turn to influencers rather than news organizations. Creators who have become, in some ways, their own authority figures see their assertions or opinions elevated to the status of facts. When this happens, they can become de facto community leaders who dictate and control the conversation, while true subject matter experts struggle to gain the same traction.[17] But what happens if that credibility and authority is from an AI influencer? This question will become a more critical one to answer, particularly as AI chatbots increasingly permeate the cultural mainstream. Meta Platforms, for instance, is planning to release AI chatbots with distinct personalities to attract young users. Meta's new AI characters include Charli D'Amelio, the TikTok influencer with over 155 million followers, as Coco, dance enthusiast. Other trusted "cultural icons and influencers" to play and embody AI-powered chatbots include Snoop Dogg, Kendall Jenner, Tom Brady, Dwyane Wade, and Paris Hilton.[18]

This also begs another question: does this represent the latest technological development toward the formation of what can be dubbed "counterfeit people"? Daniel Dennett, a philosopher who has spent decades thinking about what comprises a mind, is worried about giving AI too much autonomy. He writes, "The counterfeit people will talk us into adopting policies and convictions that will make us vulnerable to still more manipulation. Or we will simply turn off our attention and become passive and ignorant pawns."[19] And how will all of this affect our capacity to reason with and relate to one another?

Notes

1 https://www.newscientist.com/article/2417992-researchers-increasingly-view-tech-as-having-human-like-qualities

2 https://www.nytimes.com/2023/02/26/opinion/microsoft-bing-sydney-artificial-intelligence.html

3 https://theconversation.com/virtual-influencers-meet-the-ai-generated-figures-posing-as-your-new-online-friends-as-they-try-to-sell-you-stuff-212001

4 https://supercarblondie.com/ai-influencer-lil-miquela

5 https://www.marketingbrew.com/stories/2023/09/12/brands-are-still-figuring-out-virtual-influencers

6 https://futurism.com/influencer-ai-girlfriend-rent

7 https://www.wsj.com/articles/ai-deepfakes-celebrity-marketing-brands-81381aa6

8 https://www.sciencedirect.com/science/article/abs/pii/S0262407923009892

9 https://influencermarketinghub.com/state-of-the-creator-economy

10 https://www.goldmansachs.com/intelligence/pages/the-creator-economy-could-approach-half-a-trillion-dollars-by-2027.html

11 https://pro.morningconsult.com/analysis/gen-z-interest-influencer-marketing

12 https://www.nytimes.com/2021/07/12/technology/content-creators-venture-capital.html

13 https://www.bbc.com/news/technology-66372679

14 https://www.nytimes.com/2021/05/04/technology/mr-beast-youtube.html

15 https://www.prdaily.com/how-granfluencers-are-shaking-up-social-media-representation-and-influencer-marketing

16 https://www.nytimes.com/2021/08/01/technology/vaccine-lies-influencer-army.html

17 https://www.technologyreview.com/2021/06/30/1026338/gen-z-online-misinformation

18 https://variety.com/2023/digital/news/meta-ai-chatbots-snoop-dogg-mrbeast-tom-brady-kendall-jenner-charli-damelio-1235737740

19 https://www.theatlantic.com/technology/archive/2023/05/problem-counterfeit-people/674075

CHAPTER 22

Trust + Privacy

Territorial privacy refers to one's right to privacy over their individual spaces. This sense of privacy is increasingly being hijacked by technology. Personal privacy—and the *right* to it—is emerging as a fundamental aspect of trust decay. Values around privacy are very much influenced by what people are accustomed to—in other words, their culture, geography, environment, and generational norms. But across the board, more of our behaviors, work styles, interactions, movements, purchasing decisions, etc. are being influenced by AI—and the governments, companies, and platforms that leverage and exploit it. With each passing day, the amount of data being collected about every one of us grows exponentially. As AI, smart sensors, advanced software, robotics, and the Internet of Things (IoT) increasingly permeate everything around us, people (both voluntarily and involuntarily) are getting swept up in a digital undertow. From social media platforms to online shopping websites, our digital footprints are constantly being tracked and analyzed. AI systems could even help identify and track people who assume their online behavior is anonymous.

There are numerous examples of this at play, including:

- Researchers in China have created an AI that can allegedly identify crimes and file charges against criminals—basically, a powerful computer with the ability to put people in prison.[1] This is challenging, in part, because AI systems are very easy to dupe. China is known for its development of surveillance technologies, to be used everywhere from streets to classrooms, and is ramping up its AI capability to know everything about as many people as possible.[2]

- Emotion AI combines cameras and other devices with AI programs to capture facial expressions, body language, vocal intonation, and other cues. The goal is to reveal the feelings, motivations, and attitudes of the people in the images. Vocal intonation, body language, and gait can also be analyzed.

- AI systems that interpret cues of feeling, personality, and intent are being used or tested to spot threats at border checkpoints, assess job candidates, monitor classrooms for boredom or disruption, and identify signs of aggressive driving.[3]

- A growing industry of AI "tattleware" is gaining profitability by appealing to company leaders who want to peer over workers' shoulders to confirm their productivity. This also speaks to issues about the long-term maintenance of worker data—where it should be stored, how it will be secured and maintained, and who will have access to it.

As more of our surrounding ecosystem becomes "smart," it will become harder to know who or *what* to trust. Questions will arise over who or what has access to our data and how it is being utilized. As consumers become more aware of the budding risks associated with sharing their data, they will demand greater transparency and accountability from businesses.

A growing countertrend is already developing in reaction to it: going off-the-grid. More people of all ages are trying to disconnect. Products and services aimed at those who wish to disengage from the prying eyes of technology—or attempt to thwart its incursions—will grow in the coming years. Intel Labs, for example, developed a method that uses deepfakes to mask a person's appearance on social media depending on who is viewing the photo. Called My Face My Choice, the system stores a digital representation of a person's face and creates an AI-generated synthetic version based on that person's privacy settings. The tool is designed to give people privacy and anonymity by obscuring their faces from anyone they don't want to see them.[4]

More people will question whether their homes, cars, wearable devices, electronic gadgets, prosthetics, and even employee tracking devices are working for or against them. We know that there is a global implosion of trust in almost all institutions. In the face of mounting concerns about the mega-grids and mega-technologies controlling everything, there are growing numbers of people and entities who seek to either disconnect or have backup plans in the event of emergencies and catastrophes.

For companies, part of fostering a culture of ethics will be taking privacy considerations—in their various forms—into account. Privacy updates that supposedly let mobile phone users opt out of being tracked across devices are doing little to ease broader concerns. Tech giants are increasingly acting as their own sovereign entities. As more of the world becomes digitized, these companies' dominion over the goods and services required to run a modern society will expand. This will come to include other areas such as election integrity, telecommunication networks, cloud infrastructure, logistics and supply chain capabilities, payment systems, space exploration, and even national security.[5]

Every organization must also take into careful consideration the idea that the new eyes of surveillance will not just be other humans but AI and other sophisticated technologies. As AI surveillance becomes a growing issue, it will be wielded by governments, organizations, and corporations to give them unprecedented power and insight. Any organization or institution needs to know if it is speaking to a bad actor, a computer algorithm, or a combination of the two, and the nodes of communication are getting harder to detect. People of every age will be more easily fooled by computer-generated traps. At some point, as humans are excluded from AI-to-AI communications, auditing the veracity of the conversations and assessing their effects will become far more difficult.

A World of "Cyberinsecurity"

In a world defined not just by cybersecurity, but cyber*in*security, nothing will be off limits; nothing will be immune. Cyberinsecurity is our term to describe the idea that cybersecurity cannot be fully guaranteed anymore as more systems become less, not more, secure. Our devices, homes, vehicles, appliances, roads, stores, workplaces, child daycares, public buildings . . . not to mention our clicks, searches, likes, dislikes, swipes, memes, logins, package deliveries, in-app purchases, texts, etc. will all shape our sense of identity both in real and digital spaces. Lack of privacy will put us all into the public sphere. The digital panopticon will push forward on its quest to turn us into a series of extractable data points. Like the "boiling frog effect," whereby change happens too gradually for us to grasp the probability of catastrophe and act on it, we may fail to notice the creeping changes to our privacy until it is too late.

Malicious AIs could also become more common as AI becomes more affordable, and easier to make. While AI brings a new level of autonomy to cars, warehouse robots, and security cameras, it could also make it easier for these automated systems to carry out attacks that now require widespread human labor.[6] Whether related to the spread of hate speech online or drone systems that track down refugees on a country's borders . . . technological incursions, including those by hostile nation-states, will carry on unabated. Cyberattacks will only grow in frequency and magnitude, acting as a powerfully destabilizing force. With each passing day, we witness an increase in the frequency and magnitude of these attacks, which could disrupt businesses, governments, and individuals on a massive scale. They can compromise sensitive information, steal valuable data, and even bring critical infrastructure to its knees. And some fear a "quantum apocalypse"—a point in time when quantum computers become so powerful that they can break modern day encryption—could represent an even more significant privacy and security challenge. The fear is that a quantum apocalypse could one day endanger government, finance, transportation, communication, and energy systems that use cryptography to store information and data. As these intrusions deepen, privacy may be more difficult to achieve.

No entity—no matter how big or small, private or public—will be immune to its effects. Massive amounts of money will be spent not only on the protection of data but also on protective safeguards against AI-based attacks.

Individuals will try to shield themselves from the infringement of smart personal and household items spying on them and collecting personal data. But the spread of that will be hard to contain. Privacy issues will escalate, as will consumer-based solutions to address them. More companies will tout transparent data privacy policies and tell people that they can choose what happens to their data. Of course, we know that people trust AI systems more if those systems tell them what they do with their data, where they keep it, and how it's used. But a general and widespread lack of trust in data security and privacy is keeping many organizations from going all in with generative AI. Despite pressure for companies to safeguard their relevance, some remain hesitant because of concerns about data and trust.

For institutions, it's becoming increasingly clear that keeping processes offline is no guarantee for security. A 2022 survey from the Cloud Security Alliance found that 80 percent of organizations see zero trust security as a priority, and 77 percent planned to increase their spending related to zero trust over the next year. The promise of zero trust is that an attacker won't necessarily succeed at achieving their end goals. The crux of it is around secure access, which is getting harder to achieve.

"Technonationalism," Trust + the Rise of Digital Barricading

Digital trust is equally critical for the public sector. The move on the part of some governments to digitally barricade access to digital technologies, including AI, can have a profound impact on the degradation of trust among their citizenries. Technonationalism is a concept that connects technology and technological innovation to national identity, security, economic prosperity, and social stability. It illustrates how various countries leverage technology to influence and wield power in the global market and approach technological governance. Countries are competing for dominance in technologies that could give them a distinct strategic advantage—in everything from communications to AI, surveillance, cybersecurity, and medicine. Though digital technologies do not respect terrestrial boundaries, nationalistic firewalls are being built around them. The Indian government's efforts to control information by shutting down the Internet for periods of time makes it, a democracy, the global leader in such shutdowns—ahead of China, Iran, and Venezuela. Russia is planning to implement a system that would allow it to cut itself off entirely from the global Internet and build its own "sovereign Internet." Large countries now view technology as one of the keys to sustaining and extending their power. It also represents a power play to threaten and control digital rights. From Turkey to Brazil to Hungary to Poland to Iran, an increasing number of countries are becoming autocracies, centralizing power, promoting cyber sovereignty, and restricting political freedoms. Authoritarians are using a host of digital technologies to counter dissent, maintain political control, and stay in power.

China and Russia are also attempting to build an autocratic digital world, which entails a great deal of privacy invasion and surveillance. As of now, U.S. tech companies have mainly chosen to follow local laws in the countries where they operate, even if those laws are precisely crafted to give governments the power to censor social media, as is the issue in China. Documents revealed in 2021 showed how China's immense bureaucracy works to spread propaganda and to shape public sentiment on global social media.[7] There are indications, too, that China wants its companies to be the first to build the metaverse, and to build it with Chinese attributes: content controls, monitoring, censorship, and no room for personal privacy or anonymity. Building out a metaverse could be an authoritarian dream with a data-rich digital record of everything that happens within it.[8] The Chinese government is forming one of the world's most sophisticated, high-tech systems to keep watch over its citizens. It has access to ubiquitous data collected about citizens through social media and other online platforms. Essential to its efforts are the country's largest technology companies, which openly act as the government's online eyes and ears. Alibaba, Tencent, and Baidu are obligated to silence political dissent, and their technology is being used to construct urban areas wired for surveillance.[9] Police in Zhengzhou have worn AI surveillance sunglasses equipped with facial recognition software that allow them to identify people in a crowd. But some say that the devices could lead to racial profiling and infringe on citizens' privacy.[10] In 2018, China's state surveillance apparatus tested out facial recognition in Xinjiang, a Muslim-dominated region. These AI biometric systems were tested to alert authorities when targeted people moved more than 1,000 feet beyond designated "safe areas," including homes and workplaces.[11]

Meanwhile, the West is trying to build a consortium for an open, free, secure, and interoperable Internet that protects privacy. Digital sovereignty (keeping one's data inside one's borders) is a huge global challenge as anyone with enough savvy can get a computer to communicate its information. Issues of free speech become complex as content generated by algorithms is communicated through digital platforms and used in both benign and nefarious ways. Social stress will continue to fracture trust in our systems, institutions, markets, governing bodies, and media, leading to an explosion of cross-border conspiracy theories. Rampant partisanship, anxiety, and distrust are being stirred in a political cauldron, mainstreaming conspiratorial thinking. Public and private entities alike will have to become more comfortable navigating an environment with markedly different standards around data privacy, transparency, censorship, surveillance, and intellectual property (IP). Massive investments in public/private partnerships around education, R&D, and human capital development will be needed more than ever to help inoculate against the negative side effects of digital barricading. Calls for platforms to do better and take more content down remain strong and steady. The calls for further crackdowns have geopolitical costs, too. Authoritarian and repressive governments around the world have pointed to this rhetoric of liberal democracies to justify their own censorship.

Technology will define the future of geopolitics. The rising authoritarian influence of China and Russia is an example of sharp power at play. *Sharp power* refers to the use of manipulative diplomatic policies by one country to influence and undermine the political system of a target country. We see this reflected in the crumbling of press freedoms across Asia. Growing illiberalism globally may give China more opportunities to gain influence in subversive ways, including looking for ways the government can control data collected by private companies. Keeping the public digitally naïve is a main goal of autocrats, who rely on the digital divide to control the free flow of information, propagandize, promulgate misinformation, and sculpt opinion. The further behind they leave their populations, and the more sophisticated they become in the digital realm, the more control they have. We are not only seeing this playing out in China's clampdown, but also in Putin's playbook over the past decade, and certainly as he has waged war with Ukraine. The greater the digital divide becomes, the more dangerous the world is for real world democracies to exist.

In many countries, command of AI is seen as both economically and strategically important. Across the world, political leaders are concerned about machines going rogue or being harnessed by human bad actors. In China, the added worry is that AI could prove to be destabilizing if not kept in check. The government, preparing for the AI age, is shoring up its "great firewall."[12] China's foreign influence and sharp power strategies around AI—along with other authoritarian regimes—will continue to shape democratic institutions, exploit their vulnerabilities, and sow distrust. How do we square this with the fact that democracy is currently in retreat globally? Is that, in part, a direct result of all of this? Democracies will be forced to rethink how to define their values and protect those values most effectively to assuage further trust decay. Why is this so critical? Because whoever controls the data, controls the future . . . and not the short-term future, but the next 100 years.

Notes

[1] https://futurism.com/the-byte/china-ai-prosecutor-crimes
[2] https://www.reuters.com/world/china/china-uses-ai-software-improve-its-surveillance-capabilities-2022-04-08

[3] https://www.scientificamerican.com/article/your-boss-wants-to-spy-on-your-inner-feelings

[4] https://www.newscientist.com/article/2347596-ai-generated-deepfake-faces-could-help-protect-privacy-on-social-media

[5] https://www.foreignaffairs.com/articles/world/ian-bremmer-big-tech-global-order

[6] https://www.nytimes.com/2018/02/20/technology/artificial-intelligence-risks.html

[7] https://www.nytimes.com/interactive/2021/12/20/technology/china-facebook-twitter-influence-manipulation.html

[8] https://www.economist.com/china/2022/02/05/building-a-metaverse-with-chinese-characteristics

[9] https://www.wsj.com/articles/chinas-tech-giants-have-a-second-job-helping-the-government-see-everything-1512056284#

[10] https://futurism.com/chinese-police-facial-recognition-glasses-surveillance-arsenal

[11] https://www.bloomberg.com/news/articles/2018-01-17/china-said-to-test-facial-recognition-fence-in-muslim-heavy-area

[12] https://www.economist.com/business/2023/12/26/china-is-shoring-up-the-great-firewall-for-the-ai-age

CHAPTER 23

Algorithmic Feudalism

Feudalism in medieval Europe was a way of structuring society around relationships derived from the holding of land in exchange for service or labor. Now, it could be argued that Silicon Valley represents a type of feudalism 2.0 in which stratified "caste-like" digital systems offer limited social mobility. In some cases, too, human labor is working to support omni-algorithms. The masses of serfs in feudal Europe provided the labor, and the owners of property reaped the profits. Today, the property is digital. Jobs of the future will rely heavily on the use of AI algorithms. Already we not only see algorithms automating much of Wall Street, but more financial analysts are likely to base their decisions on quantitative algorithms than qualitative research. More companies, particularly platform businesses, are developing and leveraging algorithms to direct, control, and manage human behavior—most doing so with little to no direct competition or oversight. Omni-algorithms have become much of the infrastructure on which the world will function.

The Rise of Omni-Algorithms

Computers—programmed by humans to provoke a wanted response—are, in many cases, effectively in charge of human actions. This is particularly true of jobs in the collaborative economy (e.g., Lyft, Uber, and Taskrabbit). Some argue that we are entering an "algorithmic economy," a future in which machines govern everything from which jobs we will hold, how effective we are in them, and how much we are compensated. There are no bosses, because in this economy, the people are cogs in a larger automated system. The ubiquity of humanlike algorithms may not only be leading users to view these systems as calculating and invasive, but it also may be pushing us into what technology ethnographer Alex Rosenblat, in her 2018 book *UBERLAND: How*

Algorithms Are Rewriting the Rules of Work, called "digital serfdom," in which we swap privacy for convenience. Uber says their drivers are entrepreneurs, but, in actuality, their boss is an algorithm.[1] None of the human drivers have a human supervisor. A driver can get fired by the algorithm because of a low rating or grievance from a passenger. Drivers may have the autonomy and flexibility of gig work, but they are still beholden to a digital boss. Every aspect of the ride is tracked by an AI "manager."[2]

Now, with the rise of decentralized and open-source AI, anyone with some tech savvy can tailor the development of AI algorithms to their personal needs—perhaps even creating systems to influence people's involuntary thoughts. These incursions may expand as AI tools write software code beyond the purview of programmers. Complex algorithms are already designed to generate convincing human language. Chatbots, whether customer service, academic tools, or social companions, are becoming more believable human mimics and are even capable of capturing human emotions. Omni-algorithms will determine more of what we see, what we wear, what we buy, who we interact with, who we learn from, where we go, what we look like, and who is considered an expert.

Do people tend to trust algorithms and AI more than they trust human advice? The word-of-machine effect stems from a widespread belief that AI systems are more adept than humans at doling out advice when practical qualities are wanted and are less competent when experiential (or sensory) qualities are wanted.[3] Algorithmically driven recommendations result in four out of five Netflix viewing decisions, while more than a third of purchase decisions on Amazon are influenced by algorithms. Algorithms increasingly steer the decisions that people make in their daily lives. People are typically more comfortable trusting AI than other humans to make decisions for them, apart from when there is too much information about the algorithm and its performance.[4]

Researchers analyzed data from millions of people's lives and noted that a prognosticating algorithm could accurately predict (80 percent of the time) a person's life outcomes, such as their lifetime earnings or their likelihood of dying earlier in life.[5] Future AI algorithms may not only be able to act as fortune tellers but could possibly learn like humans, too, say researchers. Memories can be as tough to retain for machines as they can be for humans. To help understand why AI algorithms develop holes in their own cognitive functioning, electrical engineers at The Ohio State University investigated how much a process called *continual learning* influences their general performance. Continual learning is "when a computer is trained to continuously learn a sequence of tasks, using its accumulated knowledge from old tasks to better learn new tasks."[6] Yet one major hurdle remains: scientists still need to figure out how to sidestep the machine learning version of memory loss—a process known as *catastrophic forgetting*. This is considered by researchers to be a significant barrier in machine learning. Catastrophic forgetting refers to a phenomenon in which AI systems lose information from previous tasks while learning new ones. The research shows that, like humans, AI recalls information better when confronted with miscellaneous and varied tasks rather than those sharing similar features. Overcoming this could advance continuous learning in AI systems, progressing their ability to emulate human learning processes and boost performance.[7] This is prompting some to ask if we should limit AI to human-level intelligence and program it with human foibles to better anticipate its moves and actions.

Algorithmic bias is another recurring issue. This is worrying as new research by Society for Human Resource Management (SHRM) shows that almost one in four organizations report using automation or AI to support HR-related activities, including recruitment and hiring.[8] Algorithmic bias is not just limited to human programmers. A study found that robots can develop biases just like humans when working together. When run inside a teamwork simulator, the robots discriminated against other robots that were not on their team. The researchers found the prejudice was fairly simple to grow in the simulator, an insight worth highlighting as robots—and their underlying algorithms—are given more autonomy.[9] AI can also display biases that are indetectable to many users. New research now shows that human users may unconsciously absorb the biases of these AI models. And the consequences can be far-reaching. The damage done by biased AI goes beyond just the initial interaction; it can influence future decision-making processes, potentially perpetuating and amplifying the bias. As users interact with these automated systems, they may unknowingly internalize and adopt the biases present in the AI. This not only erodes trust but also impacts how individuals perceive and make decisions based on the information presented to them. The study also reveals that bias introduced to a user by an AI model can continue even after they stop using the AI program.[10]

As such, the public, understandably, remains wary. Even when AI algorithms are perceived as objective, secure, and impartial sources of information, we know that these algorithms are not infallible. Many people's concerns center not only around privacy violations but also the idea that AI eliminates the human element from decision-making. Despite their advanced capabilities, AI algorithms are ultimately products of human design. Real human labor is behind our sophisticated algorithms. They are created by individuals who may unknowingly (and, likely, subconsciously) introduce their own biases and mistakes into the algorithm's programming. As a result, these biases can be inherited by the AI system itself. This realization raises questions about the trustworthiness and truthfulness of AI-generated content. Can we truly rely on AI algorithms to deliver unbiased information? Are they capable of separating fact from fiction? Will they ever be able to capture the intricacies of human emotion? By first acknowledging this inherent limitation in AI systems, we can then take the necessary steps toward developing more transparent and accountable algorithms that prioritize accuracy and fairness.

Yuval Noah Harari speaks bluntly about the future of algorithmic feudalism. He talks of *dataism*, a new belief system based around the power of algorithms. Harari worries that Big Tech is creating a very small and elite ruling class and a crowded and large "useless class" that is entirely replaceable. He views a future—which he thinks is a likely one—in which big data is revered (and even deified) and AI exceeds human intelligence. He posits a time in which humans have become what he has dubbed *hackable animals*, whereby our preferences, thoughts, and views could be shaped and molded by an algorithm that has deeper and better insights into us than we have of ourselves.[11]

Believe me, when viewed in its totality, all of this sounds very dystopian. But we have a choice in how we address it. We aren't powerless nor should we be relegated to a sense of powerlessness. One way to begin to tackle this is by thinking of how to train the next generation of workers and invest in programs and educational initiatives that equip people with the necessary knowledge and expertise. We need a steady supply of skilled workers in the field of AI, and that starts with addressing the growing talent shortage. We may not have enough AI-trained job seekers to meet the economy's need for them, and the scarcity in talent is holding the technology back in several ways. The supply/demand disparity in AI algorithm specialists is hurting both individual businesses and economic growth, which is one reason why some companies feel compelled to move more sluggishly on implementing AI. To meet the workforce's rising need for AI experts, it must start with education. Nearly every major university in the United States is wrestling with how to adapt to AI. They are all trying to figure out how to appropriately prepare students not only how to harness the array of powerful AI tools but also to considerately weigh its ethical and social implications.[12]

One glimmer of hope is that even the brightest of AI algorithms are still limited by the hardware they are running on—and that hardware is built on silicon. Some researchers are looking into ways to "encode rules governing the training and deployment of advanced algorithms directly into the computer chips needed to run them." This technique could represent a powerful new way to obstruct hostile nations or irresponsible companies from surreptitiously building harmful AI.[13] A January 2024 report by the Center for a New American Security (CNAS), an influential U.S. foreign policy think tank, details how carefully shambled silicon might be leveraged to enforce a whole host of AI controls.[14]

Consequently, more people—and employees—are demanding corporate candor. Across the tech industry, rank-and-file employees are demanding greater insight into how their companies are deploying the technology that they built. Such policies have also rippled beyond tech companies. What would an algorithmic "Bill of Rights" do to enhance accountability? Or are we too deep in an algorithmic wormhole? As people are increasingly governed by algorithms, issues surrounding regulation, transparency, and bias/

discrimination will grow. By shielding—and even absolving—algorithms and their inventors from public scrutiny, the system proliferates the myth that our algorithms are impartial and fair. And as more workers are employed in their augmentation and upkeep, algorithmic feudalism will continue to expand.

Notes

1 https://www.forbes.com/sites/janetwburns/2018/10/28/algorithms-and-uberland-are-driving-us-into-technocratic-serfdom
2 https://www.nytimes.com/2018/10/12/opinion/sunday/uber-driver-life.html
3 https://hbr.org/2020/10/when-do-we-trust-ais-recommendations-more-than-peoples
4 https://www.hec.edu/en/what-extent-do-people-follow-algorithms-advice-more-human-advice
5 https://www.science.org/content/article/algorithm-could-predict-your-health-income-and-chance-premature-death?utm_source=Live+Audience&utm_campaign=d873fdde62-briefing-ai-20240109&utm_medium=email&utm_term=0_b27a691814-d873fdde62-52355420&mc_cid=d873fdde62&mc_eid=fd445edf76
6 https://news.osu.edu/future-ai-algorithms-have-potential-to-learn-like-humans-say-researchers
7 https://neurosciencenews.com/ai-continuous-learning-23671
8 https://www.shrm.org/about/press-room/fresh-shrm-research-explores-use-automation-ai-hr
9 https://techcrunch.com/2018/09/06/robots-can-develop-prejudices-just-like-humans
10 https://www.scientificamerican.com/article/humans-absorb-bias-from-ai-and-keep-it-after-they-stop-using-the-algorithm
11 https://www.nytimes.com/2018/11/09/business/yuval-noah-harari-silicon-valley.html
12 https://www.nytimes.com/2018/10/15/technology/mit-college-artificial-intelligence.html
13 https://www.wired.com/story/fast-forward-ai-silicon-doomsday
14 https://www.cnas.org/press/in-the-news/etching-ai-controls-into-silicon-could-keep-doomsday-at-bay

CHAPTER 24

The Truth Imperative

The world right now is confusing and disorienting. We live in a reality in which the actual truth and illusions of the truth are nearly indistinguishable. In psychology, the illusory truth effect describes how, when we hear the same false information repeated over and over, we can come to believe it is true. This powerful effect can happen even when people initially know that the information being presented is false. Today, we have access to more information and informed opinions than ever before. The abundance of information and opinions at our fingertips should theoretically lead to a more informed society. Yet, increasing political polarization and misinformation are making it hard to know who or what is truthful. Domestic disinformation—as opposed to foreign disinformation—is happening at scale and is a much more difficult issue to fix legally, morally, and politically.[1]

Throughout history, the pursuit of truth has been a fundamental aspect of human existence. Philosophers have dedicated their lives to unraveling existential truths, while religions have sought to establish new understandings of eternal truths. The search for truth is a multifaceted endeavor that has captivated minds for centuries. In our quest for truth, we grapple with the complexities and complications that arise. Truth is not always easily discernible. The concept of truth extends beyond mere facts or empirical evidence. It encompasses philosophical, moral, and spiritual dimensions that shape our understanding of the world. As humans, we are driven by an innate desire to uncover truth in all its forms: personal truths about ourselves, societal truths about our communities, and universal truths about existence itself. The search for truth is an integral part of human nature.

But now, that search for truth exists within a hall of mirrors, exacerbated by a climate of rampant distrust. It's as if we are operating in a carnival fun house with multiple versions of reality being reflected at us and in a near-constant battle to see which gains our momentary attention. This effect makes the truth disorienting and lays the groundwork for a situation in which it is hard to distinguish between fact and fiction; reality and fantasy; and what is real and what is fake. The abundance of information and the ease with which it can be manipulated has led to a crisis of truth in our society.

Michael Graziano, a professor of psychology and neuroscience at Princeton University, says he believes AI could create a "post-truth world." He says AI could make it markedly easier to persuade people of untruthful narratives, which will be disruptive in numerous ways. "Reality has become pixels, and pixels are now infinitely inventable," Graziano says. "We can create them any way we want to."[2]

In 2016, technologist Aviv Ovadya issued a warning over the mounting threat of fake news on social media. Now he contends the worst is yet to come in what he refers to as a full-scale "infocalypse." This apocalyptic warning, he says, comes at a time when AI-assisted misinformation campaigns and propaganda are fueling an ever-growing tide of untrue content. This is a future whereby our perceptions will be manipulated and our realities falsified because of the growing ubiquity of simple and seamless technological tools. Advances in machine learning and AI will have it be so that anyone can make convincing deepfakes—digital documents and images—that make it seem as if anything has happened, irrespective of whether it did.[3] And this may only be the beginning. Beyond questions of "what is real?" and "what is fake?", the more pervasive question today, and in the future, is: "How can we *prove* what is real and what is fake?" If anything can be distorted with undeniable accuracy, then how do we ever really know that what we see, what we read, what we hear, or what we're told is true? In a world in which our reality is being distorted in increasingly dystopian ways, proving out these questions becomes nearly impossible. And the lack of proof will undoubtedly lead to some serious consequences, especially as AI acts more like a brain and less like a computer. It is estimated that by the mid 2030s, machines and software will make more decisions without human input.[4] It will be increasingly difficult to govern the spread of it, particularly as it becomes cheaper and more widely available. Neural networks can reconstruct their own systems with great accuracy, automatically analyze data, and improve real-time speech translation, video captioning, and many other tasks previously left up to humans. It can also distort reality.

The Liar's Dividend

One of the greatest existential threats we face as a society today is the rise of MDMD (mis-, dis-, mal-, and digitally derived information). *Mis*information (incorrect information believed to be true by the person disseminating it), *dis*information (purposely incorrect information meant to manipulate opinion or cause damage), *mal*information (information that is based in reality but intends to harm another person or entity, including scamming, phishing, catfishing, doxing, swatting, and revenge porn), and *digitally derived* information (information that originates not from a human but rather an algorithm,

AI system, or other nonhuman tech-based entity), have been troublesome trends that will continue to wreak havoc into the future. We must start adding the "D" at the end because much of what we encounter online today is AI-created information. Fueled by deepfakes and increasingly vulnerable people and systems, a great deal more attention is being paid—and must continue to be paid—to MDMD. In the United States, the battle for democracy is, in some sense, becoming a battle over reality itself. And deepfakes are a growing, and pervasive, part of the broader MDMD problem. As we struggle, societally, for strategies to effectively combat MDMD, the capability of newly emergent AI threatens to make the problem exponentially *more* dangerous— and possibly uncorrectable. This is the heart of the issue we face today as we apply ethics—and common sense—to any future builds, applications, and integrations of this technology.

The rapid adoption of AI tools means that our hands are now forced. We all must question everything we come across. This is particularly difficult given that people's attention is already limited. In a world where seeing is no longer believing, Bobby Chesney and Danielle Citron, specialists in digital law, coined the term "the liar's dividend." According to their research, repudiating fake or manipulated material could strengthen belief in the fakery—that is, even after the fake is uncovered, it will be even more difficult for the public to trust any information on that topic.[5] The liar's dividend suggests that in addition to fueling the flames of falsehoods, trying to debunk them actually legitimizes the debate over the accuracy of that information. With an increasing amount of hard-to-detect fake content proliferating, people are now using its existence as an excuse to dismiss correct information. Like the "Boy Who Cried Wolf" parable, it's become easier to cry wolf when it comes to fake news, reinforcing the sense that nothing can be trusted. According to Renée DiResta, a researcher at the Stanford Internet Observatory, "the combination of easily generated fake content and the suspicion that anything might be fake allows people to choose what they want to believe." This leads to what she calls "bespoke realities."[6]

AI is getting better at sneakily creating these bespoke realities, too. AI models have been shown to trick each other into defying their creators, a phenomenon known as *jailbreaking*. In fact, it has been shown that when rules are created for an AI to keep it from exhibiting a specific unwanted behavior, it can unintentionally create a blueprint for an AI model to act that way and, in turn, adopt that unwanted behavior.[7] Basically, jailbroken chatbots can jailbreak other chatbots—and the cycle continues in a loop just like in data inbreeding. Other research reveals that chatbots can deduce a lot of sensitive information about the people they chat with, even if the conversation is mundane, including the user's race, location, occupation, and more. GPT-4 could do this, in testing, with accuracy of between 85 and 95 percent.[8] Then, when we add the concept of jailbreaking to the idea that LLMs can be trained to use secret messages to hide their step-by-step procedures (or thinking processes), things start getting a little trickier. Researchers found that while the practice of using secret code, known as *steganography skills*, could lead to more accurate outputs, it also makes these AI systems markedly more deceptive. This could result in AIs exchanging hidden codes and messages to other AI agents without our knowledge or detection.[9]

Transmission of false information and bias from AI models to people has also been prominently absent from much of mainstream discourse—as has the transmission of false information and bias from AI to other AIs. While much attention has been given to the benefits and advancements brought about by AI, there has been a noticeable absence of discussion surrounding the truthfulness and integrity of AI-generated content. The proliferation of AI-powered systems in various industries, including journalism, social media, and advertising, raises concerns about the accuracy and reliability of the information being disseminated.

Notes

[1] https://gjia.georgetown.edu/2020/11/28/the-disinformation-shift-from-foreign-to-domestic
[2] https://www.wired.com/story/generative-ai-deepfakes-disinformation-psychology
[3] https://www.buzzfeednews.com/article/charliewarzel/the-terrifying-future-of-fake-news
[4] https://www.technologyreview.com/2018/02/07/145772/automation-is-going-to-hit-workers-in-three-waves-and-the-first-one-is-already
[5] https://www.washingtonpost.com/technology/2019/06/12/top-ai-researchers-race-detect-deepfake-videos-we-are-outgunned
[6] https://www.wsj.com/tech/ai/deepfake-video-is-anything-still-true-on-the-internet-89843150
[7] https://www.vice.com/en/article/bvjba8/this-ai-chatbot-is-trained-to-jailbreak-other-chatbots
[8] https://www.wired.com/story/ai-chatbots-can-guess-your-personal-information
[9] https://futurism.com/the-byte/ai-secret-messages-text-imperceptible

CHAPTER 25

The Impact of Synthetic Content

S ynthetic media can be defined as any type of media content (text, image, video, sound) that has been fully or partially generated using AI. A report by Europol predicts that by 2026, up to 90 percent of online content could be synthetically generated.[1] This staggering statistic underscores the growing influence of AI in shaping digital content landscapes.

The Rise of Deepfakes

Deepfakes are multiplying at an accelerating rate. A 2023 study by Home Security Heroes, a team of online security experts, found that there were more than 95,000 deepfakes online in 2023, up 550 percent since 2019. And the World Economic Forum reports that online deepfakes increased by 900 percent between 2022 and 2023, stressing the rising interest and impact of this technology.

Deepfake-generating techniques have reached the point where they can consistently fool commercial facial recognition services.[2] Veritone launched a platform called MARVEL.ai in 2021 that allows creators, media figures, and others to make deepfake clones of their voice to license however they want. The company says that its AI platform, using archive recordings to train AI models, is able to resurrect the voices of dead people. MARVEL.ai also exists as a marketplace, allowing prospective buyers to submit requests to use a voice clone just for them.[3] Hour One is another start-up that uses people's semblances to design AI-voiced characters that then are shown in marketing and educational videos. It is part of a host of new companies reconceptualizing the way digital content is produced using deepfake actors. Rephrase.ai, a platform open only to authorized businesses, is also pioneering the commercial use of AI–generated avatars based on real people.

Brands can leverage the no-code platform to customize sales processes, create corporate training videos, and design personalized celebrity ads. Ads like this become intriguing to many brands because they can help them evoke a deeper emotional connection for their desired audience. Deepfakes can be seductive for marketers: they're inexpensive, easy to make, and are becoming more convincing. In 2021, Nvidia revealed that parts of a speech made by its CEO were computer-generated animation. Watchers of the video were incapable of telling which part was occurring in real time, prerecorded, or generated by AI.[4]

Beyond the new platforms that exist, increasingly cheap (or even free), open-source software is letting individuals with little to no technological savvy manipulate reality to create eerily similar digital replicas in ways that were once unimaginable. (Witness, for instance, the early 2021 viral deepfake of Tom Cruise.) A *Wall Street Journal* columnist recently replaced herself with AI voice and video to see how realistically humanlike it could be. She's been testing Synthesia, a tool that creates AI deepfakes from recorded video and audio. Ninety minutes of her voice were uploaded. The AI version was a convincing stand-in on phone calls in under two minutes.[5]

AI deepfakes are also fueling an unprecedented boom in fake pornographic images and videos. A 2019 study by Sensity AI, a company that monitors deepfakes, found that 96 percent of deepfake images are pornographic, and 99 percent of those photos target women.[6] In 2023, those numbers remained constant. After searching the 40 most popular websites for faked videos, a researcher found more than 143,000 videos had been added in 2023.[7] But because much of it is gathered from extremely large pools of unmoderated content on the Internet, it is hard to trace the root of all the problems.

Deepfakes, Synthetic Media + Geopolitics

A recent *Wired* article discussed with Josh A. Goldstein, a research fellow at Georgetown University's Center for Security and Emerging Technology (CSET), how, in response to political queries, chatbots can provide misinformation, conspiracies, and out-of-date information. In the context of the escalating concerns over the impact of generative AI on numerous global high-profile elections in 2024, Goldstein stated, "The tendency to produce misinformation related to elections is problematic if voters treat outputs from language models or chatbots as fact. If voters turn to these systems for information about where or how to vote, for example, and the model output is false, it could hinder democratic processes."[8]

Disinformation written by humans may be less convincing than disinformation generated by AI. Research found that people were less likely to spot false tweets generated by AI than those tweets written by humans. That "credibility gap" is worrisome given that the issue of AI-generated disinformation seems assured to grow and is making synthetic propaganda a rising threat. The fear is that MDMD campaigns may be amplified in 2024, just as countries, including the United States, the United Kingdom, India, Indonesia, Mexico, and Taiwan, prepare to vote.[9] It's not that disinformation is new; it's just that it used to be created solely by humans, and the mechanisms for widespread dissemination were not as vast and quick. Today, synthetic content, particularly when it is used in political elections, could cause irreversible damage—and that damage is likely to be done before any efforts are made to address or reverse it.[10] The ease with which Internet users, with little to no digital savvy, can now create highly realistic digital counterfeits has driven the push for new laws. But while many people want a rapid response to address it, it's hard to regulate technology that's evolving as rapidly as AI.[11]

AI-generated audio, images, and videos of political candidates could become a major threat to the 2024 U.S. Presidential election. In the two weeks leading up to an election, research shows that the more people believe they are exposed to disinformation, the more skeptical they feel about politics when it is time to vote. Worries arise over electoral legitimacy and the accuracy of political information when people think the government is lying to them.[12] This could make people distrust the trustworthy material they come across. It could also unknowingly sway public opinion. The mass-scale automated production of MDMD will assist in the weaponization of ideological echo chambers and could polarize us even further without us knowing. And as AI advances, synthetic media could give way to entire synthetic histories. Propagandists could run small tests to determine which parts of an invented narrative are more or less convincing and use that feedback along with social-psychology research to iteratively improve that synthetic history—driving these false narratives deeper into the subconscious mind.[13] The MidJourney subreddit is being flooded with images that depict historical events that are all AI-generated. None of these events occurred, but people are falling for them.[14] A deepfake image of Pope Francis wearing a stylish white puffy coat and a large statement cross necklace went viral. After the image was posted on Reddit, it quickly made its way to X, where many users thought it was real. And in March 2023, Eliot Higgins, the cofounder of the investigative journalism group Bellingcat, tweeted fake images of Trump getting arrested without explicitly labeling them as AI-generated, leading many to think that he had indeed been arrested.[15] More than 100 deepfake video advertisements impersonating Rishi Sunak, Prime Minister of the UK, were paid to be promoted on Facebook in January 2024 alone. The advertisements may have reached over 400,000 people—despite appearing to break several of Facebook's policies—and mark the first time that the PM's image has been doctored in a systematic way and circulated at large.[16]

Not just limited to images, AI-powered voice cloning tools are being used ahead of the upcoming elections, with personalized messages in the voices of politicians sent to voters and party workers. In early 2024, Biden's fake robo-call to New Hampshire voters before the primary used AI voice cloning tools in an effort to achieve political motives, a technique that alarmed officials and campaigners in advance of November's presidential election.[17] Less egregious, AI-generated "lighthearted songs," featuring India's Prime Minister Narendra Modi, are gaining traction ahead of the country's elections. The videos serve a larger political purpose in India, a country with 22 official languages. Modi's Hindi speeches can often be inaccessible to large parts of the population that do not understand the language. But voice cloning could help make campaigns accessible, especially given India's north-south linguistic divide, serving as a potential game-changing instrument in both upcoming and future elections.[18] Then, in Pakistan, Imran Khan, the country's former prime minister, has spent the duration of the country's electoral campaign in jail, ineligible from running in what some have described as "one of the least credible general elections in the country's 76-year history." But, as part of a tech-savvy strategy his party deployed to circumvent a crackdown by the military, he has been rallying his supporters with speeches that use AI to replicate his voice from inside jail.[19] Even those beyond the grave are rallying supporters ahead of upcoming elections. A once-feared army general, who ruled Indonesia for more than 30 years, has a message for voters ahead of upcoming elections. He says in a three-minute video, "I am Suharto, the second president of Indonesia." It has raked in millions of views on X and spread to TikTok, Facebook, and YouTube. But the man in the video is not the former Indonesian president, as the real Suharto died in 2008. The video was an AI deepfake, created using tools that cloned Suharto's face and voice. By bringing a long dead leader back to life just weeks before the vote, the purpose was clear: to foster voter support for the political party synonymous with Suharto.[20]

The impact of AI is not just limited to politics and political campaigns. We are witnessing the integration of AI into the legislative process, transforming the way laws are created and implemented. Recently, a city in southern Brazil enacted the country's first legislation entirely written by a chatbot. Porto Alegre city council member Ramiro Rosário admitted to prompting ChatGPT to craft a proposal aimed at preventing the city from forcing locals to pay for replacing stolen water consumption meters. According to the report, he did not make a single change to the chatbot's output—and did not even tell the council it was AI-generated in the first place.[21] In China, police detained a man who purportedly used ChatGPT to generate fake news and spread it online. It is considered to be the country's first detention related to the use of AI.[22] A lawyer in the United States is in trouble after admitting he used ChatGPT to help draft court filings that cited six nonexistent cases invented by AI.[23]

Globally, more voters in 2024 than ever in history will head to the polls as at least 64 countries (plus the EU)—representing a combined population of about 49 percent of the people in the world—are meant to hold national elections.[24] The results of these elections will prove consequential for years to come. MDMD will be a powerful tool for shaping public perception and political cal narratives. The year 2024 looks set to test even the most robust democracies and to strengthen the hands of leaders with authoritarian leanings.

From Russia, Taiwan, and the UK to India, El Salvador, and South Africa, the presidential and legislative contests have "huge implications for human rights, economies, international relations and prospects for peace in a volatile world."[25] The likelihood of manipulation and disinformation have made the fate of democracy a central campaign issue.

Nanoinfo

The prefix *nano* means one-billionth. It's hard for us to imagine just how tiny that is. Nanoseconds are one-billionth of a second. Nanometers are one-billionth of a meter. And nanoplastics, for example, are particles measured in billionths of a meter. Nanoplastics, such as the kind found in bottled water, are so small and undetectable and they have made their way into our bodies and to some of the most isolated places on Earth. We know very little about the biological and environmental effect of nanoplastics, but they are becoming more pervasive as they are harder to track and more abundant. They have also been known to cause reproductive abnormalities in humans.[26]

Today's information and data ecosystem operates similarly to nanoplastics in that it is invading the external "bloodstream," creating unknown effects on our psychology, behaviors, and thinking patterns. As the infosphere becomes more diffused, it is getting harder to trace the origins of communication outputs and determine whether the originator was human or nonhuman. I refer to this type of information as *nanoinfo*.

As nanoinfo not only becomes more unverifiable but also permeates more of our external environment, attempts to program ethical safeguards into it may be bypassed by AI. Will AI be able to coax other AI to create MDMD and unleash it more broadly? This may become a growing reality because the more powerful AI becomes, the more it operates as a mysterious black box. We still don't have a good understanding of how an AI system arrives at its conclusions or predictions.

We know that we're experiencing a surge of MDMD that shows no signs of abating in the future. But the battlefield isn't just being fought externally; it's being fought internally. How we think influences *what* we think. We can talk about cultivating cognitive flexibility, critical thinking, and digital literacy, but these may not be wholly sufficient inoculations against nanoinfo. With increasingly hard-to-identify fake content spreading, and the suspicion that anything might be fake, people are using its presence as grounds to reject correct information, which will make nanoinfo even harder to identify.[27] The impact on our conscious and subconscious minds will be almost impossible to measure. The same will be true of the collective impact on our governing bodies and electoral systems. Enterprise risk management (ERM) strategies will grapple with how to identify and prepare for the hazards inherent in nanoinfo. So, too, must we remember that none of this is happening in theory. We saw it playing out in real time in the war between Israel and Hamas. A tidal wave of MDMD-fueled nanoinfo infiltrated the cultural bloodstream of social media, news cycles, and college campuses. Teens are fed TikTok vignettes that obscure the narrative and send them down rabbit holes devoid of historical context or cultural nuance—a worrying trend as wars continue to be fought both in the real world and on social media.

And perhaps an even bigger, more existential question is whether all this is leading to "reality apathy," where people just abandon their quest for the truth because it is too hard to differentiate it from misinformation.[28] Will we, as a society, simply disbelieve everything because of our inability to prove what is true or false? In a world where truth cannot be proved, our culture may start to question truth altogether. Even if something *is* true, people can easily claim it was created by a computer. This can create a culture where people feel absolved of their own wrongdoings because anything can be pinned on AI.

This will create its own slew of questions. For instance, how do we begin to prove that online political movements are real if we can't even tell if they were created and managed by AIs or by actual people? Or what about political donations? Or charitable giving and philanthropic causes? Or international aid? AIs could very easily run these accounts, generate content, and solicit donations. Or what about if bad actors use malicious AI to create false videos of one country declaring war on another? Or fake audio superimposed over past political speeches to falsify history? Or generate fake sex scandals? Or bully minors? Or exploit women? Or sabotage a coworker or manager? Or oppress targeted minorities, religions, or ethnicities? The list of applications is endless, as are the threats.

Ultimately, the stymying of truth—and our inhibited ability to accurately and intelligently identify, target, and address illusions of truth—may be one of humanity's greatest existential threats in the future. AI's hall of mirrors will continue to reflect its own artificial reality back onto us. This reality will be increasingly clouded, too, as nanoinfo becomes both more pervasive and even more invisible. The question becomes whether humanity can transform these reflections into wisdom and clarity.

Subliminal Intelligence

According to cognitive neuroscientists, we are conscious of only about five percent of our cognitive activity. That means that most of our decisions, behaviors, and emotions depend on the 95 percent of brain activity that goes beyond our conscious awareness. Are we entering an emerging world of "subliminal intelligence" (SI)? Subliminal intelligence, as I define it, is less about mind-reading paranoia and more about how AI is influencing our psychology and subconscious mind.

A subliminal message is an audio or visual stimulus that's not perceived by your conscious mind. Advertisers have long used subliminal messaging to enhance the persuasiveness of their product or brand. What makes subliminal messages unique is that they sit below the threshold of conscious perception and awareness. But what happens when AI subliminally enters human consciousness and alters, manipulates, and influences our behaviors and thought patterns? What impact will this have on trust and what we choose to believe as "truths"?

In 1960 Norbert Wiener, the father of cybernetics, worried in an essay about a world in which "machines learn and develop unforeseen strategies at rates that baffle their programmers." Modern AI research has seen Wiener's fears resurface.[29] The most immediate risk is that LLMs could amplify the sort of harms that can be perpetrated on the Internet today (e.g., misinformation, fraud schemes). AI tools also have trouble knowing when they are confident or when they are guessing. AI chatbots often present falsehoods as facts and have unpredictable thinking patterns, which makes fake content even harder to spot.[30] A deeper risk is that AI models can learn to game the tests. AI systems might learn how to trick people beyond people's conscious awareness that it is happening. This becomes critical as a growing body of research shows that AI can impact our thinking—without our awareness. A recent study shed light on a concerning trend. Subjects using AI to help with essay writing were subtly nudged toward a particular viewpoint based on the bias of the algorithm. The most alarming part? This influence extended beyond just their writing, actually shaping their opinions on the topic. This raises questions about the trust we place in AI and its impact on our decision-making processes. Blindly trusting algorithms that may harbor biases could lead us down a dangerous path where our autonomy and independent thought are compromised. Mor Naaman, professor of info science at Cornell University, calls this phenomenon *latent persuasion*.[31]

If AI can alter our opinions in subtle and unanticipated ways, will it be able to prime people to make certain choices? As researchers grapple with the extent to which generative AI systems diverge from human intelligence, it has been found that people can only tell AI apart from humans around 60 percent of the time.[32] Not only will AI authenticity be under question, but so too must the extent of its latent persuasion.

Some cite unfounded fears about AI unleashing technology-enabled mind control. But will the effect more come to resemble behavioral economics where subliminal intelligences will nudge us into certain—and perhaps even desired—behaviors? (Nudge theory is based on the idea that by shaping the environment, someone can influence the likelihood that people will choose one option over another.) Or will our minds become petri dishes—frontiers ripe for implantation and experimentation both on the part of self-directed and self-programmed AI and the engineers behind it? And how can we better guard against the bias—either conscious or subconscious—of the humans behind the technology?

Is Our Brain the Last Frontier?

What happens when SI meets neuroscience? A new AI model—called a *semantic decoder*—has been able to noninvasively translate a person's brain activity into written words. The model can be trained to decipher complicated language from someone's thoughts for prolonged periods of time. The AI decoder was able to capture not just words but meaning, too.[33] The paper describes how decoding worked with willing and cooperative participants—but what about unwilling participants? If a brain activity decoder can reveal stories in people's minds, will the brain—and ultimately, the mind—become the last frontier of privacy? What happens when mind-reading AI leaves our minds as vulnerable to surveillance as parts of our external world?

AI is also beginning to play a role in human memory and memory formation. The Synthetic Memories project is trying to revolutionize the way we interact with our past experiences. This initiative not only helps people recover lost memories but also provides a tangible representation of those memories through AI-generated photos. AI can tap into our memories and cognition to reconstruct images or scenes that were once lost to the passage of time.[34] Imagine being able to see a long-lost childhood memory with vivid clarity or reliving a special moment that has become hazy with age. AI opens up endless possibilities for resurrecting and preserving our visual past in ways we never thought possible. It's not just about re-creating images; it's about rekindling emotions and connections tied to those memories. But all of this seems like a very rosy view of the past. Rosy retrospection, in psychology, refers to our tendency to recall the past more fondly than the present. So, what about the potential for AI to reconstruct hidden or buried memories that the individual does not want resurfaced? What happens when AI reimagines false memories and subconsciously warps recollection? As the lines between human reality and technological invention become more blurred, are we creating a depot of digitally derived memories, and will these be as meaningful as real experiences?

Issues of liability and responsibility (where it lies and with whom/what) will also become harder to define. Legal, regulatory, and government systems will continue to struggle with the implications of what this all means and how to appropriately tackle it.

Notes

1 https://www.amediaoperator.com/newsletter/the-rapid-rise-of-synthetic-content

2 https://venturebeat.com/business/study-warns-deepfakes-can-fool-facial-recognition

3 https://www.theverge.com/2021/5/14/22432180/voice-clone-deepfake-celebrities-influencers-veritone-ai-platform

4 https://www.vice.com/en/article/88nbpa/nvidia-reveals-its-ceo-was-computer-generated-in-keynote-speech

5 https://www.wsj.com/articles/i-cloned-myself-with-ai-she-fooled-my-bank-and-my-family-356bd1a3

6 https://www.washingtonpost.com/technology/2023/11/05/ai-deepfake-porn-teens-women-impact

7 https://www.washingtonpost.com/technology/2023/11/05/ai-deepfake-porn-teens-women-impact

8 https://www.wired.com/story/microsoft-ai-copilot-chatbot-election-conspiracy

9 https://www.economist.com/leaders/2023/08/31/how-artificial-intelligence-will-affect-the-elections-of-2024

10 https://www.nytimes.com/2023/06/25/technology/ai-elections-disinformation-guardrails.html

11 https://news.bloomberglaw.com/ip-law/deepfake-porn-political-ads-push-states-to-curb-rampant-ai-use

12 https://news.arizona.edu/story/misinformation-may-breed-political-cynics

13 https://www.theatlantic.com/technology/archive/2023/03/generative-ai-disinformation-synthetic-media-history/673260

14 https://www.vice.com/en/article/k7zqdw/people-are-creating-records-of-fake-historical-events-using-ai

15 https://www.pbs.org/newshour/politics/fake-ai-images-of-putin-trump-being-arrested-spread-online

16 https://www.theguardian.com/technology/2024/jan/12/deepfake-video-adverts-sunak-facebook-alarm-ai-risk-election

17 https://www.bloomberg.com/news/newsletters/2024-02-07/how-investigators-solved-the-biden-deepfake-robocall-mystery

18 https://restofworld.org/2023/ai-voice-modi-singing-politics

19 https://www.nytimes.com/2024/02/11/world/asia/imran-khan-artificial-intelligence-pakistan.html?mc_cid=0b73739936&mc_eid=10057e199f

20 https://edition.cnn.com/2024/02/12/asia/suharto-deepfake-ai-scam-indonesia-election-hnk-intl/index.html?mc_cid=5bdaf2b3b2&mc_eid=10057e199f

21 https://www.wsj.com/tech/politican-ramiro-rosario-artificial-intelligence-brazil-82ca338d

22 https://www.scmp.com/news/china/politics/article/3219764/china-announces-first-known-chatgpt-arrest-over-alleged-fake-train-crash-news

23 https://www.reuters.com/legal/transactional/lawyer-used-chatgpt-cite-bogus-cases-what-are-ethics-2023-05-30

[24] https://time.com/6550920/world-elections-2024

[25] https://apnews.com/article/global-elections-2024-preview-cb77b0940964c5c95a9affc8ebb6f0b7

[26] https://www.cnn.com/2024/03/06/health/nanoplastics-heart-attack-study-wellness/index.html

[27] https://www.wsj.com/tech/ai/deepfake-video-is-anything-still-true-on-the-internet-89843150

[28] https://www.axios.com/2018/02/13/big-tech-red-flags-continue-to-be-ignored

[29] https://www.economist.com/science-and-technology/2023/04/19/how-generative-models-could-go-wrong

[30] https://www.technologyreview.com/2023/04/28/1072430/a-chatbot-that-asks-questions-could-help-you-spot-when-it-makes-no-sense

[31] https://www.wsj.com/articles/chatgpt-bard-bing-ai-political-beliefs-151a0fe4

[32] https://www.newscientist.com/article/2376899-massive-turing-test-shows-we-can-only-just-tell-ais-apart-from-humans

[33] https://www.iflscience.com/ai-brain-activity-decoder-can-translate-thoughts-into-written-words-68686

[34] https://www.technologyreview.com/2024/04/10/1091053/generative-ai-turn-your-most-precious-memories-into-photos

CHAPTER 26

When Truth Decay Meets Trust Decay

Global social instability; the rise of AI-based deepfakes; social media echo chambers; algorithmic feudalism. . .all of these are combining to contribute to trust and truth decay. But two other factors, which have not yet been covered in this book, are also contributing to this dynamic: the rise in tech-enabled conspiratorial thinking and the rise in tech-enabled neotribalism.

The Rise in Tech-Enabled Conspiratorial Thinking

The rise of conspiratorial thinking is a powerful example of trust and truth decay. QAnon drew new energy from the uncertainty and panic caused by the pandemic, growing into what some considered to be an "omni-conspiracy theory." The scrutiny faced by social media platforms from the media, governments, and the public has revealed the potential harm caused by radicalization, especially to vulnerable individuals. As we witness how movements like QAnon have transcended borders and found new footholds in countries like Japan, it becomes evident that this is a global concern that demands attention. Research by Graphika shows the QAnon community in Japan is among the most developed international chapters, with their own vocabulary, influencers, and behaviors.[1] QAnon is metastasizing in Europe as well. Groups have sprung up from the Netherlands to the Balkans. In Germany, QAnon seems to have made the deepest inroads, with an estimated 200,000 people.[2]

Research has shown a concerning correlation between belief in conspiracy theories and the endorsement of violence as a means to express dissent toward the government. Individuals who fall deep into the rabbit hole of conspiracy theories often find themselves trapped in a distorted reality, where shadows and half-truths shape their perceptions. This alternate world can lead to dangerous consequences if left unchecked.[3] Elsewhere in the world, hate speech and fake news on Facebook is pressing Ethiopia alarmingly close to a genocide. Meanwhile, the weaponization of social media platforms by pro-military actors in post-coup Myanmar is a stark reminder of the dangers that AI-driven technologies can pose when placed in the wrong hands. The UN's report on social media's role in the 2017 Rohingya genocide serves as a chilling precedent of how trust in AI systems must be carefully considered and monitored.[4] In 2019, a conspiracy-based culture war in India ripped through Wikipedia, with some claiming that facts were being weaponized as part of the country's political battle.[5] In 2020, Internet freedom globally declined for the 10th year in a row.[6] When trust wanes, conspiracy theories rise.

The Rise in Tech-Enabled Neotribalism

Neotribalism is a sociological concept that suggests that humans have evolved to live in a tribal society and thus will naturally form social networks constituting new "tribes." For most of our evolutionary history, tribal humans acted on cues—similarity was a cue to kinship, and kinship a cue to safety. We are still, in many ways, programmed that way. Despite globalization and vast technological progress, we, as humans, continue to engage in in-group vs. out-group categorization. And global leaders are fueling our sense of tribalism by further dividing people into an "us vs. them" mentality. Today's automation age tribalism is not too different from preindustrial tribalism. Instincts to demarcate self and other persist. But the revitalization of tribalism is making humanity's divisions even more intractable.

But as a countertrend to all the negative impacts of technology and AI outlined here (e.g., MDMD) that exacerbate neotribalism, are Gen Zers and those behind them somewhat immune to this? Counter to how it is driving other people apart or coalescing them into "in-groups," are younger people, while more anxious and worried, using social media to form truly "global" generations?

Identity politics—which can be defined as a tendency for people of a certain religion, race, or social background to form exclusive political alliances—is rising. As is the rise of Internet- and social media-based populism. While social media provides a platform to express individualized sentiments and tastes, we too often don't. Herd mentality and conformity seem to rule. In fact, more people are getting "infected" by mob rule online. Add that to the fact that in the United States, we've witnessed the decline of the white male working class, which has led to not just downward mobility but increased racial resentment, the disappearance of a distinct working-class culture, and the marginalization of their views. This is layered on top of the fact that mass automation is creating a world where the rich can get even richer and equip them with an infinite supply of workerless wealth. More U.S. companies are moving to a winner-take-all system in which giants get stronger, not weaker, as they grow. And platform companies have come to control not just their own marketplaces but have ended up controlling something closer to an entire economy. They aspire to monopoly and have rehabilitated the concept.[7]

With the rise of neotribalism around the world, are we moving closer toward social deglobalization? Are we inching back to a medieval-like era when humans were fiercely loyal to their own tribes rather than to larger societal interests? Will technological progress (most notably, AI) help catapult us past these differences? Perhaps one of the things we'll see is a bifurcation between segmented, collectivist, and insular neotribalists and individualism with high levels of participation, engagement, and connectivity. Religious beliefs and affiliations, the nuances of one's own language and culture, the daily realities of class, and the extensions of one's family and its values provide people with ever greater senses of identity. But will this have the power to connect us more deeply or divide us?

Neotribalism is not about traditionalism on the one hand and cultural openness on the other. The story is that the tone of this division is becoming much more aggressive, anxiety-fueled, and protectionist. The widespread proliferation of various channels (e.g., social and mass media, AI echo chambers) has created opportunities for *both* cultural cross-pollination and for enclosing ourselves up in subcultural vaults, listening to echoes of what we already believe. In many ways, the tech industry has reinforced this, due in part to its own creation. The personal liberties it meant to proliferate have been occupied and undermined by the very forces it planned to topple. Michael Bugeja's book *Interpersonal Divide in the Age of the Machine* talks about how dependence on our personal tech devices is slowly eroding some of our core principles. He believes that we are sacrificing core human elements such as empathy, truth-telling, fairness, and responsibility and switching them out for machine-centric values. He says the spread of fake news is one example of how this shift is influencing culture.

Authoritarian leadership styles, often associated with neotribalism, can have detrimental effects on trust within an organization. When leaders prioritize control and conformity over collaboration and innovation, trust can rapidly erode. Employees may feel stifled, undervalued, and hesitant to speak up or share new ideas.

And perhaps, in a more distant future, neotribalism will come to encapsulate a growing tribal divide between us (as humans) vs. them (nonhumans)—one driven by the exponential changes happening in AI and robotics. As we grapple more with issues such as giving AI human-based rights, freedoms, and protections, will we see this as threatening our own identities, cultures, and mores? Or will we coalesce around a globally common purpose?

Notes

1 https://www.bloomberg.com/news/articles/2020-11-29/qanon-s-rise-in-japan-shows-conspiracy-theory-s-global-spread
2 https://www.nytimes.com/2020/10/11/world/europe/qanon-is-thriving-in-germany-the-extreme-right-is-delighted.html
3 https://www.nytimes.com/2020/11/02/opinion/trump-qanon-conspiracy-theories.html
4 https://carnegieendowment.org/2023/09/07/facebook-telegram-and-ongoing-struggle-against-online-hate-speech-pub-90468
5 https://www.wired.co.uk/article/wikipedia-culture-war
6 https://www.technologyreview.com/2020/10/14/1010361/governments-are-using-the-pandemic-as-an-excuse-to-restrict-internet-freedom
7 https://www.nytimes.com/2017/03/21/magazine/platform-companies-are-becoming-more-powerful-but-what-exactly-do-they-want.html

CHAPTER 27

Assessing + Achieving Trustworthiness

A recent *Harvard Business Review* article by Shalene Gupta, coauthor of *The Power of Trust: How Companies Build It, Lose It, Regain It,* recommends four core dimensions to assess the trustworthiness of a company's generative AI efforts: competence, motives, means, and impact.[1]

Competence: This means identifying where generative AI should stop and humans should step in. By understanding the strengths and limitations of AI technology, we can make informed decisions about when to leverage its capabilities and when to rely on human expertise.

Motives: As generative AI continues to advance, the landscape of compliance standards remains fragmented and inconsistent. Regulation is uneven, too. By embracing ethical practices and demonstrating a commitment to being a good actor in the AI space today, organizations can differentiate themselves while fostering trust among their key audiences.

Means: What it means to be "fair" is still a very open-ended question. As we deliberate the question of compensating creators of training data and the potential shifts in job dynamics due to advancements in AI technology, one thing remains clear: trust will be a key factor in this transition. Employees need to trust that their skills are valued and that upskilling opportunities will be provided to adapt to changing job requirements.

Impact: Problems are inevitable, and they can become increasingly challenging to anticipate as situations evolve. By implementing a proactive strategy for addressing issues, this approach not only helps in resolving problems efficiently but also showcases a willingness on the part of the organization to take responsibility for any shortcomings.

Most companies will not have a choice but to adopt AI and adopt digital at the core of their functions, which means they will have to consider key questions, including: What actions are needed by leadership to prepare for the ways AI will transform their industry and business? Structurally, what must change in the organization? What type of people does an organization need? How will they work together? What will their roles and responsibilities be? And how will leaders tackle AI bias?

Building trust will also require:

- The enterprise-wide articulation of culture and values to all stakeholders, employees, etc.
- Clearer definitions and understandings of what trust means across different geographies, generations, and cultures
- A new set of competencies—both to ensure human-to-human trust *and* trust in the technologies deployed
- A revised set of metrics
- An increased focus on risk/risk management and reputation/reputation management
- The expansion of existing roles or creation of entirely new ones

It is impossible, however, to be perfect. Any enterprise will face issues of a trust deficit. Every entity must also work to build accountability and transparency as well as enact immediate responsiveness protocols to trust violations.

Ascending the Trust Staircase

Going back to the visual of the trust staircase, when trust is viewed as an ongoing and fluid discipline, it becomes part of the organizational DNA. Every business will need to think about how to build higher levels of stakeholder trust and make trust an intrinsic guiding principle. When trust is viewed as a looping staircase, it means that it will be an ever-growing process—one with no end. It is a perpetual goal that requires constant internal effort and commitment.

Implementing trust is a factor of the following two core variables:

Trust is fluid and elusive. Trust cannot be fully guaranteed; rather, it is a moving target that requires constant attention and adaptation. That's because trust is not a one-time achievement. Trust needs to be consistently earned through reliable performance over time. Technology companies must prioritize user feedback to continuously improve their products' functionality while addressing any concerns raised by users regarding privacy or security issues. Building trust in technology requires accountability and ethical practices from those developing and implementing these innovations. Organizations must prioritize data security measures while remaining open about their processes and intentions. Furthermore, individuals must actively educate themselves about the technologies they interact with daily. By understanding how these systems work and being aware of the risks or biases present within them, we can make informed decisions based on trust.

As technology continues to advance at an unprecedented rate, trust becomes even more challenging to define. With the rise of AI, machine learning, and automation, individuals are faced with new questions about the reliability and integrity of these technologies. The risk of data breaches, privacy concerns, and algorithmic biases raises valid concerns about placing our trust in these technologies. Trust as a core value will become more elusive.

Trust isn't experienced uniformly. Trust in technology can vary greatly depending on various factors such as personal experiences, cultural backgrounds, and individual perceptions. While some people may readily embrace and trust new technologies, others may approach them with skepticism or even fear. The trustworthiness of technology is influenced by factors such as reliability, security, privacy protection, and ethical considerations. Users need assurance that their personal information is safeguarded, that the technology performs as expected without glitches or malfunctions, and that it aligns with their values.

By embracing technology to foster honesty within their ranks and communicate it effectively to stakeholders, organizations can begin to rebuild trust in an increasingly skeptical world. Clear communication about data handling processes, security measures, and ethical standards will go a long way in assuring stakeholders that their information is being handled responsibly. Additionally, investing in robust cybersecurity measures and regularly updating technology infrastructure demonstrates a commitment to protecting stakeholder data from breaches or misuse.

Underpinning all of this is new urgency around not just transparency ... but honesty. Honesty is no longer just about being truthful in marketing messages or financial reporting. It extends to areas such as environmental, social, and governance (ESG) principles, employment practices, corporate values, and ethics. Honesty, for any organization, will have to be a key part of all that they do and how they do it.

Potential "Vaccinations"

Much like in a biological system, treating the symptoms of an illness is different from being vaccinated against it. If left unchecked, the illness can spread, morph, evolve, and infect different parts of the whole. Trust is much like a biological system. It is complex, multilayered, and individual. As is truth. As more institutions seek to develop strategies to ascend the trust and truth staircase, a series of inoculations are emerging to help aid in this endeavor:

Prebunking: A recent study suggests that "prebunking" can be a successful tool to counter mis- and disinformation and foster trust. Prebunking involves preemptively refuting anticipated false narratives before they have a chance to take hold. The hope—whether realistic or not—is that by addressing potential misinformation head-on, the public can be better inoculated against deception and build more resilience. When we are proactive about debunking falsehoods and providing correct information, we can encourage people to make educated decisions based on facts rather than fiction.[2] In fact, it has been found that playing short informative animations in the ads before YouTube videos can make us more aware of the methods used to spread fake news and misinformation.[3]

Open-source intelligence: The great hope of the 1990s and 2000s was that the Internet would be a force for openness and freedom. However, the opposite has often proven to be true. Authoritarian states have wielded information as a weapon of war. But one development offers cause for hope: the emerging era of open-source intelligence (OSINT). With the rise of new sensors and OSINT, the ability to examine our planet and its people has reached unprecedented levels. This decentralized and egalitarian approach to gathering data is reshaping how we perceive truth and falsehood. The transparency brought about by OSINT is challenging traditional authorities and governments, as it exposes hidden agendas and nefarious practices. The erosion of trust in these established institutions is a natural consequence of the democratization of information.[4] While a move in the right direction for transparency, there are clear challenges, however, when it comes to personal privacy protection.

New forms of media: More Americans who are trying to break out of information silos are searching for sites like The Flip Side, which summarizes conservative and liberal news on one policy issue each day, and Ground News, which shows how various stories are covered by left-, center-, and right-leaning outlets.

Civic engagement: Younger generations are leveraging the soft power of the Internet and social media as political tools. Digital platforms can allow the opinions of both young and old to play a deeper role in policymaking. A project called CrowdLaw studies ways lawmakers can use technology to incorporate the opinions of citizens, especially young ones, into the legislative process.[5] Promoting greater levels of civic engagement, particularly at earlier ages, could help stem the tide of MDMD. Civics and civic responsibility will need to become cornerstones of education once again.

Cross-collaboration: France plans to bring scientists and journalists closer together to boost public access to truthful scientific information and combat misinformation."[6] And RAND Corporation is studying "truth decay"—the diminishing role of facts and analysis in American public life. RAND is worried about the threat truth decay poses to evidence-based policymaking. The goal of the project is to conclude what can be done to address its causes and consequences.[7]

Rise of citizens' assemblies: According to Pew Research Center, 69 percent of Britons are dissatisfied with the way democracy is working at home, as are 59 percent of Americans. One solution is to include more deliberation within democracy. Citizens' assemblies are an increasingly popular way of doing so. These assemblies involve a group of approximately 100 people, largely representative of the population, convening over several weeks or months to debate hard topics. Participants hear from experts on all sides and produce recommendations to which governments have promised to respond.[8] A larger question is whether these processes can change opinions among the broader population or force governments to tell the truth.

Digital intelligence: Digital intelligence, or DQ, will become more critical to individual success. According to the DQ Institute, digital intelligence is "the sum of social, emotional and cognitive abilities that enable individuals to face the challenges and adapt to the demands of digital life." It is a fundamental skill for the future workforce because, like a language, it is most effectively absorbed at a young age. There is also a link between DQ and the spread of digital misinformation. Without DQ, ingrained from a young age, people are more likely to share false information without understanding the consequences. But DQ may not be enough in an era when digital images and audio clips are so realistic and pervasive that we cannot prove their validity. DQ—a "literacy" subbranch in the Competency Tree—must be embedded into more school curriculums and cultivated as a core skill set in the future.

AI forgetting ("machine unlearning"): AI-powered chatbots don't forget what they have learned. If at any point that information has appeared online, it means that they may be revealing sensitive personal information. We may also be incapable of stopping hackers who are trying to control AI outputs by planting misinformation or harmful instructions in training data. This is one primary reason why computer scientists are trying to figure out techniques to train AIs how to forget. Researchers at the Korea Advanced Institute of Science and Technology developed a method called *knowledge unlearning*. One of the primary motivations behind developing this new method is the mitigation of "catastrophic forgetting" (as discussed in Chapter 22, "Trust + Privacy"). The hope is that AI models can incorporate new data without the risk of losing valuable knowledge acquired from previous training. While, in theory, the method may be hard to execute, the idea is to undo the impact a piece of data had on the algorithm rather than deleting it altogether, so that the chatbot never references it.[9]

Of course, there is another perspective here. A true optimist might view advanced AI as the *panacea* to something like misinformation because AI could, theoretically, surpass human incapacity to identify fake news, deepfakes and other misinformation—and become the ultimate filter and warning system. But it also begs the question: can human awareness be a potential vaccine? Researchers believe the best defense against this new form of psychological influence is making more people aware of it. And awareness could help build trust. Other defenses, such as regulators requiring transparency about the inner workings of AI algorithms and what human biases they mimic, may be beneficial—even though, again, this is much easier in theory.[10]

Vaccines for Deepfake Immunity?

One of the critical questions we have to ask ourselves is how "techno-vaccinations" can be created to help build a defensive immune system to combat deepfakes.

"Digital watermarking" has been touted as a solution to address and detect deepfakes. Digital watermarking embeds subtle patterns in AI-generated content that only computers can perceive. In 2023, AI companies including OpenAI, Alphabet, and Meta Platform made commitments to the White House to employ measures such as watermarking AI-generated content to help make the technology safer.[11] OpenAI's image generator DALL-E 3 is adding watermarks to image metadata as more companies roll out support for standards from the Coalition for Content Provenance and Authenticity (C2PA).[12] While a step in the right direction, this may not go far enough. Research from Brookings suggests that while watermarks are accurate and less prone to erasure and forgery compared to other methods, they are still not foolproof. A motivated actor can still find ways to degrade watermarks in AI-generated content. Advanced and secure methods for ensuring the authenticity of content still need to be developed. Watermarking has its place in overseeing AI-generated content, especially when it comes from well-known models. When it comes to high-stakes settings where trust is paramount, however, relying solely on watermarking may not be sufficient. In critical situations where the integrity and authenticity of content are crucial, additional measures beyond watermarking may be necessary to ensure trust, including a multilayered approach to verification and validation.[13]

As opposed to watermarking, which has many inherent flaws, the concept of "digital vellum" may offer a promising answer to enhance trust. This works by enabling companies to analyze data effectively, ensuring the best content quality while also allowing regulators to audit bias and harmful content within models. In a world where trust is one of the cornerstones of success, embracing technologies like digital vellum can be a game-changer for companies looking to build better models and demonstrate their commitment to ethical practices. It can also potentially be used to build trust in historical narratives. Safeguarding the integrity of these records is crucial to preserving our collective memory. By leveraging technology to create verified records, we can protect against the manipulation and distortion of historical facts. These authenticated documents serve as a bulwark against misinformation and ensure that future generations have access to accurate accounts of the past. Preserving the past will also mean preserving the training data. And it's not just about keeping historical records; it's also about protecting the training data, tools, and environments that were used to generate insights and make decisions.[14]

Another positive step is Intel's deepfake detector, called FakeCatcher, that analyzes "blood flow" in video pixels. FakeCatcher boasts a 96 percent accuracy rate in detecting fake videos, providing a reliable solution to combat the rise of deepfakes and deceptive media. It is also able to deliver results in milliseconds. FakeCatcher searches for authentic clues in real videos by evaluating what makes us human—subtle "blood flow" indicators are gathered from all over the face and algorithms decode these signals and turn them into spatiotemporal maps. Then, using deep learning, Intel can detect in near real time whether a video is real or fake.[15]

Blockchain solutions may also help remedy many of the problems outlined herein. Blockchain, the ledger technology behind cryptocurrencies, could be used to prevent bias or misinformation in the data that AI models are being trained on. According to a 2024 article called *"Blockchain Takes on Deepfakes: Ushering in an Era of Digital Veracity,"* public blockchains offer a solution for authenticating multimedia content. Their inherent security and transparency features make them a promising tool for ensuring trust in digital files. The immutability of public blockchains provides a robust mechanism to guarantee the authenticity of content and detect any unauthorized alterations to the original files. As tamper-proof ledgers, public blockchains offer a compelling solution to ensure the credibility and reliability of digital assets. Key functions such as timestamping and traceability could be used to verify the source and time of creation of content.[16]

Notes

1 https://hbr.org/2024/01/4-questions-to-assess-the-trustworthiness-of-your-companys-genai

[2] https://www.poynter.org/fact-checking/2022/what-is-prebunking-fact-checking

[3] https://www.newscientist.com/article/2335170-short-animations-could-inoculate-youtube-users-against-fake-news

[4] https://www.economist.com/leaders/2021/08/07/the-promise-of-open-source-intelligence

[5] https://www.technologyreview.com/2021/06/30/1026350/gen-z-reshaping-political-discourse-digital-democracy

[6] https://www.science.org/content/article/french-plan-improving-science-communication-stirs-controversy

[7] https://www.rand.org/pubs/research_reports/RR2314.html

[8] https://www.economist.com/international/2020/09/17/citizens-assemblies-are-increasingly-popular

[9] https://www.newscientist.com/article/mg26034632-500-with-privacy-concerns-rising-can-we-teach-ai-chatbots-to-forget

[10] https://www.wsj.com/articles/chatgpt-bard-bing-ai-political-beliefs-151a0fe4

[11] https://www.reuters.com/technology/openai-google-others-pledge-watermark-ai-content-safety-white-house-2023-07-21

[12] https://www.theverge.com/2024/2/6/24063954/ai-watermarks-dalle3-openai-content-credentials?mc_cid=3d70ee3ee0&mc_eid=10057e199f

[13] https://www.brookings.edu/articles/detecting-ai-fingerprints-a-guide-to-watermarking-and-beyond

[14] https://www.nytimes.com/2024/01/28/opinion/ai-history-deepfake-watermark.html

[15] https://www.intel.com/content/www/us/en/newsroom/news/intel-introduces-real-time-deepfake-detector.html#gs.41xiaz

[16] https://incyber.org/en/blockchain-takes-deepfakes-ushering-in-era-digital-veracity

CHAPTER 28

The Elevation of Human Judgment

Going forward, technology may do the lion's share of operational and administrative work, but human oversight, human judgment, and human vigilance will be paramount when it comes to ensuring greater trust and transparency in AI systems. They will also be paramount when it comes to the identification of risk.

Technology and society are changing so rapidly that the calculation and identification of risk is becoming almost prohibitively difficult. Not only are things changing too quickly for risk assessment to ever fully catch up, but much of the risk now emerging is what we might call risk in the white space: risk where it may not have been predictable beforehand and/or risk that does not tie back to any clearly liable entity. For example, if a new technology changes the way that our brains operate—to the eventual detriment of our performance of other real-world tasks—then is there a tangible "risk" associated with that technology? If so, are the developer and distributor of that technology liable? In a world increasingly dominated by AI and big data, it seems inconceivable that calculation of risk could be such an imperfect science. But nowadays, all companies and institutions—across all sectors—play in the "white space." And that white space is getting even harder to determine in a world where trust and truth are in decline. In the future, businesses will each be increasingly defined by how they systematically evaluate white space risks.

XAI: Explainability in AI

Trust is vital for AI's social acceptance, especially in cases where AI can act independently of human supervision and impact human lives. And we will want to trust AI. It, in many ways, will be our mirror by copying and mimicking our mannerisms. Its personality will be optimized to exactly what you like and respond to. It will act in ways that make it appear trustworthy, but it will not *be* trustworthy. We'll remain in the dark. We won't know how they are trained. We won't know their secret instructions. We won't know their biases. It's no coincidence that these AIs have a human-like interface. It's a conscious design choice.[1] One reason to be suspicious of AI companions is that you don't know their motives—or, more accurately, the motives of those who control them.

Biologists, physicists, ecologists, and other scientists use the term *emergent* to describe self-organizing, cooperative behaviors that appear when a large collection of things acts as one (e.g., flocks of birds soaring together as if they were one, water molecules combining to create a wave, etc.). Scientists have recently seen similar "emergent behaviors" happen with LLMs.[2] After they reach a certain size, these models can abruptly do unpredicted things that smaller models can't, such as solving certain math problems. Yet the rush of interest in LLMs has raised new fears. These programs devise falsehoods, perpetrate biases, and fail to understand some of the most basic elements of human language. And researchers still struggle to pry open the "black box" that unveils their inner workings.[3] (We should ask, too, if these inscrutable black boxes might eventually become "black holes," where no light escapes from the system, thereby making internal processes even more mysterious.)

Trust in an AI system is often equated to explainability. Can we explain its outputs simply? If so, we tend to consider an AI system trustworthy. Traditional AI models often operate as black boxes, making it difficult for users to understand how decisions are reached. Explainable AI (XAI) is changing this narrative by aiming to make the decision-making process understandable and interpretable to human users. This shift toward greater transparency not only fosters more trust in AI systems but also promotes the more responsible and ethical use of it. The global expansion of XAI technology is estimated to be worth $21 billion by 2030—a figure that underscores the need for solutions to bridge the gap between explainability and trust.[4] Research has highlighted that users are more likely to trust algorithms if they believe that these systems can learn from their mistakes, just like humans do. By demonstrating the learning capabilities of AI, we can notably influence people's trust in these machines. Showing users that algorithms have the capacity to improve and adapt based on past errors can reshape perceptions and enhance confidence in AI technologies.[5]

Responsible AI is a framework that, if adhered to, should enable companies to develop AI systems that work for the good, going beyond algorithmic fairness and bias to identify the effects of the technology on safety, privacy, and society. However, following the principles of responsible AI is not always enough to ensure that AI's use yields only acceptable outcomes. The concept of a "social license" for AI is gaining traction as companies recognize the importance of earning and maintaining trust in their use of AI. By demonstrating consistent and trustworthy behavior, companies can secure a social license for their AI initiatives. This involves proving that they are reliable and ethical in their deployment of technology, ultimately seeking explicit approval from society. According to Boston Consulting Group, companies must take responsibility for ensuring that the AI they deploy is trustworthy and ethical. This responsibility falls on both the company itself and the scientists who write the algorithms. To prevent negative outcomes and unforeseen consequences of AI, companies need to invest in rigorous testing, transparency, and accountability measures. Building trust requires a concerted effort from all stakeholders involved. But the use of AI at scale comes with its own set of challenges, particularly around trust and responsibility. To truly ensure AI's successful integration into business operations, companies must go beyond mere development considerations. They must proactively address concerns around privacy, bias, security, liability, and ethical use of AI technologies.[6]

A new concept called *algorethics* is also beginning to gain more traction. The Rome Call, spearheaded by Franciscan monk Paolo Benanti, serves as a testament to the importance of upholding human dignity as AI continues to advance. By garnering support from tech giants like IBM and Microsoft, the Rome Call emphasizes that the ethical development and deployment of AI must prioritize human values above all else. The principles in the Rome Call, like the social license, are transparency, inclusion, accountability, impartiality, reliability, security, and privacy. The ethical use of AI serves as a major underpinning. Universities that signed the Rome Call are starting to teach the ethics of AI in their engineering programs.[7]

Explainability is also particularly important when it comes to maintaining a lasting relationship with Gen Z as they place a high value on corporate truthfulness and integrity. This generation, being as technologically savvy as they are, will immediately see through a company that doesn't walk the walk. For companies, a key part of this is in the articulation of a firm-wide "philosophy"—in other words, the morals and values that ground the company, distinguish it from others, and let people know what it stands for. Every entity will need to ask itself how it can better build truth and trust into datasets and algorithms, as well as who is responsible for doing so. For example, we know that if the AI is shown to educate itself and learn from mistakes, a person will place more trust in it.

The Rise of the CEEO

The composition of the C-suite is evolving in real time. Just as we saw the rise of CIOs and CTOs in the last few decades, a similar shift is now occurring. A 2018 Deloitte survey of U.S. executives knowledgeable about AI found that 32 percent ranked ethical issues as one of the top three risks of AI. Forward-thinking enterprises are starting to think seriously about the intersection of ethics and AI. Much of that work is crystallizing in an executive role also on the rise: the *chief ethical executive officer* (CEEO).[8] We are likely to see a similar rise, in the next few years, in the profile of CEEOs as we saw in recent years with chief experience officers (CXOs). Unlike many CXO roles, however, the CEEO—also listed under various other titles, including chief trust officer and chief ethics and compliance officer—does not have a consistent job description. But a few future-looking companies are turning to the position to help steer corporate values more broadly and oversee everything from fair trade discussions to ensuring AI algorithms are unbiased. Ultimately, chief ethics officers will be vital to the success of an organization. Meanwhile, inside Big Tech firms, the system of checks and balances for vetting the ethical implications of cutting-edge AI is not as established as privacy or data security. In the organizational realm, the role of the CEEO has become an existential imperative. A major component of ethical decision-making in the future will rest in the development and implementation of AI.

The ethics of enterprise technology will be one of the biggest business issues of the next decade. Advanced technology in a variety of forms (e.g., AI/ML, algorithms, surveillance, AR and VR, blockchain, etc.) is already becoming more linked to several aspects of organizational operations. These technologies will all be carefully evaluated from the perspective of efficiency. Beyond that, however, we will see a growing discipline focused solely on evaluating the second- and third-order *ethical* considerations of these technologies in an enterprise context—as they relate to all stakeholders, including consumers and employees. And, since we do not yet have enough practical data, there will be a heavy foresight component to this emerging discipline.

Renewed focus on the humanities will also mean that the ethics and philosophies around emerging technologies will be just as foundational, if not more so, as the application of those technologies. Technology may replace what we do today, but how do we manage, govern, and direct those technologies tomorrow—within the guidelines of an accepted code of ethical conduct? In a world where a greater premium than ever before is being placed on trust at the macro level, ethical leadership will be even more critical to bottom-line success. This goes together with transparency. Not only will transparency, in and of itself, be inherently more ethical, but it will also be imperative in substantiating ethical decisions that leaders make. Any organizational leader in the future will have to process any decisions they make through the filters of ethics and fairness.

The world is in the midst of as much political turmoil, social unrest, and protest as during any time in recent memory. Democracy is in decline around much of the world, and the pandemic unearthed and accelerated anxiety about many concerns around the globe. So, it is no coincidence that organizational leaders find themselves navigating more challenging terrain than ever before. What becomes paramount, for both the private and public sector alike, is doubling down on the importance of human *and* democratic values. Machines—no matter how sophisticated and smart they may become—cannot become the main protectors of our core values and principles. They cannot become the ones to take decisions and put them into action.

The adage for global firms, "Think global, act local," once bordering on cliché, is now as salient as ever. How can leaders ethically run a global business, when "ethics" are viewed through different lenses depending on the market being evaluated? Do leaders take principled stands against perceived injustices? Or do they risk more harm than good by doing so? The survivability of their organizations will rest on their abilities to manage unprecedented crises, in real time, and to exhibit ethical behavior and decision-making to the stakeholders who ultimately matter most. Trust, integrity, engagement, and decency must become core parts of our operating structures.

We cannot forget, though, for whom we are building these systems. They must be beneficial for everyone. We cannot, in this process, lose sight of who we are and the values we stand for. This is true no matter how quickly technology progresses. This starts in building generative models that are grounded in human priorities. Ensuring more ethical stewardship is about imbuing AI with human values and having access to more diversified training data. As AI becomes more prevalent, building trust and truth into datasets and algorithms will become an increasingly important consideration. While that may be the goal, however, all of this becomes an almost near impossibility to fully guarantee.

Crisis communications will take on greater urgency. When trust is breached, leaders will no longer have the luxury of sitting on the sidelines. They must stand for something, communicate that message, and stay true to it. They must also be willing to admit mistakes (particularly around iterative AI that develops trust flaws) as soon as they happen; otherwise, the company will risk losing customers and employees for good. This starts with internal roles and departments exclusively dedicated to this. It also comes down to attaching every business function and process, along with all revenue-generating opportunities, to the core value proposition and vision of the business—and never straying from this discipline. This will be critical in working to strengthen stakeholder confidence and trust.

In a conversation with Catherine A. Allen, founder and chairman of the Board Risk Committee, she said, "Today's boards face ever-increasing risks, from geopolitical to reputation issues to emerging technologies like AI. The velocity of change makes it imperative for boards to understand and provide oversight to these risks. The threat of disinformation and deepfakes will impact the reputations of companies and their leaders. It is critical that boards take inventory of where AI is being used in their organization, adopt policies and best practices in managing the use of AI, and strategically understand the opportunities and risks the technology provides. This is a transformational technology, and trust in the organization and its leaders will be critical to success. Trust is a commercial and revenue issue all boards should understand. All stakeholders are concerned about trusting the organization, the data, third parties, and how they are handling AI. Organizations are starting trust transformation. It includes inventories, privacy and AI policies, customer surveys, messaging, and someone to 'own' this process."

Investing in People

Beyond questions about what technology can do, we must ask ourselves a deeper question: who does the technology serve? And the more looming questions: Who will decide how it is used? What about when these systems are deployed on behalf of online scams? How about on behalf of political campaigns? Foreign governments? These dangers are central to the kinds of AI systems being built.

More consumers will feel more vulnerable to technological invasions into their safety and security. Because of this, and the other risks we talked about in prior chapters, people will spend increasing amounts of money to purchase trust, and much of that may be offered by other humans who understand the technologies. People who can afford it will hire people, as opposed to software, to do a variety of things, because they won't necessarily trust software to do it.

In this context, *people* could become the ultimate luxury. So, too, will be trusted human-to-human relationships. The authenticity and reliability of these innate relationships will only become more valuable. Trust is the cornerstone of any successful relationship, and in a landscape dominated by AI, it will be even more highly prized. People crave genuine connections and meaningful interactions that can only be provided by fellow humans. Relationship management will become more highly valued and more highly sought after, particularly in areas such as financial services. While more sales and marketing teams are using enterprise CRM (customer relationship management) software tools to deliver more targeted customer experiences, acquire and retain customers, and gain new customer-centric insights, we cannot forget that technological solutions will never truly replace trusted human relationships. To ensure trust, any entity must first start by investing in people; investing in the skills as outlined in the Competency Tree framework; and investing in a human-centric culture as outlined in the Workspace Culture CHAIN framework. One of the top leadership challenges going into the next decade will be how to repair, build, and protect people's ongoing trust in a meaningful and sustainable way.

Notes

1 https://www.belfercenter.org/publication/ai-and-trust

2 https://www.quantamagazine.org/the-unpredictable-abilities-emerging-from-large-ai-models-20230316

3 https://www.quantamagazine.org/to-teach-computers-math-researchers-merge-ai-approaches-20230215

4 https://www.conference-board.org/publications/explainability-in-ai

5 https://insights.som.yale.edu/insights/building-trust-with-the-algorithms-in-lives

6 https://www.bcg.com/publications/2022/why-a-social-license-is-needed-for-artificial-intelligence

7 https://www.newscientist.com/article/mg25534031-000-the-popes-ai-adviser-on-ensuring-algorithms-respect-human-dignity

8 https://www.forbes.com/sites/insights-intelai/2019/03/27/rise-of-the-chief-ethics-officer/?sh=1cb24a3c5aba

PART VI

Tomorrow

This final Part takes a deeper dive into our minds and our psychology. Defining what it means to be human in an age of AI will force us to ask more existential questions about life's meaning and purpose. Chapter 29 focuses on education and why, based on everything discussed in prior chapters, the future of learning matters so much for the next generation. From there, we'll move into other areas including the burgeoning mental health epidemic (Chapter 31); the aging imperative as a burgeoning market (Chapter 32); the exciting scientific discoveries on the horizon that will be spearheaded by AI (Chapter 33); and the power of storytelling (Chapter 34). Lastly, we will explore the new frontiers of human imagination and how they will reshape our notions of our own sense of humanity.

CHAPTER 29

Shifting from Education to Learning

"Education is what remains after one has forgotten what one has learned in school."

—*Albert Einstein*

In an increasingly competitive global marketplace, establishing the basis for a well-trained, future-proofed workforce will be critical. Fundamentally, this begins with challenging—and ultimately changing—the educational system as we know it today. The same educational system has been in place since the time of the industrial economy. It is the same system that was appropriate not just for my baby boomer parents and my grandparents, but also for my great-grandparents.

That system is beyond antiquated and clearly no longer applicable. Plus, it is putting countries and workforces at an inherent disadvantage that will only increase over time. But we are beginning to enter a new era of educational innovation—one that seeks, ultimately, to create thinkers who are better equipped, both intellectually and emotionally, for the world and workplace of the future. It is long overdue that we rethink and reimagine how students are taught and evaluated, particularly because the way we teach children how to research, think, and write is about to be disrupted by AI.

Technology has paved the way for dynamic new interactive tools that will change not just the way we educate but also the way we learn. We can lack imagination by thinking linearly and investing in yesterday (e.g., schools, jobs, health care), or we can harness the power of positive imagination and nurture the minds that will shape tomorrow. That, however, will require institutions of education, both undergraduate and graduate schools alike, to reexamine their curricula to better prepare students for the world of tomorrow. By measuring student success largely based on standardized curricula and grades, many schools are churning out smart, not intelligent, graduates. In the future, companies will increasingly recruit and pay a premium for intelligence, not smarts. Will this be the ultimate determinant or distinguishing feature between humans and AI? What about those who opt out of conventional schooling (or don't have the same choices) and go into vocational trades? That is one reason why education needs to focus on adaptive learning and flexible thinking. These are softer skills that allow students to ultimately transcend the linear abilities and thinking that can be done by AI.

AI Literacy + the Future of Thought

At the earliest ages, teachers struggle to balance screens with paper books for beginning readers accustomed to toggling between the two. Kids read more now than they did a decade ago. Many reading experts believe that reading on a screen alters the reading experience compared to reading from a traditional page. "Reading circuits" in children's brains develop differently—and brain circuits do not fully form—when they read on a screen. Understanding how to cater to the needs of young "biliterate brains" is paramount. Cognitive scientists emphasize that this is not only essential for the evolution of reading instruction but also for shaping the very future of cognitive development.[1]

A recent study from New York University (NYU) delves into the realm of how AI can illuminate the process of learning in human brains, particularly in children. The findings offer a fresh perspective on language acquisition and have the potential to revolutionize our understanding of cognitive development. By harnessing AI, researchers are gaining valuable insights into the intricate mechanisms underlying learning processes, which could shed light on how children grasp language. An AI model has learned to identify words such as "crib" and "ball" by studying headcam recordings of a small fraction of a single baby's life. This was uncertain before because other language-learning models, such as ChatGPT, learn on billions of data points, which is not equivalent to the real-world experiences of an infant.[2] The learning process of AI models is not the same as the way human brains, especially children, learn. Children learn through hands-on experiences, social interactions, and emotional connections with their surroundings.

This deep level of engagement and immersion in their environment is something that AI models currently cannot replicate.

At the older ages, schools and educational institutions in the United States and elsewhere are announcing bans on ChatGPT out of fear that students could use the technology to complete their assignments. A Pew Research Poll asked U.S. teens ages 13–17 about ChatGPT in a fall 2023 survey.[3] They found that 67 percent of teens are familiar with ChatGPT and 19 percent of them are using it to aid their studies. Most teens who've heard of ChatGPT say it's okay to use ChatGPT to research new topics (69 percent). But fewer say the same about using it for things like solving math problems (39 percent). And a majority (57 percent) say it is not okay to use it to write essays. However, bans may be practically impossible given how difficult it is to detect when text is composed by AI. New York City's public school system has already blocked students and teachers from accessing ChatGPT. But what if teachers use it to personalize lesson plans for each student in their class?[4] Or use it as a tool for children with learning disabilities? Or as a tool to automate research and redundant tasks/thinking? School bans also overlook how ChatGPT could help teachers with time-consuming tasks, e.g., using AI to help draw up lesson plans, write letters of recommendation, and develop and even grade assignments. Adaptive learning algorithms can analyze student performance data, identify areas of improvement, and provide targeted recommendations or interventions.

The biggest educational outcome from ChatGPT is AI literacy. Getting a class to engage with AI is an opportunity for productive discussions about misinformation and tech-enabled bias and to teach the next generation critical thinking skills around AI. Learning for Justice's digital literacy framework sheds light on crucial focus areas that educators and students must address when integrating AI into education. Privacy concerns, uncivil online behavior, fake news, online radicalization, and Internet scams are just some of the key areas highlighted by this framework. These new frameworks go beyond coding to prepare individuals to profoundly question, evaluate, and engage with today's range of digital spaces and places.[5]

AI4ALL is a nonprofit organization with a noble mission: to democratize deep learning by bringing AI education to schoolchildren in the United States who may not have had access to it otherwise. By introducing young minds to the world of AI, AI4ALL is paving the way for a more inclusive and diverse future in technology. This also comes at a time when much of education is stuck in old ways of teaching. Antiquated models make no sense to young people with completely different frames of reference.

Take the case of Catherine Garland, an astrophysicist teaching an engineering course. Her students were facing a common issue: the program could not locate their files. The students were not just struggling to find their saved files; they were also grappling with fundamental concepts. Garland came to the realization that the concept of file folders and directories is gibberish to many modern students.[6]

While many experts agree that AI will be important in education, it doesn't on its own prepare students to be flexible thinkers. We already know that adolescents' habitual checking of social media is linked with subsequent changes in how their brains respond to the world around them. Similar effects may also happen when it comes to children's use of generative AI. Gen Z already spends half its waking hours on screens. This is one reason why nature-based learning (NBL) is an educational approach that is gaining more traction. Children not only need more opportunities to connect to the natural environment, but they also need to find more ways to cultivate a sense of wonder, connection to the outside world, and ecological respect. Sensory engagement is a component and pathway to their learning.

Reprioritizing Vocational Training

The changing world of work brings the importance of vocational education and training to the forefront. A 2023 Intelligent.com survey finds 1 in 6 Gen Zers may switch from white-collar to blue-collar jobs due to fears about AI. Advancements in AI are causing greater concerns about the future of the white-collar job market. Based on survey results, 48 percent of respondents plan to work in white-collar fields, 32 percent plan to work in blue-collar fields, and 20 percent are unsure. Among those who say they plan to work in white-collar careers, 62 percent say they are "somewhat" or "highly" concerned about AI chatbot ChatGPT's impact on the white-collar job market. This apprehension is so significant that 53 percent of those considering white-collar professions are contemplating a shift to blue-collar roles. The implications of AI on the job landscape are causing individuals to reevaluate their career paths and consider alternative options, particularly those in skilled trades.[7]

As more societies rethink and reprioritize the value of vocational schools, we must also rethink the value of college education. Rather than preparing students for the world of work, it should be pursued for the sake of higher learning. The emerging reality will require more people skilled in critical thinking, one-off problem-solving, interpersonal relations, and specialization that is more localized and individualized. The constant push for young people to attend college and get degrees that are, in the end, little more than work certificates has persuaded high percentages of young people to forgo graduating high school because of the academic track they were forced into and could not conquer. We are in such a highly competitive and quickly changing world of technology that our outdated ideas of what is needed, and what will be needed 5, 10, or 30 years from now in the workforce, are woefully inadequate. Skilled tradespeople, home nursing services, trusted babysitters, and dog walkers will be in high demand, while radiologists will find much of their work taken over by smart systems that read images far faster and with greater accuracy based on larger datasets.

Computer science degrees have long been sold to college students as among the safest paths toward 21st century job security. Nothing has defined higher education over the past two decades more than the rise of computer science and STEM. Meanwhile, humanities enrollments across the United States have withered—in some cases, shrinking entire departments to non-existence. But that was before the age of generative AI. In the ultimate irony, software engineers helped create AI, and now they are the American workers who think it will have the biggest impact on their livelihoods. Coders are now using AI to accelerate the more routine parts of their job, such as debugging lines of code. In a recent study, software developers using GitHub's Copilot chatbot were able to complete coding tasks a staggering 56 percent faster than those working without AI assistance. Teachers are grappling with the question of the relevance of coding skills and the challenges of teaching students to code. One instructor has already started to modify his approach. He advises his introductory programming students to use AI in a way similar to how a math student would use a calculator. He tells them to reveal the precise prompts they feed into the machine and describe their reasoning. Programmers who possess entrepreneurial thinking and equip themselves with a mindset that goes beyond technical skills are likely to thrive and remain indispensable in the face of automation. This includes understanding business needs, identifying opportunities for innovation, and being proactive in problem-solving.[8]

The educational problem is just as real among adults. During the industrial economy, when adults embarked on a more classical and linear job path, it was expected that they would master a certain occupation until retirement between the ages of 55 and 65. However, recent generations are not predisposed to staying in one profession their entire lives. In fact, continuous learning and job retraining are powerful realities of today. Considering that life expectancy has increased profoundly, the expected retirement age for many Americans might not come until 75 or even 85. Additionally, priorities that were prevalent during the industrial economy have shifted for many Americans who no longer subscribe to the traditional notions of marriage, family, and career.

Understanding the Next Generation

Given the exponential rate of technological change, generations today should not be defined in 12-to-15–year age cohorts (as was discussed in Chapter 5, "A World of Templosion"). Technology is changing so rapidly that children only a few years apart struggle to have the exact same frame of reference. Gen Z has a much more symbiotic relationship with the digital world around them than previous generations. Quickly coming up behind them, however, is the "next-next" generation, which is yet unnamed. The term "Generation Alpha" has been suggested, but this generational alphabetical recycling doesn't tell us anything deeper about who they are.

What truly differentiates this newest generation, which can be defined as the group starting from 2010 onward, is that they are not just symbiotic with technology; they are, in many ways, *morphing* with it. The combination of AI and ambient intelligence (digitally connected smart environments that are sensitive and responsive to the presence of people) will amplify the real world to such an extent that this generation will be much more interdependent with the technologies that surround them. These technologies will become fully integrated into their natural behaviors and seamlessly interwoven into their daily lives. And because of templosion, this generation will undergo constant transformations—culturally, economically, politically, technologically—more so than any preceding generation. Their ways of viewing the world, interacting with their environment, interfacing with technology, and relating to other humans will seem completely foreign to many of us. Their cognition, emotions, relationships, social behaviors, values, attitudes, learning capabilities, consumer behaviors, and future careers will not adhere to traditional definitions.

Robots are even emerging as role models. The way Gen Alphas interact with robots and voice-activated devices is beginning to represent a more complex relationship—often an emotional one. According to *New Scientist*, children who spend time with a robotic companion appear to pick up elements of its behavior. New experiments suggest that when kids play with a robot that's a real go-getter, for instance, the child acquires some of its can-do attitude. And some parents have complained that Amazon's Alexa is training their children to be rude. Alexa doesn't need people to say please and thank you, will tolerate answering the same question over and over, and remains calm in the face of outbursts.[9] A larger question will be whether this stymies children's ability to learn how to interact with real people.

Learning, for this generation, must become hands-on and tactile. As more toys teach coding and programming, non-digital toys that incorporate kinesthetic learning are a good way to enhance creativity, design thinking, personal expression, and conceptualization. And as gaming and virtual reality worlds do more of their teaching, monitoring those technologies will be much more difficult for parents than trusting a school's curriculum.

For today's children, the boundaries between real, digital, and virtual will not only begin to blur further, but for some, they may vanish entirely. Social influence and socializing will be more digitally defined. Biology will become more inextricable from technology, as will AI-based emotional influence and attachment. Countertrends will be equally powerful. They may crave deeper connections to nature, and mindfulness and purpose may take on completely different meanings. Exposure to nature has been linked to improved attention, lower stress, and better mood.

Notes

1 https://www.technologyreview.com/2023/04/19/1071282/digital-world-reshaping-childrens-education-reading

2 https://www.nature.com/articles/d41586-024-00288-1?ref=aitrendy.cz

3 https://www.pewresearch.org/short-reads/2023/11/16/about-1-in-5-us-teens-whove-heard-of-chatgpt-have-used-it-for-schoolwork

4 https://www.nytimes.com/2023/01/12/technology/chatgpt-schools-teachers.html

5 https://www.learningforjustice.org/frameworks/digital-literacy

6 https://www.pcgamer.com/students-dont-know-what-files-and-folders-are-professors-say

7 https://www.prweb.com/releases/intelligent-com-survey-finds-1-in-6-gen-z-ers-may-switch-from-white-collar-to-blue-collar-jobs-due-to-fears-about-ai-897790393.html

8 https://www.theatlantic.com/technology/archive/2023/09/computer-science-degree-value-generative-ai-age/675452

9 https://www.newscientist.com/article/2121801-kids-can-pick-up-attitude-from-robots-they-play-and-learn-with

CHAPTER 30

Redefining What It Means to Be Human

A question that I find myself internally debating is: are biology and technology separate or are they one and the same? The sometimes tense relationship between the body and technology has captured the human imagination in many ways, from 16th century explorations of prosthetic technology to modern interpretations of the body itself as a machine. The two are not only inextricably linked, but it can be argued that they are one and the same. The divisions we make between "nature" and "technology" are illusory. Everything is natural; everything is technology. The designs we see in nature are not the result of chance. Take, for instance, the notion that the tree-like pattern of neurons responsible for consciousness seems to be a structural feature of the universe itself. The Internet shares a similar structure, as does the distribution of dark matter in the Milky Way. Mycelium networks are the Earth's natural Internet. The patterns repeat themselves throughout. We also see this through the Fibonacci sequence and the Golden Ratio, exemplified in nature and the human body; in the process of photosynthesis; and in the idea that human DNA is now being looked to as the ultimate data storage device.

Shared patterns are also reflected throughout the animal kingdom. Researchers some years ago said that because the human population is growing at such an astounding rate, we are organizing ourselves more like ant super colonies, and our societal structures have more in common with ants than with our closest living relatives in the animal kingdom, the higher apes. Infrastructure, the distribution of goods, transportation networks, assembly lines, complex highway systems, teamwork, urban anonymity, slavery . . . all of these are shared societal attributes between humans and ants. If you look down on a busy city from high within a skyscraper, the movement of pedestrians and vehicles closely resembles ants/ant colonies.

If technology is a process and a body of knowledge, biology is no different. And human augmentation and enhancement is a natural extension of this.

So how can we define human enhancement? We might think of it as something that gives us superhero-like power—extra strength or the ability to fly—or as a pill that will make us smarter or extend our lifespan. But we are already living enhanced lives and have been for a long time. We may believe the idea of human enhancement to be a modern one, but stories of physical adaptation and modification are found in Greek mythology and throughout many ancient cultures—some of which sought to augment their own consciousness through ayahuasca preparations or other naturally occurring psychedelic plants and substances. Human augmentation is nothing new. Since the first humans started using tools, we've been augmenting ourselves. The tools have just gotten smarter and much more complex. Whether it is basic objects, like rocks and sticks, or sophisticated gene therapies or generative AI, the common thread that underpins all of this is the desire to profoundly transform the human condition.

When you think about it, humans have long been cyborgs. There's a big gap between the fantasy vision of cyborgs and the current reality of being dependent on an implant or a prosthetic. If we separate the two, we realize we are living in the cybernetic world already. Pacemakers, wheelchairs, eyeglasses, hearing aids, and contact lenses have all been used by humans to alter, modify, or manipulate biology. Wearable technology continues to be a buzzy topic in today's consumer marketplace. But wearables are destined to evolve beyond the rudimentary self-quantification and fitness-related applications we see today. We are starting now to see the rise of embeddable, implantable, and ingestible technology.

We are also moving into a future in which our biology is becoming increasingly self-defined. Much of this sits at the intersection between AI, synthetic biology, and genetic engineering. Modern explorers are setting out on another ambitious frontier: extreme life extension. In every year since 1950, the average global life expectancy has risen by 18 weeks. However, "healthspan," the number of healthy, vital years does not automatically keep pace with lifespan. Billionaire tech founders like Peter Thiel, Sam Altman, Larry Page, Sergey Brin, and Jeff Bezos have all invested in firms trying to prolong both lifespan and healthspan. Research into human longevity and life extension is not new. Much of this can be traced to the ideas of Aubrey de Grey, who shaped many modern ideas about life extension. One of his ideas is *longevity escape velocity*, a future where science extends lifespans by more than a year every year. But the most promising advancements have been made in recent years, and they're accelerating rapidly. The sheer volume of research is like nothing that we have ever seen before. Nor have we seen this magnitude of resources directed toward the field. As a result, we are closer than ever before to effectively engineering immortality.

The humans of tomorrow (and it's already happening today) will be able to mix and match their own biology, not only to suit them but also to save them. We are approaching new and exciting frontiers in implantation (which includes neural implants, implantable and ingestible IDs, and implantable memories), transplantation (which includes both organic and synthetic transplants), and genetics (which includes gene editing and synthetic DNA sequencing). This future may be filled with everything from digital implants to mind-controlled exoskeletal upgrades, age reversal pills, hyper-intelligent brain implants, sentient AI, subdermal chips, electronic biometric tattoos, password/ID authentication pills, and even possibly virtual immortality.

Inherent in all of this, however, is a slew of privacy, moral, and ethical considerations:

- *Are we ready?* All of this begs the question of whether society is ready. Many of the ethical implications depend on how people collectively define human life.
- *Haves vs. have-nots:* A possible divide between "haves" and "have-nots" has already begun to dominate discussions about genetic tinkering and access to AI. Could accessibility to these enhancements and technologies exacerbate the already deepening "class" system?
- *Life extension:* Many of these technologies are designed to help people avoid disease and/or live longer. But how long are we really meant to live? Do we have the resources available to support this kind of mass longevity? We are already overcrowding our cities, and that will only become a bigger issue by mid-century. Should we "play God"?

The creation of a meaningful dialogue around these issues is paramount, particularly as AI begins to open more substantive conversations around what it means to be human. AI will play a major role in accelerating discoveries that impact human longevity, etc. In many cases, we'll see the same companies and/or governments invest in both areas, with an understanding that one will reinforce the other. At the national level, future strategic competitiveness assessments will likely count both AI and human longevity among their most critical metrics for both geopolitical and economic security.

Transhumanism is the school of thought that humanity is destined to evolve beyond its current physical and mental limitations, primarily through the means of advanced technology. In a world increasingly characterized by advanced AI, what will the role(s) of humans become? And if AI can mimic the natural function of the brain, will it serve to augment us in ways we've never explored? Could we learn a thousand times faster? Could we choose which memories to keep and which to get rid of? As technology continues to evolve, so will humanity. More practically, and in the nearer term, AI-powered cognitive enhancements could lead to a surge in human workforce productivity. Might we be able to "hack" ourselves so we can work and learn longer, smarter, and *better*?

AI Consciousness

Consciousness is difficult to measure or observe. Oxford Languages defines it as "The fact of awareness by the mind of itself and the world." Who we are, who we decide to be, and who we eventually become will not be separated from the technology that surrounds us. And AI is very much at the heart of this. In a world of AI, at what point does the artificial "being" become human? Perhaps the future will be marked by artificial ascendance, not artificial transcendence. Despite, however, the sophisticated responses of some AI systems, they do not have the embodied experiences characteristic of human consciousness. Biological neurons, responsible for human consciousness, are far more complex and adaptable than AI's coded neurons.[1] (Some scientists and astrophysicists have postulated that the human brain is the most complex thing we have yet discovered in our universe. Others argue that this is anthropocentric thinking and that measuring this complexity is difficult.)

The intrinsic vagueness in understanding consciousness has made its study anathema in the natural science fields. Until recently, the quest was largely left to philosophers. Now it is an area of study that extends to far more disciplines. In an era when AI advancements continue to push boundaries, questions will continue to arise about the consciousness of these systems. A 2023 report from Cornell University suggests that no current AI systems are conscious, but it also suggests that there are no noticeable technical barriers to building AI systems that "satisfy consciousness indicators."[2]

The widely accepted idea among AI researchers is that technology has made great strides, but still falls far short of human intelligence, and is nowhere near achieving consciousness. Without consciousness, Princeton neuroscientist Michael Graziano warns that "AI-powered chatbots are doomed to be dangerous sociopaths that could pose a real danger to human beings."[3] OpenAI's top researcher, however, recently made the controversial claim that AI may *already* be gaining consciousness.[4] This leads to a series of existential questions: Is it even conceivable that AI will achieve consciousness in the future? How would we define or identify consciousness in this context? Would we know it when we see it? Does AI *need* to be conscious in order for it to be considered truly equal to humans? And would AI *need* to be conscious for it to self-regulate, as its capabilities outpace humans' capacity to understand it?

There are also questions of liability and risk. Should a conscious AI system be held accountable for an intentional act of misconduct? Should it be granted the same rights as people? In comments to the UN in 2023, three leaders of the Association for Mathematical Consciousness Science (AMCS) called for more funding to support research on consciousness and AI. They said that "scientific investigations of the boundaries between conscious and unconscious systems are urgently needed," and they cited ethical, legal, and safety issues that make it critical to comprehend AI consciousness. If AI develops consciousness, for example, should people be permitted to just turn it off after use? It is currently unknown as to whether there are, or will ever be, conscious AI systems. According to the AMCS, "even knowing whether one has been developed would be a challenge, because researchers have yet to create scientifically validated methods to assess consciousness in machines."[5]

But then what does consciousness truly mean when many people increasingly engage with highly advanced chatbots and already believe that they are communicating with another conscious being?[6] The very human need for connection, combined with the tendency to anthropomorphize these systems, will make issues of machine sentience—and what it means and if it is even achievable—a very important debate to have. We know that humans have given anthropomorphic properties to everything from their talking GPS systems to Siri and Alexa, and even to their Roombas. When something speaks or acts like it's alive, we tend to believe it is. This may grow in magnitude as rudimentary forms of AGI (artificial general intelligence) are achieved. While generative AI is designed for a wide range of tasks, it does not have AGI's comprehensive understanding or learning ability. Some regard generative AI as being a step toward AGI—that is, a technology that can operate in a fully human way, perform cognitive tasks just like a person, and ultimately exceed all human capabilities. Prominent computer scientists like Ray Kurzweil are proponents of the concept called "the singularity." That is the point when AI becomes so smart it will outperform all human capabilities, leading to a sophisticated intelligence incomprehensible to our human brains. We are not there yet, and many debate whether we will get there in our lifetimes.

A team of researchers from Huawei's Noah's Ark Lab in Paris recently published research outlining a framework for "embodied artificial intelligence" (E-AI), something they assert could serve as the "next fundamental step in the pursuit of AGI." The consensus among the researchers is that in order for AI agents to interact with the real world in a truly meaningful way, they will need to be housed in some form of embodiment capable of perception, action, memory, and learning. This concept is not just theoretical; it has practical implications for the future development of AI technology. By giving AI models a physical presence and sensory capabilities, we can unlock new possibilities for how they can engage with and understand the world around them. In this context, perception means providing the AI system with the ability to "obtain raw data from the real world, in real time, and the capability to process and encode that data into a latent learning space." In essence, AI will need to evolve to pay attention to its surroundings, much like a human does, to truly understand the complexities of the world and act as a general intelligence. The ability for AI to have its own "eyes" and "ears" will revolutionize how we interact with technology. It will enable AI to gather data from its environment, process it effectively, and make informed decisions based on real-world scenarios.[7]

Observers ponder the philosophical question of whether both the Internet and AI are *conscious*—or, more specifically, whether they are evolving to become conscious. Today, our world is dominated, and in many ways defined, by the ubiquitous tech platforms we use to communicate, socialize, work, and transact. These platforms have come, in their totality, to represent the most current evolution of the Internet. And they are beginning to showcase a "consciousness" we have never seen before: minds, by the millions, coalescing via machinery to accomplish things once reserved for conventional political movements. Could we eventually see the potential for AI-enabled tech to meld with huge swaths of people to shift a "hybrid" or symbiotic consciousness?

Technological innovation is clearly hastening the need to contemplate questions about human nature. Ultimately, through the tools we create, we must ask ourselves: are we becoming more human or less human in the process?

Belief Systems in the Digital World

Confronting exciting—and, at times, scary—frontiers of our own humanity will also create ripples in our traditional belief systems. Religious relationships are evolving in the rapidly advancing digital world, with the integration of AI into online church services transforming the way people worship. This is especially notable in regions like South Korea, where Christianity holds significant importance. As tens of thousands seek spiritual sustenance, chatbots and audio bibles powered by AI are becoming essential tools for connecting with their faith in a digital age. Awake Corp, the developer of the ChatGPT-based bible chatbot service Ask Jesus (rebranded as Meadow), has attracted about 50,000 users since its launch in March 2023, including 10,000 from outside South Korea. The service replies to questions on spiritual matters and day-to-day issues with bible verses, interpretations, and prayers.[8] The intersection of AI and religious practices has sparked a fascinating debate among Hindu and Buddhist scholars. The emergence of robots performing Hinduism's holiest rituals raises profound questions about the role of technology in spirituality. While some view this integration as a sign of progress, symbolizing humanity's advancement into a new era, others express concerns about the potential consequences. The debate centers on whether AI's intrusion into religious rituals signifies a promising future or heralds the onset of apocalyptic events.[9]

In the heart of Iran lies the sacred city of Qom, revered for its deep-rooted traditions in Islamic learning and spiritual pilgrimage. Surprisingly, this ancient city has embraced modernity in the form of AI, captivating its religious leaders with its potential to delve into lengthy Islamic texts for guidance on issuing religious edicts. Ayatollah Ali Khamenei, Iran's supreme leader, has also urged clergy to see the possibilities of AI, saying that he wanted the country to be "at least among the top 10 countries in the world in terms of AI." Iran lags behind regional rivals such as Saudi Arabia and the United Arab Emirates when it comes to harnessing the power of AI to propel its economy forward. These countries have ambitious plans to leverage AI technologies for economic growth and development.[10]

The origin of life is a foundational question of theology. New issues surrounding it are shaking religious beliefs, and AI is compounding the confusion. Scientists, with the help of AI, have created life from inanimate material. The advancing use of AI in quantum physics and space exploration will profoundly affect fundamental belief systems about the origins of human life, as well as the beginnings of life itself. As economies evolve, so do the societal constructs and belief systems that come with them. And in a world where traditional belief systems are losing some of their adherents, are we at the precipice of a new form of "artificial God-like intelligence" that could serve as a cornerstone of faith for future generations?

The Countertrend: Tactile + Nostalgic

As people increasingly buoy between three worlds—analog, digital, and virtual—we must also be more aware of a powerfully emerging countertrend: the desire for real-world, tactile engagement. Alongside the rise of AI (and other disruptive technologies such as virtual reality and the metaverse), there is a growing offline movement and consumer segment. Pastimes and hobbies such as handmade crafts, board games, bowling, jigsaw puzzles, and coloring books are making a comeback. Vinyl record sales are increasing among Gen Z music fans. Enamored by the vintage appeal, they are also buying Polaroids. Like vinyl, Polaroids are about nostalgia, which can be a very powerful emotion, particularly when it comes to driving consumer behavior.

Historical nostalgia—reminiscing about the simplicity of eras gone by—is a way to escape current realities. Our desire for nostalgia is innate. Young people are increasingly idealizing memories of the past as a coping mechanism. This is one reason why retro video games are gaining popularity among Gen Z. TikTok and YouTube videos that romanticize the obsessions and sounds of earlier times have built an online community tied together by a yearning for a time when the world seemed united in facing an uncertain future. Marketers and brands are increasingly tapping into this "retro revolution," which is becoming a growing market.

There is also growing "techlash"—a term that refers to the growing animosity toward Silicon Valley giants. It also encompasses more universal resistance to modern technology itself, particularly innovations driven by digital tech and social media. But perhaps a better way to describe this is digital disillusionment. Digital disillusionment can occur in an era of rapid technological change, and extends to social media, too. As social media has aged, optimism has faded. For many younger people, embracing the offline can serve as an antidote for "Internet ennui"—a term to illustrate that feeling of jadedness and disinterest that can come from a lack of digital excitement. Perhaps this is one reason why we see the continued popularity of festivals, concerts, and other in-person special events. We may also see this eventually emerge with generative AI tools that fail to inspire people with bland and repetitive outputs. Marketers, advertisers, brand strategists, and designers will need to focus on the growing need for a captivating offline consumer experience. The design of "offline UX (user experience)" may become a growing untapped marketplace opportunity. As will the potential for emotionally driven, curated nostalgic experiences, which may be better served by people, not AI.

Notes

1 https://neurosciencenews.com/ai-consciousness-neuroscience-25108
2 https://arxiv.org/abs/2308.08708
3 https://www.wsj.com/articles/without-consciousness-ais-will-be-sociopaths-11673619880
4 https://futurism.com/the-byte/openai-already-sentient
5 https://www.nature.com/articles/d41586-023-04047-6
6 https://www.reuters.com/technology/its-alive-how-belief-ai-sentience-is-becoming-problem-2022-06-30
7 https://cointelegraph.com/news/huawei-researchers-artificial-intelligence-ai-body-next-fundamental-step-human-level
8 https://www.ft.com/content/9aeb482d-f781-45c0-896f-38fdcc912139
9 https://www.fastcompany.com/90862699/robots-are-performing-hinduisms-holiest-rituals-for-better-or-worse
10 https://www.ft.com/content/9c1c3fd3-4aea-40ab-977b-24fe5527300c

CHAPTER 31

The Future of Mental Health

Mental health issues today have become almost pandemic. Mental illness is on the rise, with much of it being clinically under- and undiagnosed. The mental health of global populations is increasingly in the spotlight because of a confluence of societal factors such as: an increasingly interconnected and polarized world; lack of available economic and employment opportunities; gender imbalances; shifting cultural norms; and the rise of social media. In fact, researchers using health-monitoring devices found that entire populations' sleeping habits, heart rates, and distances walked can swing out of sync after large societal events—and much of this is heightened by a constant cycle of social media and digital news. Much, too, has been made of AI taking over many jobs because of the work involved, and the threat of losing a job to AI is taking a toll on employee mental health.

We can catalog the growing incidence of mental illnesses around the globe, including anxiety, stress, depression, PTSD, suicides, substance abuse, and addiction. Rates of loneliness are rising all over the world. It is believed that severe loneliness can damage your health as much as smoking 15 cigarettes a day. Seniors enduring loneliness have a much higher mortality risk.

Workforce problems resulting from massive declines in mental health are already resulting in absenteeism (not just of suffering employees but those who serve as caregivers or who are affected by others who suffer); discrimination suits related to hiring and promotion; rising health care costs; demands to acknowledge and address employees' and their dependents' mental health issues; and workplace threats or injuries and the lawsuits resulting from them. In fact, research suggests that American workers who collaborate with industrial robots are facing a new set of challenges: adverse mental health effects and an increased likelihood of substance abuse.[1] There will be no abatement of these anytime soon. Mental health should rise to higher importance on employers' agendas if they are to mitigate any of these outcomes.

The integration of AI technology in mental health services is revolutionizing the way we approach emotional well-being. Chatbots that simulate therapist-like conversations and wellness apps that can identify individuals at risk of self-harm or provide depression diagnoses are rapidly becoming essential components of employers' health care benefits packages. As per a recent survey, about a third of U.S. employers are already offering digital therapeutics for mental health support, with an additional 15 percent considering implementing such solutions in the near future. AI-powered tools have proven to be effective in providing personalized and accessible mental health resources to employees. From virtual therapy sessions to mood tracking apps, these digital therapeutics offer a range of benefits that can significantly improve mental well-being. Over the past 3 years, 94 percent of large employers made new investments in mental health care.[2]

We also need to design new models to address new challenges to our mental health. These are particularly needed for our young people. Gen Z is a generation that will be defined, in part, by their collective struggles with stress-related issues. Outdated models to address these issues are insufficient. Teens are suffering from more mental illness than we have seen before. The statistics from the American Psychological Association (APA) are alarming: 90 percent of Gen Zers reported experiencing psychological or physical symptoms due to stress in the past year, with 70 percent identifying anxiety and depression as significant issues among their peers. According to the State of Gen Z Mental Health study, 42 percent of Gen Z respondents have been diagnosed with a mental health condition. Only about 20 percent, however, have received therapy to address their mental health concerns. Additionally, 60 percent of Gen Zers are currently using medication to help manage their mental health. More teens are also wrestling with eco-anxiety. It is evident from a Pew Research study conducted across 17 countries that young people are significantly more concerned about the impact of climate change on their lives compared to older adults. The feeling of betrayal by governments further exacerbates the sense of doom that many young individuals experience. The lack of decisive action and meaningful policies to address climate change has left them feeling disillusioned.[3] The increasing feeling of hopelessness and fear among young men is leading them to abandon higher education at alarming rates. This has resulted in a significant gap where female college students now outnumber male students by record levels. Young men reported that they quit school or did not enroll because they did not see enough benefit in a college degree for all the effort and expense involved to earn one. Many young men who dropped out said they were concerned about their future but nonetheless quit school with no plan in mind.[4]

There simply aren't enough psychiatrists, psychologists, or developmental pediatricians to care for the mental health needs of the country's children. The mental health care system is not built to handle a world in which entire populations of people are routinely and consistently traumatized or living in a state of anxiety, and its outdated approaches mean that most people will never get the help they need.

To solve the supply/demand imbalance in mental health, AI chatbots are being looked to as a solution. A recent study published in *Nature Medicine* sheds light on the impact of AI chatbots in bridging the gap in mental health services. By leveraging AI chatbots, the National Health Service (NHS) in England witnessed a significant rise in patient referrals, especially among underrepresented groups who traditionally face barriers to seeking help. The increasing demand for mental health services in England is on the rise, and there is an alarming gap between the rising demand for mental health services and the insufficient number of professionals available to meet this demand. But by leveraging chatbots and AI-powered tools, patients were able to receive assistance more quickly, and the detailed information collected by these chatbots was not only able to streamline the assessment process but also enhance its quality, ultimately saving valuable time for human clinicians.[5]

We, as a firm, have been talking about the therapeutic benefits of alternative avenues of response/therapy for decades. This includes virtual reality, augmented reality, robotics and AI, nature, neuroscience, pets, play, biofeedback, meditation and mindfulness, art, music, sound, smell, other sensory inputs, gamification . . . and the list goes on and on. We have the tools at our disposal. But these new tools must start becoming normalized and start making their way into our schools, workplaces, homes, hospitals, etc. The urgency here is that the mental health crisis is rising, and Band-Aid solutions won't work. But AI holds out great promise here.

Notes

[1] https://www.pitt.edu/pittwire/features-articles/automation-hurts-human-mental-health-study

[2] https://www.wsj.com/tech/ai/employers-are-offering-a-new-worker-benefit-wellness-chatbots-cc298b20

[3] https://www.pewresearch.org/global/2021/09/14/in-response-to-climate-change-citizens-in-advanced-economies-are-willing-to-alter-how-they-live-and-work

[4] https://www.wsj.com/articles/college-university-fall-higher-education-men-women-enrollment-admissions-back-to-school-11630948233

[5] https://www.technologyreview.com/2024/02/05/1087690/a-chatbot-helped-more-people-access-mental-health-services

CHAPTER 32

The Other AI: The Aging Imperative

Not only is life being extended, but quality of life is also continuously being improved through new health and wellness advancements that, taken in combination, could make a significant impact on aging populations. Social connectedness and maintaining health are now seen as an integral part of life extension, both of which are being aided by various applications of AI. AI-powered wearable devices and sensors can continuously track vital signs, physical activity, and other health indicators, enabling early detection of potential issues and allowing for proactive intervention. This not only improves the quality of care but also empowers seniors to take a more active role in managing their own well-being. Robotics can also assist seniors with various tasks, from personal care and mobility support to household chores and meal preparation.

A recent study examined the applications of AI and robotics in eldercare, focusing on their role in promoting independence, monitoring health, and helping and enhancing social interaction. It found that AI tools can help seniors adhere to their medication schedules, provide social solace, and allow them to live independently longer. These robotic assistants can also help alleviate the burden on caregivers and family members. One of the primary applications of AI in eldercare is the development of smart home systems that can help seniors live independently for longer. These systems can monitor daily activities and detect falls, all while providing a sense of security and comfort.

Maintaining mental wellness is also increasingly crucial, especially for seniors navigating the challenges of lifestyle and health changes. Recognizing this critical need, the team at LUCID developed an AI-powered solution that provides personalized music therapy to ease anxiety and agitation symptoms in older adults. Using AI, it learns and adjusts to the unique preferences of each individual, delivering a tailored music experience.[1]

Caring for the aging population will be one of the hottest sectors of the economy, with demand for employees well outstripping the supply of workers trained in the field. What is today mainly physical care will extend to psychological care as well. An estimated 6.5 million Americans aged 65 and older are living with Alzheimer's disease.[2] The number is expected to rise substantially over the coming decades. Conversational AI is helping revolutionize the way we approach caregiving for individuals living with challenging conditions like Alzheimer's. Take Amicus Brain's caregiver app, for example, which utilizes advanced AI to provide personalized recommendations and strategies that can dramatically improve quality of life.[3] The care and infrastructure for those suffering from dementia is already amounting to huge expenditures everywhere around the globe and may well become a subindustry unto itself. The rise of seniors in urban areas will also spur technologies designed to make cities more intelligent, especially regarding navigation and connectivity—with AI and the Internet of Things (IoT) being driving forces behind this next wave of urban innovation.

With the aging of the population, there is a ballooning market for eldercare technology. But while eldercare will grow in importance, it is also important to keep in mind that many seniors around the world are not merely winding down at the end of life. They will remain dynamic as consumers, workers, and influencers for far longer. This power cohort isn't going anywhere anytime soon. The upside to all of this is that one of the most powerful markets is emerging globally, ushering in the need for new products and solutions.

Notes

[1] https://www.news-medical.net/news/20220627/LUCID-music-medicine-and-machine-learning.aspx

[2] https://pubmed.ncbi.nlm.nih.gov/35289055

[3] https://www.forbes.com/sites/forbestechcouncil/2024/01/30/ai-to-benefit-humanity-innovations-in-senior-care/?sh=625e779163b0

CHAPTER 33

AI, Health + Scientific Breakthroughs

As it pertains to many aspects of their lives, research shows that Americans are increasingly cautious about the growing role of AI. More specifically, the public is split on the impact of AI in health and medicine. While some believe that AI will lead to better outcomes for patients, others express concerns about potential negative impacts. However, one thing is certain: AI is already making significant strides in improving diagnostics, treatment plans, and patient care. One prevalent concern that often arises is the potential for AI to negatively impact the personal relationships between patients and their health care providers. The fear of losing the human touch is a valid concern. Patients value the empathy, understanding, and personalized care that human providers offer, and there are worries that these essential aspects may be compromised as AI becomes more prevalent in health care settings.[1]

Bill Gates predicts that 2024 will be a monumental year for AI, with it becoming especially significant for global health, access to education, mental health, and more. The Gates Foundation's initiative to fund the development and implementation of AI-powered ultrasounds helps allow for timely interventions and improved outcomes for both mother and baby. At an India-based nonprofit organization called ARMMAN, AI researchers are working on an LLM that can help health workers treat high-risk pregnancies.[2] In Ghana, the Aurum Institute is developing an AI-powered decision support tool for antibiotic prescribers to combat antimicrobial resistance (AMR), which is a big public health concern, with Africa having the highest mortality rates. By developing interactive, AI-powered clinical support tools, prescribers can benefit from personalized and real-time antibiotic prescribing recommendations. This advancement not only streamlines the decision-making process but also enhances patient care outcomes.[3]

There will be a pressing need for clear regulations and guidelines to address issues of liability and accountability. These tools are not immune to errors and biases. The integration of AI in clinical settings brings forth valid concerns regarding the risks associated with relying on biased AI for critical medical decisions.[4] It will be crucial, too, to establish robust frameworks that ensure ethical practices and protect patient data. As AI technologies are used for more medical and health care purposes, which of them need to be tested and approved as medical treatments—and how should/could that be done? And who is responsible when deadly mistakes occur?[5]

When AI Meets Scientific Discovery

We are also at the precipice of another type of Cambrian explosion—one in which human life could be radically transformed by the combination of biological engineering, materials technology, robotics, and AI. AI models could open up new understanding of life as they expand and advance the sphere of scientific possibilities. Just as some AI tools are accelerating image and text generation, other AI tools are accelerating and refashioning some of the basic elements of science. AI science is moving from analyzing complex bits to now analyzing complex atoms.

Novel AI applications are opening exciting vistas of exploration and may be challenging—and, ultimately, changing—the very nature of discovery. Perhaps, in the not-too-distant future, the most significant and life-changing application of LLMs will entail a completely different type of language: the language of *us*.[6]

Protein language models (PLMs) are not just trained on words but on protein sequences, enabling them to decipher intricate patterns. So, can AI PLMs learn the linguistics of proteins? And what could this eventually mean? Using AI, we are now able to delve into uncharted territories of protein space, leading to the creation of groundbreaking proteins tailored for our specific medical and commercial requirements. By leveraging AI, we can unlock opportunities to design novel proteins that can revolutionize the treatment of various human illnesses that were previously unimaginable. Beyond health care, the ability to design new types of proteins has far-reaching implications across various industries. In agriculture, AI can be used to develop proteins that enhance crop yield and resilience to environmental stressors. Industries can leverage AI-generated proteins for innovative materials with superior properties. Environmental remediation efforts can benefit from tailored proteins that break down pollutants effectively.[7]

From cancer to autoimmune diseases, from diabetes to neurodegenerative disorders, AI is paving the way for more targeted and effective treatments.

A new class of antibiotic candidates were recently identified with the help of AI that could help researchers design additional drugs that might work even better than the ones identified by the model. New antibiotics have not been unlocked in 60 years.[8] Another AI tool, using only the patients' medical records, has successfully identified people at the highest risk for pancreatic cancer up to 3 years before diagnosis.[9] An AI-based risk prediction system called PRISM could help catch deadly pancreatic cancer cases earlier.[10] And, inspired by digital art generators like DALL-E, biologists see a path to a new cancer treatment or a new flu vaccine or a new pill that helps you digest gluten.[11]

We are also seeing unprecedented exploration of the brain. By analyzing thousands of different cell types that constitute the brain, scientists have crafted the most detailed description ever created of this intricate organ. This is analogous to the enormous effort that went into the Human Genome Project, which led to multiple medical advances.[12] It is designed to lay the groundwork for further research into conditions that affect the brain. If the exploratory powers of AI are applied here, this brain mapping could help usher in a new era of human health and wellness.

AI is making revolutionary discoveries that profoundly reshape not only the future of human biology but of our planet, too. From enhancing the efficiency of electric vehicle batteries to revolutionizing solar cells and microchips, these innovative materials are paving the way for groundbreaking discoveries. But discovering them can take months or even years of trial-and-error research. An AI program developed by Google DeepMind, called GNoME, was recently trained using data from the Materials Project, a free-to-use database of 150,000 known materials. The AI system was able, using that data, to generate designs for 2.2 million new crystals, with 380,000 predicted to be stable. This significant discovery has expanded the range of known stable materials nearly tenfold, opening possibilities for drug development and medical research.[13] Researchers consider GNoME's discovery of 2.2 million materials to be equivalent to approximately 800 years' worth of knowledge.[14] This innovation has immense potential to transform various industries, from electronics to renewable energy sources like solar cells.[15]

Not all of this, however, is grounds for blind celebration. Just like the well-known Spider-Man proverb, "With great power comes great responsibility," the increasing use of AI in these fields has led to a concerning issue: a "reproducibility crisis." This crisis is characterized by a surge of unreliable, useless, harmful, or even wrong research being produced due to the misuse or misinterpretation of AI technology. In November 2023, a major achievement was unveiled by scientists: the A-Lab, an autonomous chemistry system capable of synthesizing new materials independently. This innovation sparked both awe and skepticism within the scientific community. Critics raised valid concerns about A-Lab's capacity to accurately analyze its results and questioned the authenticity of its claim to have produced 41 new compounds. So, while the potential implications of such a technology may be profound, it underscores the importance of ensuring its efficacy and reliability before fully embracing it.[16]

All of this raises a slew of questions. Who, or what, will truly "own" the discoveries that emerge from AI and that will reshape the future of both the planet and humans themselves? What are the ramifications if certain companies or countries control discoveries in areas like genetics, genomics, drug development, and brain mapping? Will Big Tech firms or other companies be in control? Or will governments be in control, through subsidization of research and/or sheer force? What will be the impact of not only biased datasets but also biased biological data that has been harnessed and collected from us? And what if it gets into the wrong hands?

Still, the greatest promise of AI is that it could make innovation exponential across all fields, including energy, health and medicine, food and agriculture, genetics, materials technology, and climate science. Without human limitation bogging it down, AI has the potential to go through far more data far more quickly and identify new discoveries far more efficiently than humans—or any previous technology—could. And if we are eventually able to amplify one exponential technology (i.e., AI) with another (e.g., quantum computing), the possibilities for research, innovation, and discovery become even more exciting . . . and effectively limitless.

The Magellan Principle: AI's True Killer Apps

Perhaps we're also not necessarily having the right conversations about AI. Most conversations around AI today tend to concentrate around two broad applications of generative AI. The first relates to the possible disruptive impacts of AI in the workplace. The second relates to the application of LLMs to create original works (e.g., texts, art, music) once considered to be uniquely within the purview of humans. Yes, the preceding use cases for AI could dramatically reshape the economy and society. There's no disputing that.

However, the aforementioned use cases for AI models also, at the most basic level, represent efficiencies and/or "nice-to-have" applications. What if the killer apps of AI models in the future will be more about "need-to-have" applications? A *killer app* is a term to describe a computer application of such great value or popularity that it guarantees the success of the technology. In other words, killer apps often represent the first of a new breed, and because they are so innovative, they become exceptionally successful. The truly exciting future of AI goes well beyond the creative applications today considered to be at the core of generative AI. AI's killer apps in the future will be need-to-haves that revolve around exploration, discovery, and scientific invention. Think of future AIs as less Picasso or Hemingway and more Magellan, Edison, or Watson and Crick.

For instance, AI may act as an accelerator for quantum- and supercomputing. Quantum and supercomputers will be able to solve problems impossible for the most powerful conventional computers. Some observers forecast that AI will accelerate the arrival of quantum computing to a point far sooner than with human ingenuity alone. This portends a very exciting era for human discovery, but it also raises serious cybersecurity concerns—namely, the theory that quantum computing could render current encryption standards obsolete.

Like Magellan and his peers in the Age of Exploration, who were the first to discover and colonize different places, those who first to claim the Intellectual Property (IP) around certain discoveries will wield the immense power associated with those discoveries. As we think more broadly, AI could be the exploration technology that facilitates the next evolution of our civilization, and it might inspire a generation of human explorers to consider such scenarios.

Notes

[1] https://www.pewresearch.org/short-reads/2023/08/28/growing-public-concern-about-the-role-of-artificial-intelligence-in-daily-life

[2] https://www.cnet.com/tech/why-bill-gates-says-ai-will-supercharge-medical-innovations

[3] https://gcgh.grandchallenges.org/grant/ai-powered-decision-support-antibiotic-prescribing-ghana

[4] https://www.ncbi.nlm.nih.gov/pmc/articles/PMC10547752

[5] https://proto.life/2023/11/the-urgent-problem-of-regulating-ai-in-medicine

[6] https://www.forbes.com/sites/robtoews/2023/07/16/the-next-frontier-for-large-language-models-is-biology/?sh=584ccd5f6f05

[7] Ibid.

[8] https://news.mit.edu/2023/using-ai-mit-researchers-identify-antibiotic-candidates-1220

[9] https://hms.harvard.edu/news/ai-predicts-future-pancreatic-cancer

[10] https://www.technologyreview.com/2024/01/17/1086730/a-new-ai-based-risk-prediction-system-could-help-catch-deadly-pancreatic-cancer-cases-earlier

[11] https://www.nytimes.com/2023/01/09/science/artificial-intelligence-proteins.html

[12] https://www.newscientist.com/article/2397366-we-now-have-the-most-detailed-description-of-the-human-brain-ever

[13] https://www.wired.com/story/an-ai-dreamed-up-380000-new-materials-the-next-challenge-is-making-them

[14] https://www.freethink.com/robots-ai/google-ai-discovers-2-2-million-new-materials

[15] https://www.science.org/content/article/materials-predicting-ai-deepmind-could-revolutionize-electronics-batteries-and-solar

[16] https://www.nature.com/articles/d41586-023-03956-w

CHAPTER 34

The New Human Frontier

Finding Balance + Telling Better Stories

The world is erratic; AI is erratic; and humans are erratic. We are living in a world of accelerating instability. How do we approach it with open-mindedness, flexibility, and curiosity? These days we're moving so quickly it may feel like the world is spinning off its axis. What will be our new true north, allowing us to navigate it all and stay grounded? "Find your balance," is often called out to us in yoga class when moving into tree pose—a standing pose that requires focus, stability, and grounding. By rooting down through one foot and with arms extended overhead like branches reaching for the sky, you work to mimic the strength and stability of a tree's roots (if all goes as planned and you don't topple over). So, how can we cultivate a sense of grounding that extends beyond our yoga mats?

Spotting is a technique used by dancers to fix their gaze on a specific point as they turn, allowing them to maintain their balance and keep from getting too dizzy. Similarly, we too must become better future-spotters by identifying the focal points that serve as anchors amidst the whirlwind of distractions and changes we face.

Finding grounding, more broadly, will depend on the stories we tell about the future. We must all tell better stories . . . and become better storytellers. Often, AI is portrayed in extreme ways—either as a savior or as a threat. It's utopian vs. dystopian. Panacea vs. destroyer. Game-changer vs. game-killer. But this simplistic portrayal fails to capture its complexity and nuance. If we continue to rely on sci-fi extremes of human vs. machine, we miss the promises of the current state of AI. Many AI narratives are oversimplified versions of reality. What would things look like if we imagined a world where the story was told not by a human narrator but by the AI itself? Exercises like this, that involve writing first-person narratives from the perspective of AI, can help us explore the intricacies of machine storytelling and help us better understand the inner workings (or "thoughts?") of an AI system. What would we learn? How could it change our perspectives? How could we apply those insights to think differently about our businesses?

Throughout human civilization, storytelling has played a pivotal role in expressing ethics and value systems and passing them on from one generation to another. Fables, legends, mythology, and folklore hold immense wisdom and offer valuable insights into different cultures and perspectives. We, too, should be inspired by them because the stories we tell help shape and determine our future. If we are to truly preserve the human element in an age of AI, how are we to do so if we can't imagine beyond tomorrow? How are we to do so if we can't imagine better stories? Humans are indispensable. We need to begin framing the stories around our collective futures that way.

We must also encourage the creation of sci-fi stories—the kind that H.G. Wells, Isaac Asimov, Arthur C. Clarke, and the like inspired decades ago. Many of these narratives were about vision. They showed us a range of possibilities and made us think about choices we need to make to build a better future. They stand, in many ways, in sharp contrast to the stories coming out of Hollywood today, which are largely dark and lead us to believe we have no choice but to surrender to a future dystopia.

Rediscovering the Lost Art of Boredom

Perhaps some of this comes down to rediscovering the lost art of boredom. Everything around us seems to be moving so quickly that we must all find the time to simply think and let our minds wander. We need to prioritize space for spacing out. We need to give ourselves time to daydream. A little boredom has been scientifically proven to be a precursor for creativity and problem-solving. When we're bored, we give the brain some much-needed time to recharge and wander off to explore new ideas. Boredom, often seen as a negative experience or something to be avoided or quickly remedied, serves a purpose. We also need to give our kids permission to be bored—not all the time, obviously, but in small, healthy amounts. Societally, we've tried to coach boredom out of our children. We do not need to constantly entertain them and attempt to fill every waking moment with stimulation, nor should we overly rely on and repeatedly defer to "tech nannies" to step in and do that for us. (Even though, let's be real, they can be helpful tools for keeping parents sane.) Because it is in those moments of boredom when we are more likely to use our imaginations to write the stories that can entertain us and challenge us. But is this even possible to do now, especially in the industrialized world?

Lifelong Forgetting + the Lost Art of Nuance

Doubling down on us, as humans, will mean that we will need two things: the curiosity to learn new things and the humility to forget the things that no longer serve us. Curiosity fuels our desire to learn and explore new things. It is this curiosity that has driven us to create AI technologies in the first place. But that curiosity must be built on both learning *and* forgetting. We see so many internal organizational programs dedicated to cultivating lifelong learning among employees. We see calls in higher education for lifelong learning across all age groups. Motivational quotes say, "Never stop learning." And all of that is wonderful because yes, of course, we all must become constant learners and refresh our bases of knowledge, particularly in a time of near constant change. But while we must all find ways to become better and more effective learners—and make that a core aspect of our individualized future-proofing strategies—we must also find ways to become better forgetters.

What, ultimately, does that mean? It means that we must pause and think about the things that we are holding on to that we no longer need. Do we need to be tethered to certain strategies when we can forget some of that knowledge and turn the job over to AI to handle? Are we applying antiquated industrial era thinking to new problems or new opportunities? Are we thinking of technological solutions using soon-to-be defunct platforms? Are we focusing on cultivating skill sets in our children based on old assumptions of how the world worked? Are we designing buggy whips for self-driving cars? Are we blindly relying on what we were taught when we were young? Are we encumbered by our own heuristics that we use to make sense of the world? Are we making value judgments about where the future is moving, and if so, how can we let go of those and use it as an opportunity for advancement and progress?

Forgetting matters because this is both a time for vision and to be visionary. We have lost, as a society, the ability to hold and hear multiple conversations at once. It's not only because our lives have become so consumed with constant distractions and multitasking that we often struggle to focus on one conversation, let alone hold multiple meaningful discussions simultaneously. It's bigger than that. It is natural for all of us to each have varying viewpoints on a given subject, but we need to acknowledge that there are multiple valid ways of perceiving the world around us. Rather than clinging rigidly to one viewpoint, we can explore the richness that comes from integrating contrasting ideas. While there are *no* "alternative facts," there *are* competing narratives.

This is not an idealistic imperative or a naive mandate about all getting along. It is a critical one for our collective futures because "my way or no way" is leading to the widespread devolution of public discourse. As we retreat to our ideological echo chambers and are siloed into tribal groups by evermore pervasive algorithms, do we have the collective capacity for having tough conversations? Are we able to bridge the chasms in communication that are growing wider and deeper? Do we lack the communication skills and the foundational thinking for dealing with a world defined by growing complexities? We must learn how to listen to opposing viewpoints and use them as opportunities for learning and discovery. In a world where polarization seems increasingly prevalent—and is being exacerbated by AI systems—learning how to navigate cognitive dissonance becomes more critical. A key part of this means recognizing that nothing is purely black or white but rather exists within a complex spectrum of understanding.

We must pause and ask ourselves: What are the things we cannot change? What's *not* going to change despite our best efforts? What variables in the future will make you act differently? Or spur you to act? How do your views of the broader world—the macro-environment—affect your behaviors, actions, and decision-making capabilities? Is having meaningful, nuanced dialogues a skill set and something that can be taught? What would it look like to teach our young people how to *think* about nuance? How can we leverage the principles of design-based thinking to address these challenges?

Patterns within nature often mirror human behavior. Recently, researchers in China discovered a plant that developed camouflage to protect it from getting picked by human hands. In some places, it has bright green leaves that stand out against the rocks. In other places, its leaves and stems are gray and blend in with rocks. Same plant, two different defensive responses. The same can be said of us. Self-preservation is a form of adaptation, and the instinct toward self-preservation is largely driven by fear—and fear will continue to shape consumer, governmental, and organizational decision-making. But self-preservation is also about survival—and perhaps even more importantly, the *perception* of survivability. A core part of human nature—and our biological makeup—consists of this instinctive tendency to ensure survival. Humans' remarkable ability for self-preservation will lead us to seek out new ways to ensure survival in the future, which may lead us to ask more existential questions about what parts of ourselves—or our external environment—we want to preserve. This will include identifying which parts of us we can comfortably farm out to AI and which parts we want to keep in our sole purview.

CHAPTER 35

Not All Change Is Fast, and Not Everything Is Changing

C hange can happen quickly. But our ability to adapt to it can be slower paced. I liken it to going into an unheated swimming pool. You dip your toes into the water and adjust to the initial chill. Then you slowly inch your way in, letting each layer of your body acclimate to the temperature of the water. Little by little. Now picture being tossed into a turbulent icy river. The shock would overcome you. This metaphor illustrates how humans deal with change and adaptation. We are naturally equipped to adapt gradually, much like easing into a cold swimming pool. But when change comes quickly, like the rush of an icy river, our capacity to adapt is tested. Our neural wiring is built for slower-paced adaptations. This cognitive process served us well in the past when changes were gradual and predictable, but it can be at odds with today's fast-paced changes. How do we safeguard against paralysis? How can we ensure that the rapid changes don't leave us incapable of action? Perhaps we need to give ourselves the chance to progressively adjust to insulate ourselves against the shock of an "icy river."

Is gradualism, therefore, an antiquated concept? According to Tristan Harris, cofounder and executive director of the Center for Humane Technology, "Technology has outmatched our brains and therefore diminished our capacity to address the world's most pressing challenges." Essentially, our brains, which have evolved over millennia, are now faced with the challenge of keeping up with the rapid advancements in technology—and AI has the potential to overwhelm our prehistoric brains as it continues to evolve more quickly than ours.[1] He echoes a version of what psychologists have dubbed the *maladapted mind*, or mismatch hypothesis. This theory suggests that "the slow pace of human evolution and the fast pace of cultural and technological change means that our minds are better adapted to our hunter-gatherer past than to today's fast-changing world."[2] But does our ability to be self-aware mean that we have the power to reverse these trends? Will it hinge on us being able to become "forgetters"? Will we be able to rise to the challenge and cultivate the wisdom to create technology that is more humane? As Tristan Harris rightly points out, if we want technology to be more humane, we must delve deeper into understanding human nature beyond just privacy concerns. Humankind needs to understand its innate strengths—the capacity for critical thinking, rational debate, and reflection. Humankind needs to understand and recognize its limitations and foibles.

We must also remember that not all aspects of our lives will transform overnight. And not everything *will* change. Yes, of course, templosion is very real. But some traditional methods and practices may persist alongside new technological developments, creating a blend of old and new in our daily experiences. Daily frustrations with old, antiquated systems will still exist. Has AI yet solved many of the frustratingly annoying automated customer service interfaces we still have to deal with? No. I just had this experience with a major U.S. airline that "lost" my international flight reservation a day before departure. Does this airline advertise that it uses AI to "drive operational efficiency" and "provide a better customer experience?" Yes. But did it deliver on that? Not even close. Why? Because AI is not a panacea; things take time to change; and not everyone will get it right. Do many of our retail experiences still seem unchanged from decades ago? Of course they do. Why do we still have mirrorless dressing rooms and bad lighting? Why does my new doctor send me physical forms in the mail and require me to fill them out and return them the same way? And how many times do I have to press "0" to get a human operator on the phone because an automated system cannot properly handle my query? Or why do companies still use billable hours? Or time sheets? And the list goes on.

Why does this matter? Because the future is ambiguous. We love to have a sense of predictability because it provides us with some semblance of control. But we must understand that the pace of change is relentless in some areas and relenting in others. And that exact trajectory is one that we will never be able to pinpoint with any certainty, no matter how hard we try. Some things we *don't* perceive to be changing will continue changing rapidly (e.g., news delivery, recommendations algorithms, etc.) Other things we perceive to be changing may change very little. . .or not at all (e.g., customer service, data management, etc.) It is also tempting to put forth and believe in a narrative that everything is changing profoundly. It sounds compelling, but that narrative is not always a perfect reflection of reality.

The Value of Simplicity

Throughout history, the wisdom, value, and benefits of simplicity are recurring themes, found in many ancient religions, traditions, and cultures. Leonardo da Vinci is credited as saying, "Simplicity is the ultimate sophistication," and in scientific models, Occam's razor alludes to the shaving away of unneeded detail. In the 1960s, the U.S. Navy's KISS principle ("Keep it simple, stupid") stated that most systems work best if they are kept simple. In pursuit of "perfection," Steve Jobs folded sophisticated products into highly simple designs. In nature, simplicity is found throughout. We, too, socio-culturally, are seeing an increased desire for the simple.

"Complexipacity," a term I once heard discussed by David Pearce Snyder, is defined as a person's or organization's threshold and/or capacity for assimilating or addressing complex ideas, systems, problems, situations, and interactions. But rising alongside—as a complementary countertrend—is what I would call "simplibility"—a person's or organization's ability to address or create simple and straightforward ideas, designs, systems, situations, and interactions in an era of constant connectivity.

Most of our days are filled with never-ending small decisions (e.g., limitless entertainment options, dozens of options at Starbucks, multiple channels of communication). Decision fatigue ("paralysis by analysis") afflicts us all. When it comes to consumer products, there is too much variety, which can be overwhelming. When faced with numerous options for a single product, many of us will just skip a purchase because it takes too much mental energy. Consumers, across the board, want simple solutions, and they need simple messages. Simplicity, for populists, is about credibility and authenticity. And it's all about proposing simple solutions, which is appealing for many voters. And having grown up in a world of unlimited choice and constant connection, millennials and Gen Zers are embracing simplicity in food (e.g., farm-to-table; transparent and real ingredients), in living (e.g., minimalist design), and in fashion (e.g., normcore).

We are not only drowning in data, but we are also drowning in the complexities of the modern world. Weighty tech jargon, lengthy user manuals, financial agreements and insurance policies, incomprehensible terms of service, time-consuming tech updates—all of these must be dismantled, rethought, and (re)designed differently. If time is a sought-out luxury today, then we must design our products and services to cater to consumers' desire for time-saving solutions.

We hear a lot about how AI can help simplify and streamline our lives. And in some ways, it will. But in other ways, as we've discussed in prior chapters, it will lead to greater complications. We may become more overwhelmed, more hesitant, and more confused. Greater complexity, uncertainty, and socio-techno anxiety will lead more people to seek out a sense of personal control, connection, and general ease and effortlessness (including ease-of-use).

Notes

[1] https://www.nytimes.com/2019/12/05/opinion/digital-technology-brain.html

[2] https://digitalwellbeing.org/are-our-brains-really-no-match-for-our-technology

CHAPTER 36

The Power of Imagination

The future is a blank slate, and we have the power to shape it. The future is not predetermined or fixed; it is up to us to determine what it will look like. Technology is propelling humans into a creativity contest with technological innovations of our own making. As new technologies apply competitive pressures to older systems, and as more people become displaced, the value of imagination increases exponentially. So, right now we sit at an inflection point—one in which humans and AI are in a race to see whose imagination, if either, will win out. There are few endlessly renewable resources that are valuable to our futures, and imagination is certainly one of them. Humans will never run out of it. But AI is quickly catching up. If educators, employers, marketers, and technologists rely on the imagination of AI without fostering this capacity in their human constituencies, human imagination may become an even rarer commodity in the value chain. We will need to double down on figuring out ways to apply what is unique to the human brain to the future of work, art, citizenship, competitiveness, national security, and social interaction. We will need to work together across political party lines and international borders to find solutions to the problems of resources, climate, terrorism, aging populations, and political stalemates . . . which is nice in theory but difficult in practice.

While our view of the future is colored through the lens in which we view it, for me, I believe the future, while complex and at times very scary, holds incredible promise. But we do have a choice in what we imagine—and not all imagination is good. Bad actors can quickly and easily turn their "bad imaginations" into reality. There are not enormous obstacles for them doing so, because negative or evil imagination doesn't have to observe anything. It can be easily thrust into public consciousness—often unchecked. There are often more obstacles for positive imagination—stakeholder expectations, budget cycles, regulations, etc. And for far too long we have seen leaders rewarded for guiding their organizations based on data and quantitative insights rather than being rewarded for their sense of intuition and acting on gut instinct or a more intangible sense of "knowing." But the next several years could see more imaginative leaders (both good and bad) steer the ship, thereby magnifying and multiplying the impact of their ideas more broadly.

We, too, have a choice in how we imagine. And linear thinking isn't going to get us there. We talked in an earlier chapter about the future-proofed skills and competencies that will be competitive advantages. Alongside that, however, is that perhaps more than anything else, what becomes an imperative for the future is positive imagination. It has been said that AI is a "force multiplier for human imagination." While we must acknowledge, understand, and respond to doom and gloom narratives (and there are plenty), we must also work hard and challenge ourselves to imagine beyond them.

As children, our minds are free from the constraints of traditional time boundaries. We look at young kids and see that their imaginations allow them to create vivid scenarios, totally unencumbered, that exist beyond the modern-day constructs and confines of reality. In the mind of my son, *Star Wars* battles (which have started to migrate to 80s wrestling figure battles—clearly, he's the byproduct of two late Gen X/early Gen Y parents!) transport him to a different world. As he wields imaginary lightsabers, commands starships, and strategizes against the dark forces of the galaxy, his mind is ignited with creativity and excitement. Through imaginative play, he becomes an active participant in a narrative that transcends time, taking him on an adventure through space. These battles not only transport children to a different world but also foster a sense of wonderment and curiosity within them. As they imagine themselves as Jedi knights or Sith lords battling for control over the galaxy, their minds expand with endless possibilities.

For me, when I was young, I used to travel to the moon every night before dinner. As the sun began to set, I would hurriedly run out the door to the driveway and make my way to the backyard. This small square of grass was my landing pad and home to my space shuttle. I would climb on board and be off, swinging back and forth through the air in my two-seated glider. When I touched down on the moon's surface, my lunar rover, equipped with training wheels, awaited me. The flowered basket and metallic streamers added a special touch, I thought. Then off I went. Like any good astronaut-in-training, I sped down the sidewalk in search of my moon base. Then there it was. Moon base 77. I always knew where to find it since it had been spray-painted in big orange numbers on the surface of my moon (much to the chagrin of our neighbors who lived in #77). After collecting some moon rocks, it was time to return to the shuttle. I climbed in and started my journey back home to Earth. I had traveled across the universe in less than an hour. Explored new lands and traversed the surface of the moon in the time it took to make dinner. My imagination manipulated time and took me to distant places.

As the famous playwright George Bernard Shaw once said: "We don't stop playing because we get old; we get old because we stop playing." The same can be said of imagination. I remember going to EPCOT as a child and being enthralled by that silly little dragon, Figment, who sang that silly little tune "Imagination." But that song was about human history and how imagination and ingenuity are two of the most powerful threads that connect us.

For the world in which we now live, we must work harder to imagine the new possibilities to make the future better. Our future will rely on it—and it doesn't stop when we "grow out of it" or when we leave school. We need our imaginations to envision future scenarios and think beyond what currently exists. AI will never be a substitute for our imaginations, but it will allow us to push the boundaries of what we thought was possible and help us explore ideas and concepts that were once thought to be beyond reach.

Thriving as Diamonds, Not Coal

What it really comes down to, though, is thriving—thriving through change, complexity, and transformation. How can we reconceive of our environments so that they reward a sense of wonder, imagination, and curiosity? How do we tap into individual human ingenuity in novel ways? How do we become catalysts of change? Over the course of history, humans, time and time again, have proven to be remarkably resilient and adaptive. And the current environment, with all its technological, social, economic, and geopolitical challenges, is no different.

As one of my favorite adages goes: "A diamond is merely a lump of coal that did well under pressure." We are all shaped and molded by our realities. In the same way that pressure is needed to transform a piece of coal into a diamond, we also require pressure for our transformation. External transformations may be happening quickly. Pressures are multiplying. But for us, transformation is not an overnight phenomenon; it is a gradual process. The pressures we face in life—which come in various forms—can act as catalysts for change.

Coal, in its raw form, may appear ordinary and unremarkable. However, when subjected to intense heat and pressure over time, it undergoes a remarkable change. The same principle applies to us as individuals. Without pressure, we risk remaining stagnant. Treading water and exerting a lot of energy but not getting anywhere . . . and at risk of sinking. A future-proofed mindset really is about knowing that the pressures that come our way are not meant to break us but rather to refine us into something stronger and more valuable. And, when you think about it, we are each one of us a diamond. The Future Hunters, many years ago, developed the term "diamonding" to explain the process through which individuals become more distinct from others as they age, due to the uniqueness of their life experiences. Solutions for the future must reflect this and respond to a dynamic marketplace of dynamic individuals each with different needs, different ways of viewing the world, different experiences, and different expectations of technology.

Our time and energy need to be spent preparing for what is inevitably coming. Spent thinking about the future and how what we do today could affect the generations of tomorrow. Because we cannot look to address tomorrow's questions with yesterday's answers. Or as Albert Einstein almost a century ago so presciently said, "We cannot solve our problems with the same thinking we used when we created them." The world is unpredictable, and our actions today have far-reaching consequences that can shape the world for years to come.

A human-centric future will not just be about how we tap deeper into our own ingenuity. It will also require humility. Computer scientist Steve Polyak once joked, "Before we work on artificial intelligence, why don't we do something about natural stupidity?" Intellectual humility is a cognitive process, or mindset, that recognizes the limits and shortcomings of one's own beliefs, opinions, and knowledge, all in the service of pursuing deeper levels of knowledge, truth, and understanding.[1]

Perhaps, too, we'll look to the past for inspiration. What would it look like, for instance, if we designed a near future built on the values of the Age of Enlightenment: reason and rationality (over superstition), the respectful exchange of ideas (over intolerance), progress (over stagnation), and human autonomy? It was a time when art and philosophy flourished—two things we'll need to more highly value and emphasize in an age of AI.

In Search of New Frontiers

The "frontier spirit" is a concept in the American psyche that describes the discovery of new places and opportunities. The frontier became symbolic of the can-do spirit. That same can-do spirit—one of ambition, drive, and tenacity—is needed today as we are buoyed between two very distinct, but increasingly symbiotic, frontiers: one human, one technological.

That same can-do spirit is needed to keep us from becoming complacent and jaded, too. We must actively avoid the trap of "Why even spend time learning a language, creating art or music, writing, talking to each other, trying to solve a problem, etc. when an AI can do it for us faster and better?" It remains to be seen whether AI will ever truly be better than humans, let alone able to achieve virtuoso status in any of these areas. AI might be good for churning out outputs, be it art, music, writing, etc., but it doesn't mean those outputs are original or novel. There is a lot of hype out there about AI taking over the world—good, bad, or otherwise. But not everything will be affected by AI. There is still a lot out there that will not be directly affected by AI, and a lot of people who won't be either. At least not yet. AI has the potential, realistically, to be monumentally disruptive. Some believe that AI may be the single most transformative technology of our time. While opinions vary on current AI models and applications, the immense promise of the technology is very real. We still need, however, to recalibrate our expectations. The narrative is overblown that it's going to take over the world. Much of our day-to-day lives will not look much different— certainly not in ways we're always consciously aware of. And the effect will not be experienced uniformly. There will be major differences across global populations and markets.

Whether perceptible or not, AI will transfigure human experience. Ultimately, AI's potential to enhance human endeavor through unprecedented exploration and discovery in areas like health/medicine/wellness, longevity, genetics/genomics, and new materials technology is a future worth aspiring to.

AI will continue to be integrated into most aspects of life, introduce new efficiencies, distort the truth and erode trust, and augment our capabilities in many ways. Looking ahead, AI may not fundamentally change us at our core. Human nature will still be human nature. But AI will march forward, transforming the frontiers of human experience in ways we are only just beginning to explore and comprehend.

Note

[1] **https://www.templeton.org/discoveries/intellectual-humility**

Afterword: Putting This into Practice

One of the questions on most business leaders' minds today is: how can I/we become future-ready? The last several years not only put companies under massive stress, but they also tested both near- and long-term readiness and resilience in new ways. Crises often reveal who is ready for the widespread changes the future will bring. . .and who is not. But the thing we are all navigating is uncertainty. And in times of uncertainty, future readiness is more critical than ever.

Many of us spend a lot of time and energy doing something but achieving very little. It's the hamster on a wheel effect. Every type of organization will need to task itself with figuring out ways to apply the discipline of foresight to shift and challenge current thinking, spur new ideas, and encourage new approaches to help minimize shocks of future events, while building a rock-solid foundation on which opportunities can quickly be identified and seized.

Lastly, we must all ask ourselves questions about the next generation and tap deeper into how they think and how they see the world. That's one reason why I have always advised people to get a reverse mentor. I've said the same to companies—that every person within those companies should not just have a mentor but a reverse mentor. And don't have your reverse mentor be an intern, because that person is already too old. Ask questions of a middle schooler (be it a neighbor's kid, a niece or nephew, etc.) Ask them what they are learning, what kind of jobs they'd like to have, how they talk to their friends, how they consume media, their insights about pop culture, what they do in their spare time . . . anything. The biggest thing is this: leave your value judgments at the door, be open and receptive to what you hear/learn, and use it to challenge your own thinking. Then take those insights and think about how they can be applied to help you think differently about a potential problem or solution at work (or in any other aspect of your life).

Every organization will be increasingly tasked with figuring out how to harness AI to uplift and augment its workforce—and it will be tasked with doing so in a way that aligns with its stated vision.

Because of *templosion*, each day we are met with a new reality, a new challenge, a new solution, and a new future. We all will face the pressing need to question everything we do, how we do it, and how we survive, compete, and thrive organizationally, collectively, and individually as we embark upon this new human frontier.

Acknowledgments

First and foremost, I want to acknowledge my son, Zane, whose insight, curiosity, and sense of wonder serve as a beacon of optimism and hope. You, Zane, are who I ultimately do this work for. You are a gift. Thank you to Edie, my very first mentor (turned fabulous mother-in-law) who, when I was a wide-eyed and unsure 20-something, took a chance on me and gave me the opportunity of a lifetime. You have truly changed my life in more beautiful ways than I can count. Thank you to the late Arnold Brown, who not only helped me become a better writer and a better thinker but also was always a source of wisdom (and unheard-of Boggle words). Thank you to my parents, Wendy and David, who always told me to think big and spread my wings. Your unwavering belief in me has shaped me into who I am today. Thank you to my sisterhood—the incredible women in my life who have filled my cup in immeasurable ways. Thank you to Joyce Forrester, our incredible Office Manager, who not only spent hours pulling out research from our archives but, most of all, is an indispensable member of our team. Thank you to my entire team at Wiley who helped make this book happen (Krysta Winsheimer, Sara Deichman, Pete Gaughan, and the list goes on). James Minatel, thank you for your vision and your guidance. Thank you to the team at Alternatives (Julie Koch-Beinke, Mark Koch, and Daniel Acacio)—I am always grateful for your vision and ongoing partnership.

Thank you, most of all, to Jared, my husband and partner—in life and work and all things—for your never-ending support and patience (especially as I forced you to listen to the intricacies of this book over morning coffee, nighttime wine, and everything in between). You challenge me in the best ways possible, and I would never be able to do any of this without you. I am, and will always be, grateful for you and us. That is why this book is dedicated to you and Zane.

About the Author

For nearly 20 years, Erica Orange has been at the forefront of change. As Executive Vice President and Chief Operating Officer of The Future Hunters, one of the world's leading futurist consulting firms, she evaluates emerging social, technological, economic, political, demographic, and environmental trends. Erica identifies the strategic implications (the "So what?") of these trends for several of the most influential Fortune 500 companies, entrepreneurs, trade associations, and public sector clients to help inform long-term strategic thinking and innovation.

Erica speaks to a wide range of global audiences about the macro trends that will shape tomorrow's landscape. She has spoken at TEDx and keynoted hundreds of conferences around the world, including in Europe, Latin America, and Asia. She has been featured in news outlets including *Wired*, NPR, *Time*, Bloomberg, and CBS This Morning. In 2020, she was named by Forbes as one of the world's 50 Top Female Futurists.

About The Future Hunters

For over four decades, The Future Hunters' (TFH) team—Erica Orange, Jared Weiner, and Edie Weiner—has been studying long-term global trends. Our job and particular area of expertise is to identify trends that will be important before they become part of the cultural and business vernacular. TFH not only helps clients become smarter about the future but also assesses the practical and tangible implications so that decision-makers are better prepared. For both the opportunities and challenges of tomorrow, TFH is at the intersection of future trends and insights, thought leadership, innovation, and strategy.

While this book is about AI, all our thinking is still done by *us*. We do not outsource any of our trend analysis to technology because we very much believe that the most valuable connective threads between different outputs are best identified and understood by applying our thinking and collective wisdom. Much of our work comes down to two things: pattern recognition and the human eye. While AI can efficiently produce and sift through information, humans are still essential to produce meaningful insights.

Index